# Lecture Notes in Business Information Processing 252

W0230428

More information about this series at http://www.springer.com/series/7911

David Aveiro · Robert Pergl
Duarte Gouveia (Eds.)

# Advances in Enterprise Engineering X

6th Enterprise Engineering Working Conference, EEWC 2016
Funchal, Madeira Island, Portugal, May 30 – June 3, 2016
Proceedings

 Springer

*Editors*
David Aveiro
University of Madeira
Funchal
Portugal

Duarte Gouveia
University of Madeira
Funchal
Portugal

Robert Pergl
Faculty of Information Technology
Czech Technical University in Prague
Prague
Czech Republic

ISSN 1865-1348          ISSN 1865-1356   (electronic)
Lecture Notes in Business Information Processing
ISBN 978-3-319-39566-1          ISBN 978-3-319-39567-8   (eBook)
DOI 10.1007/978-3-319-39567-8

Library of Congress Control Number: 2016940338

Printed on acid-free paper

This Springer imprint is published by Springer Nature
The registered company is Springer International Publishing AG Switzerland

# Preface

The CIAO! Enterprise Engineering Network (CEEN) is a community of academics and practitioners who strive to contribute to the development of the discipline of enterprise engineering (EE) and to apply it in practice. The aim is to develop a holistic and general systems theory-based understanding on how to (re)design and run enterprises effectively. The ambition is to develop a consistent and coherent set of theories, models, and associated methods that (a) enable enterprises to reflect, in a systematic way, on how to realize improvements, and (b) assist them, in practice, in achieving their aspirations.

In doing so, sound empirical and scientific foundations should underlie all efforts and all organizational aspects that are relevant should be considered, while combining already existing knowledge from the scientific fields of information systems, software engineering, management, as well as philosophy, semiotics, and sociology, among others. In other words, the (re)design of an enterprise and the subsequent implementation of changes should be the consequence of rationalized decisions that take in account the nature and reality of the enterprise and its environment, and respect relevant empirical and scientific principles.

Enterprises are taken to be systems whose reality has a dual nature by being simultaneously, on one hand, centrally and purposefully (re)designed; and, on the other hand, emergent in a distributed way, given the fact that, its main agents, the humans that are the pearls of the organization, act with free will, in a creative and in a responsible (or sometimes not) way. We acknowledge that, in practice, the development of enterprises is not always a purely rational/evidence-based process. As such, we believe the field of EE aims to provide evidence-based insights into the design and evolution of enterprises and the consequences of different choices irrespective of the way decisions are made.

The origin of the scientific foundations of our present body of knowledge is the CIAO! Paradigm (Communication, Information, Action, Organization) as expressed in our Enterprise Engineering Manifesto and the paper "The Discipline of Enterprise Engineering." In this paradigm, organization is considered to emerge in human communication through the intermediate roles of information and action. Based on the CIAO! Paradigm, several theories have been developed, and are still being proposed. They are published as technical reports.

The CEEN welcomes proposals of improvements to our current body of knowledge, as well as the inclusion of compliant and alternative views, always keeping in mind the need to maintain global systemic coherence, consistency, and scientific rigor of the entire EE body of knowledge as a prerequisite for the consolidation of this new engineering discipline. Yearly events like the Enterprise Engineering Working Conference and associated Doctoral Consortium are organized to promote the presentation of EE research and application in practice, as well as discussions on the contents and current state of our body of theories and methods.

Since 2005 the CEEN has organized the CIAO! Workshop and, since 2008, its proceedings have been published as *Advances in Enterprise Engineering* in the Springer LNBIP series. From 2011 on, this workshop was replaced by the Enterprise Engineering Working Conference (EEWC). This volume contains the proceedings of the 6th EEWC, held in Funchal, Madeira Island, Portugal. There were 34 submissions. Each submission was reviewed by three Program Committee members and 12 papers were selected after careful review for inclusion in this volume.

The EEWC aims at addressing the challenges that modern and complex enterprises are facing in a rapidly changing world. The participants of the working conference share a belief that dealing with these challenges requires rigorous and scientific solutions, focusing on the design and engineering of enterprises. The goal of EEWC is to stimulate interaction between the different stakeholders, scientists, as well as practitioners interested in making enterprise engineering a reality.

May 2016

David Aveiro
Robert Pergl
Duarte Gouveia

# Organization

EEWC 2016 was the sixth working conference resulting from a series of successful CIAO! Workshops and EEWC Conferences over the past years. These events were aimed at addressing the challenges that modern and complex enterprises are facing in a rapidly changing world. The participants in these events share the belief that dealing with these challenges requires rigorous and scientific solutions, focusing on the design and engineering of enterprises.

This conviction has led to the effort of annually organizing an international working conference on the topic of enterprise engineering, in order to bring together all stakeholders interested in making enterprise engineering a reality. This means that not only scientists are invited, but also practitioners. Next, it also means that the conference is aimed at the active participation, discussion, and exchange of ideas in order to stimulate future cooperation among the participants. This makes EEWC a working conference contributing to the further development of enterprise engineering as a mature discipline.

The organization of EEWC 2016 and the peer review of the contributions to EEWC 2016 were accomplished by an outstanding international team of experts in the fields of enterprise engineering. The following is the organizational structure of EEWC 2016.

## Advisory Board

| | |
|---|---|
| Antonia Albani | University of St. Gallen, Switzerland |
| Jan Dietz | Delft University of Technology, The Netherlands |

## Conference Chairs

| | |
|---|---|
| Robert Pergl | Czech Technical University in Prague, Czech Republic |
| Jorge Sanz | National University of Singapore, Singapore |

## Program Chairs

| | |
|---|---|
| David Aveiro | University of Madeira, Madeira Interactive Technologies Institute and Center for Organizational Design and Engineering, INESC INOV Lisbon, Portugal |
| Antonia Albani | University of St. Gallen, Switzerland |

## Organizing Chairs

| | |
|---|---|
| David Aveiro | University of Madeira, Madeira Interactive Technologies Institute and Center for Organizational Design and Engineering, INESC INOV Lisbon, Portugal |
| Duarte Gouveia | University of Madeira and Madeira Interactive Technologies Institute, Portugal |

## Program Committee

| | |
|---|---|
| Alberto Silva | INESC and University of Lisbon, Portugal |
| Artur Caetano | University of Lisbon, Portugal |
| Carlos Mendes | University of Lisbon, Portugal |
| Carlos Páscoa | Portuguese Air Force Academy, Portugal |
| Christian Huemer | Vienna University of Technology, Austria |
| Duarte Gouveia | University of Madeira, Portugal |
| Eduard Babkin | Higher School of Economics, Nizhny Novgorod, Russia |
| Florian Matthes | Technical University of Munich, Germany |
| Frank Harmsen | Maastricht University and Ernst & Young Advisory, The Netherlands |
| Geert Poels | University of Ghent, Belgium |
| Gil Regev | École Polytechnique Fédérale de Lausanne, Switzerland |
| Graham McLeod | University of Cape Town and Inspired.org, South Africa |
| Hans Mulder | University of Antwerp, Belgium |
| Henderik Proper | Luxembourg Institute of Science and Technology, Luxembourg |
| Jan Dietz | Delft University of Technology, The Netherlands |
| Jan Verelst | University of Antwerp, Belgium |
| Jens Gulden | University of Duisburg-Essen, Germany |
| João Pombinho | University of Lisbon, Portugal |
| Joop de Jong | Mprise, The Netherlands |
| Jose Tribolet | INESC and University of Lisbon, Portugal |
| Joseph Barjis | Institute of Engineering and Management, San Francisco, CA, USA |
| Junichi Iijima | Tokyo Institute of Technology, Japan |
| Marcello Bax | Federal University of Minas Gerais, Brazil |
| Martin Op 't Land | Capgemini, The Netherlands; University of Antwerp, Belgium |
| Mauricio Almeida | Federal University of Minas Gerais, Brazil |
| Miguel Mira Da Silva | INESC and University of Lisbon, Portugal |
| Niek Pluijmert | INQA Quality Consultants, The Netherlands |
| Olga Oshmarina | Higher School of Economics, Nizhny Novgorod, Russia |
| Peter Loos | University of Saarland, Germany |
| Philip Huysmans | University of Antwerp, Belgium |
| Renata Baracho | Federal University of Minas Gerais, Brazil |
| Robert Lagerström | KTH – Royal Institute of Technology, Sweden |
| Robert Pergl | Czech Technical University in Prague, Czech Republic |
| Sérgio Guerreiro | Lusófona University, Lisbon, Portugal |
| Sanetake Nagayoshi | Waseda University, Japan |
| Steven van Kervel | Formetis, The Netherlands |
| Stijn Hoppenbrouwers | HAN University of Applied Sciences, The Netherlands |
| Ulrich Frank | University of Duisburg-Essen, Germany |
| Ulrik Franke | Swedish Defense Research Agency, Sweden |

# Contents

## Foundations of Enterprise Engineering

# Organization Implementation

# Formalizing Organization Implementation

Marien R. Krouwel[1,2]([✉]), Martin Op 't Land[1,3], and Tyron Offerman[1,4]

[1] Capgemini Netherlands, P.O. Box 2575, 3500 GN Utrecht, The Netherlands
{Marien.Krouwel,Martin.OptLand,Tyron.Offerman}@capgemini.com
[2] Radboud Universiteit, Comeniuslaan 4, 6525 HP Nijmegen, The Netherlands
[3] Antwerp Management School, Sint-Jacobsmarkt 9-13, 2000 Antwerp, Belgium
[4] LIACS, Leiden University, Niels Bohrweg 1, 2333 CA Leiden, The Netherlands

**Abstract.** Our research program aims at finding building blocks that are able to deal quickly with the constant change that organizations face. In order to do so, a deeper understanding of possible organization implementation variants is necessary, as well as the implications on the operation and IT support of organizations. In earlier research, we have composed a list of Organization Implementation Variables to informedly decide upon organization implementation, enabling traceability in governing enterprise and IT transformations. This list has been validated and extended by four practical case studies and has been formalized afterwards and validated by prototyping. In this paper the resulting framework is presented which (*a*) is broader and more detailed than before, (*b*) has a sound theoretical basis, and (*c*) contains precise and validated definitions of the variables itself. This paper shows that the framework is not only suitable for organization modeling, but also has possibilities for designing software in which implementation choices can be made explicit and variable. This paper also provides insights in the implications of implementation choices on the operation of an organization.

**Keywords:** DEMO · Enterprise engineering · Organization implementation · Agile

## 1 Introduction

As strategic and operating conditions become increasingly turbulent due to factors such as hyper-competition, increasing demands from customers, regulatory changes, and technological advancements, the ability to change, often referred to as 'agility' [1], becomes an important determinant of firm success [2]. Though change occurs in organizational essence, such as products and services delivered, most of the time change deals with different implementations [3]. Our research program [4] aims at finding building blocks that are able to deal quickly with the constant change that organizations face. In order to do so, a deeper understanding of possible organization implementation variants is necessary, as well as the implications for the operation and IT support of organizations.

© Springer International Publishing Switzerland 2016
D. Aveiro et al. (Eds.): EEWC 2016, LNBIP 252, pp. 3–18, 2016.
DOI: 10.1007/978-3-319-39567-8_1

For the process level, several approaches have been proposed for describing different process variants, e.g., [5,6]. Variants of the same process describe different implementations of the same process, differing by e.g. product type or location. These variants may either coexist or exist sequentially. These dimensions for variance can be seen as types of change, each being variable in the implementation of the processes. Others have classified different types and dimensions of process change, e.g. [7,8]. However, these approaches are restricted to the process area, whereas change does not only occur on the process level but also in the organizational structure and the (supporting) means that are available. Also, the implications for the operation and IT support are not described.

For variability in IT, the Normalized Systems theory [9] describes a list of anticipated types of changes and proposes a set of building blocks that can deal with these types of change in order to avoid combinatorial effects in which change becomes harder and harder over time. This list, however, is on a very technical level and not in terms of typical organizational changes. Instead, we are looking for a list of anticipated types of change on the organizational level, including a way in which organizational changes are transparently translated into IT changes, enabling traceability in governing enterprise and IT transformations.

Other researchers have tried to bridge the gap between organization model and IT, while leaving room for different implementation variants, making the implementation variable in some dimensions, e.g. [10–12]. However, only de Jong [12] provides a framework to systematically detail some of the design decisions that are needed to specify an Enterprise Information System. Also, none of the authors make explicit how their organizational models are used to design software; traceablity or completeness of design choices is not possible.

As an alternative, in 2013, Op't Land and Krouwel composed a list of Organization Implementation Variables (OIVs) [13], based on literature and structured according to the Enterprise Engineering Framework (EEF) [14]. The EEF has the same theoretical basis as the Design and Engineering Methodology for Organizations (DEMO) [15] which has shown to offer a quick way for finding the essence of an organization as starting point for identifying local differences [16–18]. Since then, this list of OIVs has been validated and extended by four practical case studies [19–22]. It was noticed by many reviewers that the goals and concepts of this framework were not clear. Also it was concluded that the implications towards operation and IT support should be made more clear in order to avoid implicit design choices.

Within the goals of the research program, in this paper the OIV framework is presented: its goals, requirements, concepts, as well as some example contents and its implications on the operation and IT support of organizations. With this formalized framework, it becomes easier to validate whether the framework really meets its goals. One of these goals is validated by prototyping.

The remainder of this paper is structured as follows. In Sect. 2, we will outline some terms used in this paper. Next, in Sect. 3 the research approach is presented and in Sect. 4 the resulting framework is presented, including some examples. Section 5 provides the conclusions, including the implications on operation and IT, and provides directions for future research.

## 2   Way of Thinking

Weinberg and Dietz discern two distinct perspectives on any system: function and construction [23,24]. The functional perspective, or black-box model clarifies the behavior of the system in terms of (functional) relationships between input and output of the system. The constructional perspective, or white-box model clarifies the internal construction and operation of the system in terms of collaboration between its elements to deliver products to its environment. The highest level white-box model of a system, completely independent of the way in which it is realized and implemented, is called its *ontology*. The lowest level, most detailed white-box model of a system is called its *implementation model*. By *implementation* is understood the assignment of technological means to the elements in the ontological and implementation model, so that the system can be put into operation. By *technology* we understand the means by which a system is implemented. For organizations, a wide range of technologies is available, including human beings and organizational entities, ICT artifacts (e.g., phone, email, computer programs) and mechanical means.

DEMO is a methodology for the design, engineering, and implementation of organizations [15]. As the highest level white-box model of an enterprise – a goal-oriented cooperative – DEMO defines the *enterprise ontology*: the essence of an organization, fully independent from the way in which it is realized and implemented. The organization of an enterprise is a heterogeneous system, constituted as the layered integration of three aspect systems, namely the Business (B) system, the Informational (I) system and the Documental (D) system [15, p. 115]. The production of these systems concern (B) original acts (material and immaterial), such as deciding, judging and creating, (I) informational acts, such as remembering, recalling and computing and (D) documental acts, such as storing, retrieving, transmitting and copying. The ontology of any organization (B, I or D) can be expressed in a DEMO model which consists of four aspect models:

*Construction Model (CM)* represents the composition, environment and structure of the organization and consists of transaction kinds, associated (initiating and executing) actor roles, and information banks including the links between these banks and actor roles;

*Process Model (PM)* details each transaction kind according to the transaction axiom and makes explicit the waiting links between coordination acts;

*Action Model(AM)* specifies for every agendum kind the action rules to be applied by the actor roles;

*Fact Model (FM)* contains entity types with their property types, product kinds and their relationships (fact types).

DEMO is grounded in a set of theories, among which are the FI and MU theory. FI [25] is a philosophical theory about knowledge in general and clarifies the notion of (factual) knowledge and information. It also explains how factual knowledge is created from perceptions of concrete things, directed by (fact) types, which operate as conceptual sieves. MU [26] is a theory of models and modeling in general, and of conceptual modeling in particular. It also presents General Ontology Specification Language (GOSL), a universal language for specifying conceptual complexes, conceptual schemas and meta schemas. As we are building a framework to *model facts* about the implementation of an organization, both theories provide a sound basis to build the framework on.

## 3   Way of Working

The goal of this research is to design a framework for the understanding and modeling of organization implementation, based on sound theories and validated in practice. As the result is an artifact that needs to be designed, in this research we adopt the design science methodology [27] as main methodology. Where behavioral science seeks to develop and justify theories that explain or predict phenomena related to the identified business need, design science seeks to construct and evaluate artifacts designed to meet the identified business need [28]. However, as Hevner states, these methodologies cannot be separated and should be used complementary [29]. Because design is inherently an iterative and incremental activity, Hevner suggests three cycles for Design Science Research [30] which can be applied in as many iterations as needed (Fig. 1):

- the *relevance cycle* provides the requirements for the research and determines whether the resulting artifact improves the environment;
- the *rigor cycle* provides past knowledge to the project and ensures new contributions are added to the knowledge base;
- the *design cycle* is where the artifact is constructed and evaluated.

In this paper, the result of several iterations is presented. Hevner suggests a checklist for design science research [31]. We will use that checklist (Table 1) to assess progress on this design research project. In Sect. 4 we will discuss the answers to these questions.

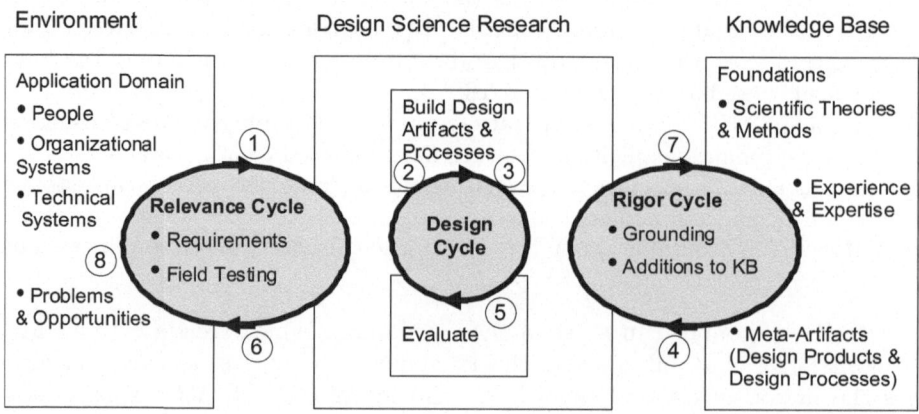

**Fig. 1.** Design Science Research Cycles [30], including references to the questions of the checklist (Table 1)

**Table 1.** Checklist for design science research [31] and section in which the question will be addressed

| 1 | What is the research question (design requirements)? | Subsect. 4.1 |
|---|---|---|
| 2 | What is the artifact? How is the artifact represented? | Subsect. 4.3 |
| 3 | What design processes (search heuristics) will be used to build the artifact? | Subsect. 4.4 |
| 4 | How are the artifact and the design processes grounded by the knowledge base? What, if any, theories support the artifact design and the design process? | Subsect. 4.2 |
| 5 | What evaluations are performed during the internal design cycles? What design improvements are identified during each design cycle? | Subsect. 4.4 |
| 6 | How is the artifact introduced into the application environment and how is it field tested? What metrics are used to demonstrate artifact utility and improvement over previous artifacts? | Subsect. 4.4 |
| 7 | What new knowledge is added to the knowledge base and in what form (e.g., peer-reviewed literature, meta-artifacts, new theory, new method)? | Subsect. 4.5 |
| 8 | Has the research question been satisfactorily addressed? | Subsect. 4.5 |

## 4   Result

In this section the result of several iterations of the OIV framework development is presented, by answering the questions of Hevners checklist (Table 1).

### 4.1   Goals and Requirements

Answering question 1, the goal of the framework is to gain insight in the implementation of an organization (either B, I or D) in order to

(a) decide informedly upon organizational changes;
(b) enable traceability and completeness in governing enterprise and IT transformations;
(c) assess to what extent IT platforms (can) support organizational implementation variability;
(d) design IT that inherently supports typical organizational changes; and, ultimately
(e) design organizations (or, better, implementations) that support typical organizational changes.

Moreover, the ontology plus implementation choices should capture all design decisions that need to be taken to come to a complete implementation model that can be put into operation. Note that the framework only concerns the 'hard' aspects that really can be chosen and changed on the short term and not the more 'soft' aspects that cannot really be changed or are very hard to change, like culture, beliefs, (shared) values or (management) style [32,33].

## 4.2   Use of Existing Theories

Answering question 4, the framework is based on existing theories in the field of Enterprise Engineering as outlined in Sect. 2. More specifically, it is built on top of the Enterprise Engineering Framework [14], fed by earlier literature research [13], and structured using DEMO [15] and the FI [25] and MU [26] theories. For the construction and evaluation, design science theories [27,28] are used, as explained in Sect. 3. The resulting framework and its concepts are presented in the next sections.

## 4.3   Concepts

In this section, the concepts of the framework are explained (question 2).

**Organization Implementation.** In the framework, by organization implementation is meant all design decisions that are taken to create the implementation model, the lowest level and most detailed white-box model, of an organization, including the assignment of technological means to the elements in the implementation model, so that the system can be put into operation.

**Variable.** In mathematics, a variable is a placeholder of some element in some set. In general, a variable is any entity that can take on different values.

**Organization Implementation Variable.** Following the mathematical definition of a variable, we will define an Organization Implementation Variable (OIV) as a placeholder for an element in the set of possible organization implementation design choices in some category. Thus, an Organization Implementation Variable describes the design freedom or restrictions in some organization implementation design category. For example, the functionary types, organizational units, work locations and authorizations, need to be decided upon before an organization can become operational. Moreover, they may be subject to change, and thus are (a) variable in the implementation of an organization. Note that an OIV is not a target variable or KPI, nor does it contain the principles that guide the decisions or the rationale behind it – an OIV belongs to the *construction* of an organization, while target variables and KPI's belong to the *function* of an organization; the principles belong to the *context* or environment in EEF terms.

Two kinds of OIVs can be distinguished: *elementary* and *cross reference* OIVs. An elementary OIV is an OIV that is not dependent on the existence of some other OIV or element in the ontology, e.g. functionary type. On the other hand, a cross reference OIV is an OIV of which the existence depends on the existence of some other OIV or element in the ontology, e.g. authorization. Therefore, a cross reference variable can be compared to a weak entity type in ER modeling [34]. More example OIVs can be found in Subsect. 4.6.

**OIV Values.** Note that there are two ways to express the value(s) of any variable:

1. by expressing the specific value or set of values by enumerating the/each value, and
2. by setting constraints, implicitly defining the value(s) of the variable.

For elementary OIVs, the first way is recommended as its value can often easily be expressed in an amount or entity. For cross reference OIVs, declaring constraints makes the resulting set more flexible, allowing for future values without having to enumerate every value explicitly.

The assignment of a value to a OIV can be modeled as a set of transaction kinds; the process of implementation design itself can be modeled in a DEMO Construction Model. The choices itself can be considered facts which are the results of transactions. They can be modeled in a DEMO Fact Model. Note that a cross reference OIV can be discerned in the FM by the presence of a *mandatory role constraint* [35, p. 315], denoted by a black dot (see legend in Fig. 2).

**Layers.** The EEF contains the layers *Parties and People* and *ICT and other means* while Dietz and Hoogervorst propose three categories for the implementation: implementation, installation, and operation [36, p. 43][1]. However, the meaning of the layers and categories was not fully spelled out, and they do not fully encompass the sourcing process as well as the assignment and scheduling of (human) resources. Therefore we propose the following layers or categories in the OIV framework.

*Implementation* contains the (non-ontological) structure of the organization such as functionary types, organizational units, work locations as well as the relations between them and with the ontological elements (mainly agendum type);
*Means* contains all technological means, including human beings and ICT artifacts – also known as silicon and carbon servers [37] – as introduced in Sect. 2, needed to operate;
*Installation* contains the (temporary or more durable) assignment of specific means to elements in the implementation;
*Operation* contains the assignment of specific agenda to specific means.

### 4.4   Construction and Evaluation Process

Answering question 3, in the design process, every OIV is defined as an entity type in a DEMO Fact Model, including definitions and examples from the EU-Rent case [38]. The example instances are used for validation by population [39, 40][2]. For every entity type, its producing transaction kind is identified and

---

[1] Note that it might be confusing that implementation itself is a category within the broader meaning of implementation. For the rest of this section, implementation is meant in the narrow definition.
[2] The term 'population' is used instead of 'instantiation' as instantiation may imply that one instance is enough, where population implies multiple instances should be used for validation.

modeled in a DEMO Construction Model. In order to enable iterations in the construction and evaluation process (questions 3 and 5), the implementations of four large European public organizations and one academic case have been modeled (for details, see Table 2), by assigning values to each of the (applicable) OIVs. This may also count as field application (question 6).

**Table 2.** Details of case studies: organization, research question, approach and results

---

**Rijkswaterstaat (RWS)** [19]

*Question* To what extent can OIVs be found in the documentation of RWS?

*Approach* Analysis of IVS90, the national supporting Information and Monitoring System of the (main) waterways and the Maritime in the Netherlands

*Results* Clearer definitions; observation instructions; 1 new OIV: Region

**Jeugdzorg Nederland** [20]

*Question* Which of the proposed OIVs can be identified in an enterprise?

*Approach* Analysis of documentation and interviews regarding the implementation of Jeugdzorg and their recently built case management system (WIJZ)

*Results* Clearer definitions; 1 new OIV: Region

**European parking law enforcer** [21]

*Question* How to build a simulation model based on a DEMO model and OIVs?

*Approach* Proposed method is applied to two cases: one fictional and one real

*Results* Clearer definitions; 2 new OIVs: agenda cluster, X-ref

**Dutch municipal subsidy providers** [22]

*Question* To what extent does the Capgemini MultiSubsidy application support the different implementations of Dutch subsidy providers?

*Approach* Analysis of documentation and interviews regarding the implementation of Dutch municipal subsidy providers and the MultiSubsidy application

*Results* Clearer definitions; no new OIVs

**EU-rent** [41]

*Question* How to construct a model to assess the support of OIVs by IT?

*Approach* Construction of DEMO CM and FM of organization implementation, validation by population with examples from EU-Rent case

*Results* Clearer definitions; CM and FM of implementation; no new OIVs

---

Additionally, a prototype has been built, based on the DEMO Fact Model (FM) as presented in Subsect. 4.6, in which the implementation, including means, installation and operation, can be configured on top of the identified transaction kinds. This helped in defining the OIVs to the level where they can be instantiated. Also, it helped gain insight in the impact on the operation. The result is a fully functional prototype in which transactions can be started and agenda are routed to authorized persons who can deal with the agenda, creating new agenda, while completely adhering to the organization implementation choices. In this prototype, no software (programming code) needs to be changed when changing the organizational implementation.

### 4.5   Additions to Knowledge Base and Practice

Answering question 7, the framework provides a more detailed insight in what organization implementation entails than earlier research does. Also, a set of Organization Implementation Variables is provided, including a method to assign a value to each OIV. This forms the foundations for a sound theory regarding organization implementation.

Answering question 8, it can be concluded from the five cases that the framework provides insight in the implementation of an organization. More specifically, we will elicit to what extent the goals of the framework are met.

(a) **decide informedly upon organizational changes:** this goal is met as a direct consequence of a detailed insight in the implementation of an organization. Although only in the case of the European parking law enforcer organizational change was proposed, the other cases show that it is possible to provide insight in the proposed change, as well as its consequences.

(b) **enable traceability and completeness in governing enterprise and IT transformations:** this goal is almost met; the detailed insight in the implementation of an organization enables traceability. Completeness is hard to claim, but the cases have only brought three new OIVs with respect to the original set of OIVs [13]. It is expected this set will not grow significantly from new case studies.

(c) **assess to what extent IT platforms (can) support organizational implementation variability:** this goal is met as confirmed by the Jeugdzorg and Dutch municipal subsidy case. However, more research is required to come to a complete method for such an IT agility assessment.

(d) **design IT that inherently supports typical organizational changes:** this goal is partly met as a first prototype is built. More research in this area will be needed in order to be able to support *all relevant* OIVs, which requires that it is clear for each OIV whether it is possible, relevant and necessary to support it in IT.

(e) **design organizations (or, better, implementations) that support typical organizational changes:** this goal is not yet met as the framework is not yet used to design implementations without combinatorial effects, i.e., such that change does not become harder over time.

### 4.6   Examples

In this section some example Organization Implementation Variable are outlined (Table 3), including some definitions and example instances (Tables 4, 5, 6, 7, 8 and 9) as well as a DEMO FM (Fig. 2) of it. This paper does not attempt to be complete as it is impossible to provide definitions for all 25 variables within the restriction of 15 pages.

**Table 3.** Example organization implementation variables

| Category | Example OIVs | |
|---|---|---|
| | *Elementary* | *Cross reference* |
| Implementation | Competence | Competence requirement |
| | Functionary type | Logical unit of work |
| | Organizational unit | Task competence |
| | Work location | Authorization |
| | Addressee | Event location restriction |
| | Juristic person | Order of working |
| Means | Human resource | Competence validation |
| | ICT artifacts | |
| | Mechanical means | |
| Installation | | Installation |
| Operation | Incidental delegation | Addressee specification |

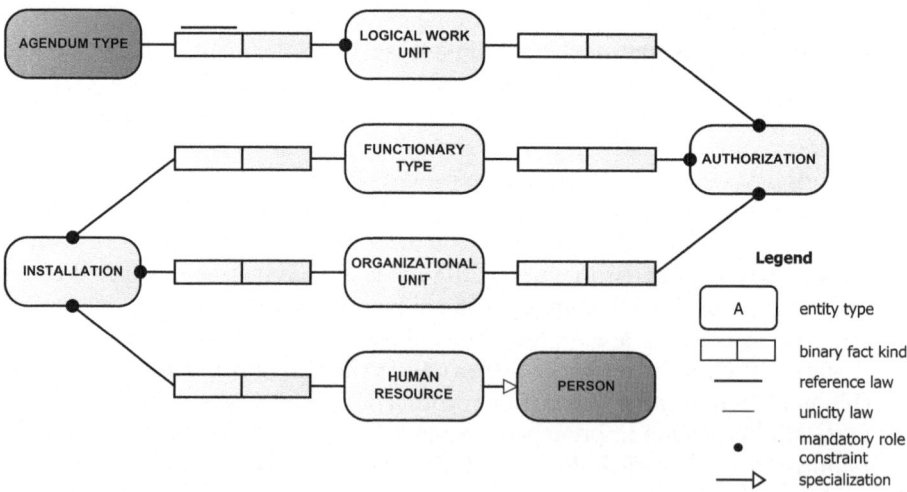

**Fig. 2.** (part of) DEMO FM for implementation design, in ORM notation [40]

**Table 4.** Functionary type

| Definition | A functionary type is a call sign intended for the assignment of agendum types |
|---|---|
| Example(s) | 1. Desk officer |
| | 2. Distributor |

**Table 5.** Organizational unit

| Definition | An organizational unit is a named element or segment of an organization, possibly with an hierarchical relation to another organizational unit. |
|---|---|
| Example(s) | 1. Sales<br><br>2. Logistics<br><br>3. Distribution, placed under Logistics<br><br>4. Transportation, placed under Logistics |

**Table 6.** Logical unit of work (LUW)

| Definition | A logical unit of work is then union of agendum types of which instances are usually dealt with by a single person as being an inseparable unit of work. Note that it is often separable, therefore the term logical is used. |
|---|---|
| Example(s) | 1. T1/pm, T1/ex and T1/st are combined in LWU 'T1 dealing' |

**Table 7.** Authorization

| Definition | An authorization is the assignment of a functionary type to a (set of) LWU(s), a(n) (set of) organizational unit(s) and a (set of) work location(s), with some responsibility (e.g. cf. RACI [42]). Note that authorization includes structural delegation, i.e., it might be possible that one functionary type is Responsible for the work, while another functionary type is Accountable. |
|---|---|
| Example(s) | 1. Desk officer is assigned to deal with T01/rq (Accountable and Responsible), in the sales unit at ABC Street 123, Leiden<br><br>2. Distributor is assigned to deal with T07/rq (Accountable and Responsible), in the distribution unit at Air Lane 23, Amsterdam |

**Table 8.** Human resource

| Definition | A human resource is a natural person who works under a contract of employ or hire agreement. Note that this includes volunteers. |
|---|---|
| Example(s) | 1. Jane is employed at RAC.<br><br>2. Chiara is employed at RAC.<br><br>3. Anthony is hired externally at RAC |

**Table 9.** Installation

| Definition | An installation is the assignment of a mean, either a human resource or a technological or mechanical mean, to a (set of) functionary type(s), a(n) (set of) organizational unit(s) and a (set of) work locations. |
|---|---|
| Example(s) | 1. Jane is assigned to desk officer in the sales department at ABCstreet 123, Leiden, Netherlands. |
| | 2. Anthony is assigned distributor in the distribution department at Air lane 23, Amsterdam, Netherlands |

**Operation.** For the operation layer, additional concepts were identified, that could not be defined as an OIV. For instance, an organization might define *info@company.com* as its general email address. Any agendum that is received on this email address needs to be routed to the right person. Often this is done by some secretary or automated system, for which the actor role *dispatcher* can be identified. This actor role needs knowledge about the possible addressees and the rules for routing general requests to a person in the organization who can deal with such a request. Note that the same reasoning holds for phone numbers and other communication channels, as well as for other agenda types that come from outside the organizations. In conclusion, additional actor roles, necessary for the implementation, installation and operation of an organization, can be identified and should be modeled in a (generic) DEMO Construction Model.

## 5 Conclusions and Future Research

The goal of this paper was to present a framework for the understanding and modeling of possible organization implementation variants, as well as to understand the implications on the operation and IT support of organizations. Using Hevners checklist, as part of looping through the three cycles of design science, we have elaborated the process, progress and preliminary results of our research;

1. the framework has as goal to gain insight in the implementation of organizations, in order to informedly decide upon organization implementation, enabling traceability in governing enterprise and IT transformations, as well as to design more agile organizations and IT;
2. the framework is built on top of several existing EE theories, fed by literature research, while DEMO is used to model the OIVs in a Fact Model, giving the framework a sound theoretical basis;
3. the framework has been evaluated against and extended by four practical case studies and one academic case study, resulting in additional OIVs and more precise definitions;
4. a prototype has been built in which the OIVs can be instantiated and its effect on the operation and IT support can be studied.

The five case studies show that the framework can indeed be used for organization implementation modeling. The prototype shows that it is possible to design software in which implementation choices can be made explicit, while allowing for future change. However, reflecting on the goals of the framework:

- The case studies are limited to public organizations. Case studies at commercial organizations should be performed in order to investigate whether they reveal new OIVs.
- Although the framework already enables assessing whether software (can) support the OIVs, it is worthwhile to investigate whether a thorough method for the assessment of IT agility can be designed.
- More research is needed to investigate whether it is possible, relevant and worthwhile to support all OIVs in software, preferably in a way that does not create combinatorial effects and consequently allowing future change without growing efforts.
- Also, more research is needed to investigate whether agile organizations without or with little combinatorial effects can be designed, enabling the agile enterprise, based on this framework.

The original framework [13] contained a layer called *ICT and other means*. In subsequent work, OIVs in this layer did not receive much attention. In fact, they are now aggregated in just two OIVs in the *Means* layer. It might be worthwhile to put more effort in finding detailed design choices in this layer, e.g. by looking at methods and modeling languages that are more focused on this layer, such as ArchiMate [43,44].

As shown in Subsect. 4.6, research in the operation layer shows that there might be some generic actor roles that should be implemented in every organization. Extending the prototype might be helpful to find all OIVs and other concepts in the operation layer. Moreover, a generic DEMO Construction Model could be made of the concepts in that layer, or maybe even for every process in the organization that is concerned with designing the organizations ontology, implementation and operation.

The prototype has not yet incorporated revocation patterns [45]. Though other researchers have put effort in translating the transaction pattern, including revocations, to software [11,46], additional research is required to investigate the impact of organization implementation (variables) on revocation, especially when implemented in software. Additionally, the topic of time outs has to be addressed, both in organization and ICT.

## References

1. Oosterhout, M.P.A.: Business agility and information technology in service organizations. Ph.D. thesis, Erasmus University Rotterdam, June 2010
2. Overby, E., Bharadwaj, A., Sambamurthy, V.: Enterprise agility and the enabling role of information technology. Eur. J. Inf. Syst. **15**, 120–131 (2006)

3. Dietz, J.L.G., Hoogervorst, J.A.P.: Enterprise ontology and enterprise architecture - how to let them evolve into effective complementary notions. GEAO J. Enterp. Architect. **2007**, 1 (2007)
4. Krouwel, M.: Towards designing modular structures for reducing non-linear effects of organizational change: research proposal. http://www.ciaonetwork.org/uploads/eewc2013/presentations/doctoral_consortium/1_krouwel.ppt. Accessed 3 April 2016
5. Lind, M., Goldkuhl, G.: Designing business process variants – using the BAT framework as a pragmatic lens. In: Bussler, C.J., Haller, A. (eds.) BPM 2005. LNCS, vol. 3812, pp. 408–420. Springer, Heidelberg (2006)
6. Hallerbach, A., Bauer, T., Reichert, M.: Capturing variability in business process models: the provop approach. J. Softw. Maintenance Evol. Res. Pract. **22**(6–7), 519–546 (2010)
7. Regev, G., Soffer, P., Schmidt, R.: Taxonomy of flexibility in business processes. In: Regev, G., Soffer, P., Schmidt, R. (eds.) BPMDS, CEUR Workshop Proceedings, vol. 236 (2006). CEUR-WS.org
8. Schonenberg, H., Mans, R., Russell, N., Mulyar, N., van der Aalst, W.M.P.: Towards a taxonomy of process flexibility. In: Bellahsne, Z., Woo, C., Hunt, E., Franch, X., Coletta, R. (eds.) CAiSE Forum, CEUR Workshop Proceedings, vol. 344, pp. 81–84 (2008). www.CEUR-WS.org
9. Mannaert, H., Verelst, J.: Normalized Systems: Re-creating Information Technology Based on Laws for Software Evolvability. Koppa, Kermt, Belgium (2009)
10. Terlouw, L.: Modularization and specification of service-oriented systems. Ph.D. thesis, TU Delft (2011)
11. van Kervel, S.: Ontology driven enterprise information systems engineering. Ph.D. thesis, TU Delft (2012)
12. de Jong, J.: A method for enterprise ontology based design of for enterprise information systems. Ph.D. thesis, TU Delft (2013)
13. Op 't Land, M., Krouwel, M.: Exploring organizational implementation fundamentals. In: Proper, H.A., Aveiro, D., Gaaloul, K. (eds.) EEWC 2013. LNBIP, vol. 146, pp. 28–42. Springer, Heidelberg (2013)
14. Op 't Land, M., Proper, H.A.: Impact of principles on enterprise engineering. In: Österle, H., Schelp, J., Winter, R. (eds.) Proceedings of the 15th European Conference on Information Systems, pp. 1965–1976 (2007)
15. Dietz, J.L.G.: Enterprise Ontology - Theory and methodology. Springer, Heidelberg (2006)
16. Mulder, J.B.F.: Rapid enterprise design. Ph.D. thesis, TU Delft (2006)
17. Op 't Land, M., Zwitzer, H., Ensink, P., Lebel, Q.: Towards a fast enterprise ontology based method for post merger integration. In: Proceedings of the 2009 ACM symposium on Applied Computing (SAC-ACM2009), pp. 245–252. ACM (2009)
18. Krouwel, M.R., Op 't Land, M.: Using enterprise ontology as a basis for requirements for cross-organizationally usable applications. In: Figueiredo, A.D., Ramos, I., Trauth, E. (eds.) Proceedings of the $7^{th}$ Mediterranean Conference on Information Systems 2012 (MCIS2012), MCIS Proceedings, University of Minho, Portugal, AIS Electronic Library (AISeL) Paper 23(2012)
19. Molly, S.: Exploring organizational implementation fundamentals in a real enterprise. Master's thesis, Antwerp Management School (2014)
20. van Bockhooven, S., Op 't Land, M.: Organization implementation fundamentals: a case study validation in the youthcare sector. In: Complementary Proceedings of the Workshops TEE, CoBI, and XOC-BPM at IEEE-COBI 2015 (2015)

21. de Laat, L., Op 't Land, M., Krouwel, M.: Supporting goal-oriented organizational implementation - combining DEMO and process simulation in a practice-tested method. In: Aveiro, D.G.D. (ed.) EEWC 2016. LNBIP, vol. 252, pp. 19–33. Springer, Heidelberg (2016)
22. Krouwel, M.R., Huysmans, P.: Observing organization implementation variables in practice: a case study on dutch municipal subsidy agents. Forthcoming
23. Weinberg, G.M.: An Introduction to General Systems Thinking. Wiley-Interscience, New York (1975)
24. Dietz, J.L.G.: Enterprise engineering - the manifesto. http://www.ciaonetwork.org/publications/EEManifesto.pdf. Accessed 3 April 2016
25. Dietz, J.L.: The FI theory - understanding information and factual knowledge. Technical report, Czech Technical University in Prague, Delft University of Technology version 2.3 (2015)
26. Dietz, J.L.: The MU theory - understanding models and modelling. Technical report, Czech Technical University in Prague, Delft University of Technology, Antwerp Management School version 1.2 (2015)
27. Simon, H.A.: The Sciences of the Artificial, 3rd edn. MIT Press, Cambridge (1996)
28. March, S.T., Smith, G.F.: Design and natural science research on information technology. Decis. Support Syst. **15**(4), 251–266 (1995)
29. Hevner, A.R., March, S.T., Park, J., Ram, S.: Design science in information systems research. MIS Q. **28**(1), 75–105 (2004)
30. Hevner, A.R.: A three cycle view of design science research. Scand. J. Inf. Syst. **19**(2), 87–92 (2007)
31. Hevner, A., Chatterjee, S.: Design Research in Information Systems: Theory and Practice, 1st edn. Springer Publishing Company, Heidelberg (2010)
32. Hayes, J.: The Theory and Practice of Change Management, 4th edn. Palgrave Macmillan, Basingstoke (2014)
33. Schein, E.H.: Organization Culture and Leadership, 3rd edn. Wiley, Hoboken (2006)
34. Chen, P.P.: The Entity Relationship Approach to Logical Database Design. Q.E.D. Information Sciences, Wellesley (1977)
35. Halpin, T.: Information Modeling and Relational Databases, 1st edn. Academic Press, Cambridge (2001)
36. Dietz, J.L.G., Hoogervorst, J.A.: EE theories Overview. Technical report, Czech Technical University in Prague (2015)
37. Tribolet, J.: An engineering approach to natural enterprise dynamics: From top-down purposeful systemic steering to bottom-up adaptive guidance control. In: 2014 International Conference on Evaluation of Novel Approaches to Software Engineering (ENASE), p. 1, April 2014
38. Object Management Group: Business Motivation Model (BMM) Specification, V1.1. OMG Available Specification OMG Document Number: formal/2010-05-01, Object Management Group http://www.omg.org/spec/BMM/1.1/PDF/. Accessed 3 April 2016
39. Dietz, J.L., Halpin, T.: Using DEMO and ORM in concert - a case study. In: Siau, K. (ed.) Advanced topics in database research, vol. 3, pp. 218–236. Idea Group Publishing, Hershey (2004)
40. Halpin, T.: Object-role modeling version 2. In: Liu, L., Özsu, M.T. (eds.) Encyclopedia of Database Systems, pp. 1941–1946. Springer, Heidelberg (2009)
41. Offerman, T.: Improving IT Supported organizational change; formalizing organizational implementation fundamentals. Master's thesis, Universiteit Leiden (2014)

42. Mike, J.M., Keller, P.J.: Business Process Mapping: Improving Customer Satisfaction. Wiley, New York (2009)
43. Open Group: Archimate 2.1 Specification. Van Haren Publishing, Zaltbommel (2013)
44. Ettema, R., Dietz, J.L.G.: ArchiMate and DEMO – mates to date? In: Albani, A., Barjis, J., Dietz, J.L.G. (eds.) CIAO! 2009. LNBIP, vol. 34, pp. 172–186. Springer, Heidelberg (2009)
45. Dietz, J.L.: The DELTA theory - understanding systems ontology. Technical report, Czech Technical University in Prague, Delft University of Technology, Antwerp Management School version 3.0 (2015)
46. Gouveia, D., Aveiro, D.: Two Protocols for DEMO Engines: PSI or Tell&Agree. CIAO DC 2015 (2015)

# Supporting Goal-Oriented Organizational Implementation - Combining DEMO and Process Simulation in a Practice-Tested Method

Lotte de Laat[1(✉)], Martin Op 't Land[2,3], and Marien R. Krouwel[2,4]

[1] ZorgDomein Netherlands, Straatweg 68, 3621 BR Breukelen, The Netherlands
mail@lottedelaat.com
[2] Capgemini Netherlands, P.O. Box 2575, 3500 GN Utrecht, The Netherlands
{Martin.OptLand,Marien.Krouwel}@capgemini.com
[3] Antwerp Management School, Sint-Jacobsmarkt 9-13, 2000 Antwerp, Belgium
[4] Radboud Universiteit, Comeniuslaan 4, 6525 HP Nijmegen, The Netherlands

**Abstract.** The increasing need for agility on one hand, and for timely and well-founded decisions on organization implementation on the other hand makes goal-oriented process simulation increasingly popular. However, a computer simulation may be of little value without a conceptual model which precedes the simulation. The Design and Engineering Methodology for Organizations (DEMO) assists in understanding and (re)designing business processes and their implementation. However, current simulation methods based on DEMO lack the notion of goal-orientation on desirable KPIs, such as service windows and reaction time. We developed a goal-oriented combined method that addresses the aforementioned issues, and tested it using both an educational and real-life case. This method helped deciding on the organization implementation, including e.g. number of FTEs and order of working, making modeling choices explicit. Combining DEMO and process simulation allows the modeler to make a well-defined balance between (a) project time and money constraints and (b) completeness of the simulation model.

**Keywords:** Computer simulation · DEMO · Organizational implementation · Goal-oriented simulation method · Enterprise engineering

## 1 Introduction

Enterprise process simulation has received increasing interest in the last years, because it offers a safe and controlled way to compare alternative enterprise implementations, and their expected outcomes [1]. However, a computer simulation may be of little value without a conceptual model that precedes the simulation [2]. Because of its claimed stability over time and its independence of organizational implementation, DEMO's ontological models have been used

© Springer International Publishing Switzerland 2016
D. Aveiro et al. (Eds.): EEWC 2016, LNBIP 252, pp. 19–33, 2016.
DOI: 10.1007/978-3-319-39567-8_2

for such a conceptual modeling of business processes [3]. However, numerical evaluation of a system is not possible when solely using DEMO models. As a consequence, DEMO modeling and computer process simulation are complementary. Therefore, it would be interesting to explore whether value can be found from a method that combines the benefits of DEMO and process simulation.

Previous research has shown that it is possible to use a combination of DEMO and simulation [2,4,5]. However, the herein proposed methods result in a process simulation of a DEMO model instead of a simulation model of process implementation alternatives. Also, to implement the enterprise ontology of a domain, many implementation choices have to be made, instantiating Organization Implementation Variables (OIVs) [6] such as delegation, order of working, and splitting or combining of roles. Current literature on DEMO and simulation does not make these choices explicit and even restricts them heavily by leaving these choices implicit. Therefore, the resulting simulation lacks significant value for supporting decision making on a broad range of implementation choices.

In this paper we propose and test the first goal-oriented method to come to a simulation process model based on a DEMO model that can support decision making in practice. We classify the method as *goal-oriented*, since the simulation model that is obtained by using the method differs per *simulation question* and *project goal* that is defined. The method therefore starts to clearly define the project goal or simulation question. Next, the DEMO models are built (or reused) with the same level of detail for internal and external actors. Then the method selects Organizational Implementation Variables (OIVs) [6], to define the degrees of freedom that are relevant for the goal at hand, and sets its range of values of interest. Finally the simulation is programmed such that, using collected data, it can answer the simulation question in terms of the selected OIVs. This method is applied on both an educational (simple pizzeria) and real-life (parking business for a large city) case.

Our method offers a way to simulate organization implementation alternatives for the same DEMO model and assess their expected outcomes. The resulting simulation model provides practically usable numerical information that supports decision making on feasible or desirable KPIs, such as service windows and reaction time, or other relevant measures such as personal or material costs. This makes the method goal-oriented, offering answers to organizational design questions. The outcomes can then be used for making organizational implementation decisions. Using organizational implementation variables, the modeler can balance between degrees of freedom expressed in OIVs, completeness of the simulation, and modeling and computational time and effort. This is a way to cope with project time and money constraints and to obtain a reusable basis for goal-oriented process simulation. In addition, this method gives the opportunity to control the Return on Modeling Effort (ROME).

The remainder of this paper is structured as follows. In Sect. 2 the problem statement of this research is given. In addition, the way of thinking and way of working is explained. In Sect. 3, the proposed method developed in this research is applied to the real-life Parking case. The results hereof can be found in Sect. 4. Lastly, the conclusions of this research can be found in Sect. 5.

## 2    Research Design

### 2.1    Problem Statement

Our research aims at investigating how to make well underpinned decisions on enterprise implementation. We adopt the definition that an enterprise is a goal-oriented co-operative [7]. In order to let an enterprise operate, it should be implemented with people and (a/o ICT-) means. The implementation of an organization is the assignment of people and (technological) means such that the system can be put to operation. Lastly, a good decision is making choices such that a set of goals is achieved. Therefore, a good organization implementation decision is defined as the assignment of people and means in the organization such that organization goals are achieved.

DEMO's ontology model can help support good implementation decision making, since it is a stable basis for an implementation model [8]. However, there are many implementation alternatives that correspond to the same DEMO model. It can be difficult to make good implementation decisions without a conceptual model behind it [4], since goals, means, and technology can change quickly over time. The *Design and Engineering Methodology of Organizations* (DEMO) [3] clarifies the essence or ontology of an enterprise. DEMO theory considers the essence of an enterprise to be the network of actors entering into and complying with commitments regarding the products or services that they bring about in cooperation, independent of the way this is organized with people and (other) means [3]. A DEMO model fully abstracts from the way objectives are realized or implemented. DEMO clarifies this on one hand by a consistent set of four ontological aspect models - hereafter called DEMO models - and on the other hand by concepts (a) for the relationship between essence and implementation with people and means and (b) for the relationship between the business organization (B-organization) and how this is realized in the Information organization (I-organization) and the Documental organization (D-Organization). Since DEMO models are implementation independent, the models stay true and stable over time, although technology, culture, and even processes may change [3]. Therefore, the DEMO models of an organization can be used as a stable foundation for considering implementation alternatives.

Previously defined transformation methods from DEMO's ontology model to implementation model have only been partly satisfactory until now. Several researchers have tried to transform a DEMO model into an implementation model or simulation model [1,2,4,5,9,10]. However, whether the proposed methods give desirable results for a broad range of simulation questions (such as different groupings of roles, or order of working) has not been researched yet. In addition, the goal of those methods is not the same as in our proposed method. Barjis [1,2] uses (discrete event) simulation, but only to visualize the DEMO models - clarifying the state of each transaction, and when a certain actor is ready to deal with an agendum. A main improvement was made by adding important operational elements like distributions and queues [5] to the basic model. However, by adding those elements on predefined places in the model, there is no guarantee that the relevant "good implementation decision making" can be supported.

Computer simulation is increasingly popular due to increasing computer power. However, in general computer simulation theory the problem of implicitly making organizational decisions is not discussed. A possible solution is to use a list of Organizational Implementation Variables (OIVs) [6]. One of the main arguments to introduce OIVs was to professionalize the work field of the business analyst [6]. In that list, the possible types of implementation choices that can be made in an organization are defined, making it possible to make implementation choices explicit and structured.

We want to develop a method that supports good implementation decision making based on a conceptual model. Our idea is that the DEMO model of an (sub)organization and the list of OIVs can be used as a stable framework to support the model building process of a goal-oriented simulation model of the organization. The developed simulation model should be (a) (partly) reusable, (b) systematically constructed, and (c) supporting explicit decision making on implementation choices. In addition, the developed method (a) takes the simulation question of interest into account, and (b) has an attractive Return On Modeling Effort (ROME).

## 2.2   Proposed Way of Thinking

As DEMO models have proven to be a stable framework independent of implementation decisions, DEMO is used as a starting point of our method. The following two axioms from the main underlying theory of DEMO, the $\Psi$-theory, are relevant for our method:

- **Operation Axiom**: People in an organization (subjects) perform two kinds of acts: Production acts (P-acts) and Coordination acts (C-acts). To focus on the acts that the subjects perform we abstract from the subjects and concentrate on the different *actor roles* they have in the enterprise. An actor is a subject fulfilling an actor role. Performing P-acts contributes to the purpose or the mission of the enterprise. By performing C-acts the actor enters into and complies with commitments about P-acts.
- **Transaction Axiom**: C-acts and P-acts occur in standard patterns, called transactions. These patterns are always started by an actor role that is referred to as *initiator* and executed by the actor role referred to as the *executor*. The basic transaction pattern for one transaction consists of five acts in the following order: request, promise, execute, state, and accept. First the initiator does the request (C-act) for production of a P-fact, followed by a promise of that P-fact by the executor. In the execution step (P-act) the executor produces the P-fact. The P-fact is presented to the initiator by the C-act state, and finally, the P-fact is accepted by the initiator. Next to these *successful* C-acts, seven other types of C-acts exists. Four if there is a problem with the transaction (quit, decline, stop, reject), and three that are involved with the revocation pattern of a transaction (revoke, refuse, allow). Finally, in practice the C-acts may be explicitly or implicitly performed.

A DEMO model of the essential level of the organization consists of four aspect models:

- **Construction Model (CM)**: represents the composition, environment and structure of the organization. The model consists of transaction types, actor roles and coordination and production bases that are connected via initiator, executor, and information links. An example of a DEMO Organizational Construction Diagram is shown in Fig. 1.
- **Process Model (PM)**: details each transaction type according to the transaction axiom. In addition to the causal links as defined in the Construction Model, waiting relationships between coordination acts are represented.
- **Action Model (AM)**: translates the Process Model into business rules that are guidelines for actors. For every agendum type, there exists at least one action rule. Additional essential rules that are not present in the Process Model can be modeled here.
- **Fact Model (FM)**: specifies the state space of the aspect models. The way objects, facts, and results are linked to each other is modeled in the FM.

Methods from existing literature that uses DEMO modeling as starting point for a simulation study [1,5] were replicated using two case studies, and tested using a set of simulation questions. The simulation questions were chosen such that they represent different types or specific areas of research, namely: (1) current system statistic, (2) what-if question, (3) DEMO unhappy flow, (4) specific goal to reach, (5) strategy change, and (6) optimization question. A main problem that should be addressed is that all currently existing methods make implicit choices about the implementation of an organization. An example is that stock can be made of semi-finished products before an order of the finished product is placed. Due to natural order of acts that is modeled in the DEMO model, it is implicitly assumed that the start of the execution of a P-act always occurs after the request of the finished product in currently existing methods. Obviously, this does not have to be true in practice. Therefore it is important to always keep track of all assumptions that are made, and by doing so making implementation choices explicit. Therefore, an *assumptions document* should always be written during the modeling process [11]. From the assumptions document it should be clear what the implications of the assumptions are.

Since so many implicit choices were found in simulation examples in literature, OIVs are used in our method. The list of OIVs aims at providing a complete list of types of variable elements in an organization, independent of the organization at hand. By knowing which elements of an enterprise are variable, the choice of value for those variables can be made explicitly. Three examples of variables from this list are given [12]:

- **Functionary type**: a functionary type is a call sign intended for the assignment of agendum types. E.g. functionary type "transporter", who can react on the agendum types paid purchase/stated and completed purchase/promised.
- **Human Resource**: a human resource is a natural person who works under a contract of employ or hire agreement.

– **Competences**: relevant competences necessary in the organization to fulfill P-acts and C-acts.

In addition to the list of variable elements in the organization, cross-references are defined. Those can be interpreted as implementation rules for the range of possible implementations. An example of such a cross reference is *functionary type y can only work at work location x*. So, although multiple work locations and functionary types exists, the set of feasible implementations should be defined.

Next to the lack of explicit choices, other problems with the previously developed methods were found. Based on a simple pizzeria case, a set of simulation questions were identified to test the existing methods. An important implication that was found is that the transformation methods are not goal-oriented. A simulation model of the organization should be goal-oriented such that it can be defined whether the obtained simulation is satisfactory. A simulation question should be defined at the beginning of a simulation project and has to reflect the goal of the project. The simulation question makes the project goal-oriented and makes every participant of the project heading in the same direction [11]. Existing methods do not define a simulation question, however the way a simulation is built highly depends on it. An example is that a company may consider to merge two departments, or the company wants to know how queuing time changes when increasing the number of costumers with 20 %. With the first question, two different company structures have to be compared within one environment. The second question implies only one structure, but a changing environment. For that reason, the elements of the simulation that can be hard coded or should be kept variable in the simulation differ. Furthermore, the methods make use of a (semi) automatic transformation from DEMO model to simulation model. This results in one possible (sub)implementation. The simple example of a pizzeria shows that a one-to-one relation between essence and implementation is not true. For example, a pizzeria has as essence to deliver pizzas. The pizzeria can choose to prepare pizzas in advance and only finish them at the moment of order entry, or the pizzeria can start from scratch at the moment of order entry. Therefore, the relation between ontology and implementation is one-to-many, since there can be an endless amount of implementation alternatives for one DEMO model. Therefore, the range of simulation questions that can be answered with one possible implementation model is limited.

Lastly, the method allows for both continuous and discrete event simulation and does not restrict the choice of simulation software or programming language.

## 2.3   Proposed Way of Working

We will now elaborate on a way of working for transforming a DEMO model into a simulation model, based on the way of thinking outlined above. The main principles behind our way of working are:

– The method is goal-oriented;
– All implementation choices are made explicitly;

- All (modeling) assumptions and choices are documented;
- The modeling time and effort can be controlled.

Based on the above principles, the results found by testing multiple transformation methods, and the boundary condition that simulation is suitable for this project (e.g., instead of static analysis or intervening in the operational situation; see [11]), the following steps are defined for our method:

**Step 1:** formulate the simulation question and plan the study, taking time and money constraints into account.

**Step 2:** make *or reuse* the four DEMO aspect models of the enterprise. The boundaries of the relevant part of the enterprise can be adapted to fit the research question.

**Step 3a:** define relevant OIVs. Not all OIVs are relevant for the simulation study. Dependent on the research question and time and money constraints, a distinction is made between relevant and irrelevant OIVs.

**Step 3b:** select a range for the relevant OIVs. If an OIV is relevant for the goal of the study, it should be given a one point solution (not variable in the study), or a range of possible solutions (variable in the study). The larger the amount of possible solutions, the harder it is to answer the research question, but the more precise and realistic the solution will be.

**Step 4:** make an assumptions document, collect data and define and design the simulation model(s). In the assumptions document the assumptions made in step 3 are noted. Furthermore, assumptions made on the DEMO model, OIVs, attributes and distributions of entities[1], attributes and entities of resources, and any other relevant choice made during the modeling process has to be denoted in this document. Entities entering the model can be based on the Fact Model. In addition, assumptions are made about agenda clusters that can be simulated as a whole. The model can now be designed based on the structure of the DEMO model, implementation choices explicitly made about the OIVs, and the assumptions document; this designed model should reflect the assumptions that are made. Finally, note that the internal and external actor roles should be considered with the same importance in this document, even though the business rules for those actor roles are not known. This indicates that assumptions about this business rules have to be made.

**Step 5:** build the designed simulation model and check validity. Does the assumptions document match with the built simulation model? Only if validity is confirmed, the modeler can continue to the next step.

**Step 6:** run the computer simulation model. Finally, the simulation model can be programmed using the chosen software/language and run for a range of simulation parameters.

**Step 7:** did the simulation answer the simulation question? If not re-iterate from step 3.

---

[1] Attributes are parameters which accompany an entity as it moves through the model [13]. An example of an attribute is the amount of pizzas that are part of the order.

## 3  The Approach in Practice

A real-life case referred to as the *Parking case* is used to test the proposed Way of Working. A city in Europe is outsourcing all its parking activities. This includes managing long and short term parking rights, parking law enforcement, parking meter control and maintenance, and all information providing activities. In this paper we focus on the law enforcement activities of the case. Law enforcement is conducted by *scan cars*, which are equipped with scanners that can match license plates with parking licenses. When no match is found between a scanned car and a valid parking license, a *scan scooter* is send to the *suspicious car*. The scan scooter is equipped with similar scanning tools, which are used by the driver to check whether there is a case of illegal parking. This step is necessary because the suspicious vehicle has the right to some time to buy a ticket (5 min), or could have been (un)loading cargo (for which a vehicle does not require a parking license). When the scan scooter confirms that no valid license ticket matches the vehicle, the vehicle will receive a fine. This fine has to be paid to the city's tax office.

The potential international contractor has to present a plan to the city how the parking activities are going to be filled in if they are contracted. The city will contract the party with the best procurement plan. The city and the contractor have conflicting incentives. The goal of the city is to maximize the percentage of fined cars of all cars in violation and maximize the number of bought licenses. The contractor wishes to fulfill its tasks at the lowest possible costs, since it receives money for the assignment in total and not per imposed fine. Therefore, the contracted party receives a payment for carrying out the project, and additionally a bonus or malus. This bonus-malus calculation is based on 2 KPI's, namely (1) the payment- and (2) the checking-rate in the different districts of the city, as estimated by the city. If both the estimated payment- and checking-rate is not above a threshold in a district, the contracted party will receive a malus for that district, and no bonus for any other district. If the estimated payment rate is above a certain threshold for all districts the contractor receives a bonus.

The DEMO model of the Parking case was made before the simulation project started. Part of the Organizational Construction Diagram that is relevant for the parking law enforcement activities can be found in Fig. 1.

In step 1 of the simulation project the goal of the project is defined. The goal of the contractor is to get more insight in the parking law enforcement area of the city in general and the potential profit that can be made. It is decided that the best way to do this is to simulate the Parking case to find the optimal implementation strategy for the case. Therefore, the following simulation question is constructed: *what is the most profitable way for the contractor to conduct the parking-law enforcement activities?*

For step 2 of the project the simulation plan of the DEMO model is reused. The part of the DEMO model that is reused is based on the *key actor roles*. Note that, in contrast with DEMO theory, no difference will be made between internal and external actor roles within the simulation project. The *parker* and *parking*

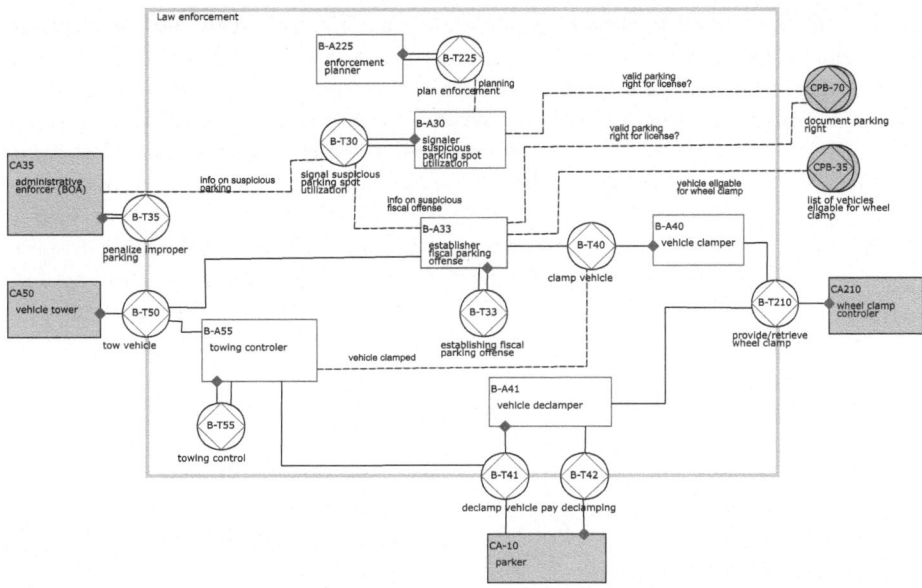

**Fig. 1.** Part of organizational construction diagram of the Parking case.

*law enforcers* are defined as the most important roles, based on the assignment and research question. From this two roles, the parker is an external actor role, since it cannot be controlled within the boundaries of the enterprise. However, the environment of the enterprise will have to be simulated to obtain any results, even though the action rules of the enterprise environment are not all known. All elements of the DEMO model that are connected (via a causal or information link) with at least one of the key actor roles are defined as relevant. Remark is that it may be that self-initiating actor roles are relevant for the project, but may not be connected with a key player. In our case study it happens that one self-initiating actor role was not present in the DEMO model that was relevant for the simulation study. A second difficulty to finding this actor role was that it was an information providing actor role (DEMO informa level), and in our DEMO model only actor roles that produce original facts are modeled (DEMO performa level).

Step 3 is the next step to come from the DEMO model to an implementation model, by defining the relevant OIVs. First the OIVs that are relevant for the simulation question are set. For example, language support is not relevant for this simulation question, since the supported languages in the organization do not influence the parking law enforcement. Now that this OIV is set to be irrelevant, it is not variable within the organization. An example of a relevant OIV is competence, since certain diplomas are needed to drive a scooter or car. However, to answer the simulation question we are looking for an answer on how many scan scooters and cars are optimal. It can be assumed that the competences needed are not an issue when contracting personal (this is denoted in the assumptions document). Therefore, this OIV is not set to be variable within the simulation. An example of an OIV that is variable within the organization is *human resource*, since the amount of personnel will vary in the simulation scenarios. However, although the amount of human resources will be variable, more detailed information on human resources is irrelevant for the simulation question in this stage of the project.

On top of the OIVs one new concept is introduced for simulation purposes: agenda clusters. Some agenda will be performed in a (undisturbed) sequence. By introducing this OIV, an important bridge between agenda and implementation is made. In the simulation, a sequence of agenda can be simulated as a whole instead of considering C- and P-acts separately as is done in previous methods. The advantage hereof is that some agenda are performed tacitly in practice, which may make them irrelevant for the simulation. Since they do not take (a significant amount of) time to take place they do not influence the results of the simulation. However, they do take unnecessary computer time to run. Secondly, the time it takes to finish an agenda may be impossible to measure. For example, a phone call is made in which an order is requested and promised. The whole length of the phone call is relevant for the performance of the organization, but it is unclear how one would measure the exact time of the request and the promise separately. However, it is fairly easy to measure the time it takes to handle a phone call, and even some administrative tasks that are correlated. Therefore, it is a natural choice to simulate some agenda together, that makes the data collection process for the simulation much more manageable. The clustering of agenda for the parking case is shown in Fig. 2. Note that clusters should be based on the Process Structure Diagram (PSD) and not the Organizational Construction Diagram (OCD), since a cluster of agenda can handle agenda related to more than one transaction or part of a transaction. Take for example the delivery of a pizza. The request of payment is simulated in a cluster together with the delivery of the pizza. However, the promise and payment itself is simulated within another cluster. The choice for a cluster can be led by the natural order of things, the possibilities for data collecting, and the time constraints of the simulation.

The choices made on the clusters, and other OIVs may impact the outcome of the simulation. Therefore, all assumptions that are made, for example that language support does not influence the outcome of the simulation, are written down in an assumptions document, which is step 4 of the project. All the choices made on relevance, variability, and level of detail lead to one or more simulation models, and the correlated data collection. The assumptions document contains all this information, including the DEMO model, and is written in such a way that there is insight in the simulation choices and the impact of those choices for anyone concerned. In every step of the simulation process, the assumptions document is filled and checked for correctness. Based on the information collected in the assumptions document, it may be that relevant information for the project becomes clear without building the simulation. For the parking case, basic statistical calculations were performed to calculate an expected chance for

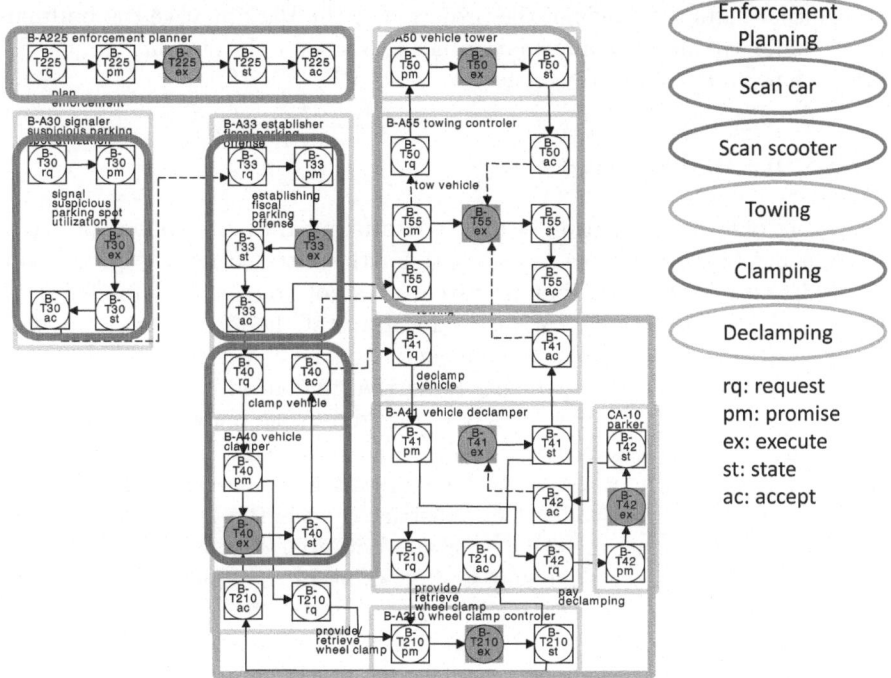

**Fig. 2.** Agenda clusters of the Parking case, drawn over the DEMO PSD.

a malus. The resulting chance was much higher than expected, and this information was used to change the plan for the simulation model slightly with respect to the output that should be delivered.

The assumptions document now contains all information to program the simulation model(s). This step is integrated with the writing of the assumptions document, because an important principle is that the built model reflects the assumptions that are made. For example, the way a queue is programmed reflects the assumption on the handling of a queue in practice. Therefore, both the assumption on the queue, and the way it is programmed are documented. In addition, the translation from DEMO model to simulation model is documented. An example is that the actor role *establisher fiscal parking offense* is implemented by both the contractor and the city. The contractor to be able to hand out fines, and the city implements this role to estimate the extent of the bonus or malus. Both implementations are documented and programmed to make an estimation of the impact of the implementations on the simulation question.

The confirmation of the correctness of the built model is step 5 of the project. It is checked whether the proposed model reflects all assumptions and business rules correctly. For the parking case Arena Simulation was used for step 6 of the project. There is no restriction in the choice of simulation program or language. The project team should choose the simulation program or programming language that suits the needs of the project. For the Parking case the built simulation model satisfied the information-need to answer the simulation question, and therefore no re-iteration was needed in step 7.

## 4    Results in Practice

By carrying out the simulation study, it was found that the chance of getting a bonus is not high enough to compensate for the extra corresponding personal costs, which implies that the bonus system does not trigger the intended incentive. This result is in contrast with the incentive of the city. At some point in time a period is reached in which the incentive of the city is counteracted by its own introduced Bonus-Malus scheme. From the simulation it became clear that this is due to two reasons. First, the potential difference between real checking-rate and the estimated checking-rate, since this may result in an 'unfair' malus. Secondly, this effect is increased since this system is in place for eight districts, and receiving a malus for at least one district cancels the bonus for any other district. For that reason, the advice for the potential contractor is to propose a new method to estimate payment- and checking-rates, which reflects the real goals of all stakeholders better.

By discussing the outcome of the simulation study with the possible contractor, it became clear that the outcome of the study was a surprise. The chance of a malus, with as consequence no bonus, was much higher than anticipated. The possible contractor only worked with the DEMO models to make a plan, before the simulation was available. DEMO models do not give numerical insight or information about the probabilities of an event. Therefore, the possible contractor was surprised about this result. This is an indication of the value that can be added by making use of simulation models as an addition to DEMO models.

Furthermore, value was also added by the data collection process which preceded the finished simulation study. An example is that a current payment rate in one of the districts is 72 %. However, the payment threshold is equal to 80 %. This is an unrealistic requirement, which is out of the power of the possible contractor. When only the DEMO models of the project would have been considered, these kind of numerical issues would not have been encountered. Due to the insights given by the simulation, the impact of those unrealistic numbers is brought to the surface and discussed with the city.

An advantage of the proposed method became clear while programming the simulation. There was only a short time period between the moment data was made available by the city and when the contract plan had to be submitted. Therefore, it was decided to build only a part of the simulation, and add more level of detail when insufficient results were found or time constraints allowed it. First, only the clusters enforcement planning, scan car, and scan scooter where programmed, with the correct variable parameters as decided upon in the assumptions document. The resulting set of simulations already gave enough insight to know that the bonus-malus system is expected to cause the wrong incentives. Due to the structure of the implementation, the remaining clusters of acts would only give another indication of additional costs. Mathematical methods could be used to give an expectation of these costs. This saved both programming time, and computer time. Since computer time was the biggest issue with this particular simulation study, this choice allowed for a successful optimization of the simulation within the available time period.

It was known that if the possible contractor would be chosen, there would be a need for a more detailed simulation study. Therefore, the simulation was built in such a way that it can be extended easily with the clusters of agenda that were not programmed yet. Calculation time would grow significantly for this renewed simulation, but the available time will not be a restriction anymore. Note that it is possible to take into account future changes in the simulation program, since the DEMO models and OIVs on the topic are clear. Therefore, not only the DEMO models are reusable, but also the simulation program. The reusability of the program can be taken into account depending on the nature of the study and the time constraints of the project.

## 5   Conclusions and Future Research

The goal of this research was to develop a goal-oriented method, based on DEMO conceptual modeling, that supports decision making on organizational implementation alternatives. Three existing transformation methods have been tested for this purpose. The main conclusion is that these methods result in the simulation of a DEMO model and do not support decision making on organizational implementation alternatives. In addition, implicit assumptions are made within currently existing methods. As a result, not all simulation question can be answered, or the resulting simulation model may even be wrong. It can be concluded that current literature focuses on providing proof that *a simulation model can be based on a DEMO model*. In this paper, the focus is shifted to combining DEMO and simulation in order to *reach the goal of the simulation study*.

The first step for improvement is to take the goal of the simulation study explicitly into account, thus making the transformation method goal-oriented. In addition, all modeling choices should be made explicitly and should be documented. A seven-step method is developed that suffices these needs. In this newly proposed method OIVs are used to bridge the gap between the enterprises ontology and its implementation. Additionaly to existing OIVs, the concept of *agenda clusters* was introduce which deals with the gap between strict separation of agenda in DEMO theory, and the fuzzy gap between agenda that may be present in practice. This full list gives the modeler the opportunity to find a balance between simulation time, project time and money constraints, and completeness of the simulation model. Although the usage of OIVs and agenda clusters bring ontology and implementation together, the DEMO model still has to be built with caution with respect to the goal of the study. Next to that, the need for agenda clusters shows that OIVs alone is not enough to bridge the gap between ontology and simulation. Whether the additional agenda clusters fulfills this need for any simulation study in general should be further researched.

In this research it became clear that the line between internal and external actor roles becomes fuzzy in a simulation environment. The answer to a simulation question depends heavily on the simulated business environment. When using a DEMO model for simulation purposes it may be an improvement to draw the boundary of an enterprise around actor roles that are important for the simulation question of interest instead of using the boundary line as a separation based on the control over the action rules of the actor role. In addition, for the simulation it may be necessary that actor roles with an information providing (informa) service should be modeled, because non-standard calculations may be necessary to answer the simulation question.

The value of the use of computer simulation is highlighted by results of the Parking case. With the use of the simulation method proposed in this paper several implementation options in terms of the number of employees could be compared. This comparison could not have been made by the sole consideration of a DEMO model or filled in OIVs. However, the impact of the use of simulation extends beyond the possibility of comparing multiple options. In the Parking case, the results of the simulation study showed that the incentives of the city and the potential contractor are conflicting. Now that this information is known, a proposal can be made based on that information to change the contract in a way that is beneficial for both the client and the contractor. In addition, numerical mistakes and unrealistic requirements from the client were identified in the process of building the simulation model. It should be noted that the value of (static) mathematical methods should not be neglected during the simulation process. Static calculations can be used as a quick way to find focus areas in the simulation study, or even to sharpen the simulation question.

The proposed method is the first step to bring DEMO modeling and computer simulation together, while simultaneously considering the goal of the study. The method has been based on the results of a theoretical case study, and tested on one real life case study. Additional testing on several cases is required to see whether the method is adequate in general. The generality of the methods proposed in current literature and in this paper were tested. Although the proposed method gave better results on the basis of the studied cases, this is no proof that this holds for all simulation questions in general. This is an additional reason that the proposed method should be tested on multiple cases. Lastly, the method proposed in this paper provides much more degrees of freedom for the modeler, because choices are made explicitly. This takes both more modeling and documentation time than in the methods from previous literature. However, the modeling time and effort to come to the simulation model can be controlled by the modeler in the proposed method. Therefore, together with the goal orientation, a good Return On Modeling Effort (ROME) can be obtained. The ROME can not be controlled in the previously defined models, since the base structure is based on a one-to-one translation of the underlying DEMO model.

Finally, during the modeling of several implementation alternatives of the different cases that were considered, the relationship between technological progress and a DEMO model was sometimes unclear. The DEMO methodology for Process Modeling and Action Modeling relatively easily introduces wait conditions, of which some appear to embody "order of working" in stead of pure (unavoidable) ontological dependencies. For example, a PSD for a pizzeria could show a wait condition between the C-act accept baking and the P-act of delivery. However, when using a food-truck with a built-in oven, it is possible to drive the order to the customer, while baking the order. This implies that the introduction of a certain technology would change the DEMO model, while the moment of baking could be interpreted as an implementation choice. Therefore, this choice might better not be made via a wait condition within the DEMO model. The question arises: how do implementation possibilities that do not exist right now, but might exist in the future, change a DEMO model? Further research should help making the DEMO methodology here more precise to prevent implicit implementation choices, which might hinder future agility.

# References

1. Barjis, J.: Enterprise modeling and simulation within enterprise engineering. J. Enterp. Transform. **1**, 185–207 (2011). Taylor & Francis
2. Barjis, J.: Automatic business process analysis and simulation based on DEMO. Enterp. Inf. Syst. **1**(4), 365–381 (2007a). Taylor & Francis
3. Dietz, J.L.G.: Enterprise Ontology. Springer, Heidelberg (2006)
4. Barjis, J.: Developing executable models of business systems. In: Enterprise Information Systems (ICEIS), vol. 3, pp. 5–13. Taylor & Francis (2007b)
5. Liu, Y., Iijima, J.: Automatic model transformation for enterprise simulation. In: Aveiro, D., Tribolet, J., Gouveia, D. (eds.) EEWC 2014. LNBIP, vol. 174, pp. 136–150. Springer, Heidelberg (2014)
6. Op 't Land, M., Krouwel, M.: Exploring organizational implementation fundamentals. In: Proper, H.A., Aveiro, D., Gaaloul, K. (eds.) EEWC 2013. LNBIP, vol. 146, pp. 28–42. Springer, Heidelberg (2013)
7. Daft, R.: Organization Theory and Design. Cengage learning, Boston (2012)
8. Krouwel, M., Op 't Land, M.: Using Enterprise Ontology as a basis for Requirements for Cross-Organizationally Usable Applications. AIS Electronic Library (2012)
9. Poletaeva, T., Abdulrab, H., Babkin, E.: Ontological foundations of multi-agent framework for organizational diagnosis. In: Kobyliński, A., Sobczak, A. (eds.) BIR 2013. LNBIP, vol. 158, pp. 170–184. Springer, Heidelberg (2013)
10. Wang, Y., Albani, A., Barjis, J.: Transformation of DEMO metamodel into XML schema. In: Albani, A., Dietz, J.L.G., Verelst, J. (eds.) EEWC 2011. LNBIP, vol. 79, pp. 46–60. Springer, Heidelberg (2011)
11. Law, A.M.: Simulation Modeling and Analysis, 4th edn. McGraw Hill, New York (2007)
12. Krouwel, M., Op 't Land, M., Offerman, T.: Formalizing organization implementation. In: Aveiro, D. (eds.) EEWC 2016, LNBIP 252, pp. 3–18. Springer, Heidelberg (2016)
13. Kelton, W.D., Sadowski, R.P., Sadowski, S.N.B.: Simulation with ARENA. WCB/McGraw-Hill, New York (2011)

# Value and Co-creation

# Objectifying Value Co-creation –
# An Exploratory Study

João Pombinho[1]([⊠]), Carlos Mendes[1], Bruno Fragoso[1],
Ricardo Santos[1], Nuno Silva[1], Elton Sixpence[1], and José Tribolet[1,2]

[1] Instituto Superior Técnico, University of Lisbon, Lisbon, Portugal
{jpmp, carlos.mendes, bruno.fragoso, ricardomssantos,
nuno.miguel, elton.sixpence}@tecnico.ulisboa.pt
[2] Instituto de Engenharia de Sistemas e Computadores,
Investigação e Desenvolvimento, Lisbon, Portugal
jose.tribolet@inesc.pt

**Abstract.** Understanding value co-creation has been identified has a critical research topic area due to the evolution on how customers design, produce and consume products/services. Moreover, there is a plethora of theory sources that address it and an apparent lack of alignment between them. In this exploratory study, we use enterprise engineering techniques, namely organizational modelling methodologies (DEMO and e3Value), to clarify the co-creation and co-design concepts. In order to do so, we extended the Flower Shop case with procedures that were identified in the literature as co-creation. The analysis of this case allowed us to objectify the co-design and co-production concepts by defining in which specific modelling patterns these concepts can be illustrated, in order to make them explicit and assert alignment with the business model. Furthermore, such analysis has supported specification of a generic co-creation (sub)organization which serves as a reference for alignment with service design and management knowledge areas.

**Keywords:** Enterprise ontology · DEMO · e3Value · Value co-creation · Co-design · Co-production · Value model · Value network

## 1 Introduction

The context involving services has dramatically changed in the last decades. Achievements in information technology allowed the development of new revolutionary services and changed how customers serve themselves before, during, and after purchase (Ostrom et al. 2015). In order to deal with, and understand these changes, new disciplines emerged. One of these disciplines is Service Science that focuses not merely on one aspect of service, but rather on service as a system of interacting parts that include people, technology, and business (Chesbrough and Spohrer 2006). Additionally, Service Science is the study of service systems and the co-creation of value in complex configurations of resources (Vargo et al. 2008).

Despite the contributions to this discipline there is still the need for further development in topics such as the 12 research priorities identified by (Ostrom et al. 2015).

© Springer International Publishing Switzerland 2016
D. Aveiro et al. (Eds.): EEWC 2016, LNBIP 252, pp. 37–53, 2016.
DOI: 10.1007/978-3-319-39567-8_3

One of these topics is understanding value creation. This topic involves the orchestration of several roles and resources in order to produce results that may be in the interest of several stakeholders. Clarifying some topics involved in this orchestration is a critical research area (Ostrom et al. 2015). We focused in three subtopics of the research priority 'understanding value creation':

– Integrating the roles of customers, employees, and technology for value creation;
– Understanding value creation in multi-actor, network, and collaborative contexts;
– Specifying the concept and operationalization of value co-creation.

Another research priority identified by (Ostrom et al. 2015) addressed in this research is leveraging service design and the respective subtopics:

– Involving customers through participatory design and co-design to enhance service experience;
– Aligning service design approaches with existing organizational structures.

These five subtopics are the fields in which this exploratory research may contribute with new knowledge. In order to do so, we propose to use enterprise engineering principles to clarify the co-creation concept. In the process we use DEMO (Design & Engineering Methodology for Organizations) white box models and e3Value models to differentiate co-creation and co-design, and to specify a generic co-design organization. A white-box model is a conceptualization of the definition of an ontological system and captures its construction and the operation, while abstracting from implementation details (Dietz, J. 2006). Therefore, we present the ontological transactions (DEMO) and value objects (e3Value) that may be involved in co-creation and co-design.

The remaining document is structured as follows. Next, we present related work, starting with an overview of related work in service science, enterprise engineering and business modelling. Then, we will use the case of a florist to highlight certain aspects relevant to our research through the creation of DEMO and e3Value models. The following section, (re)defining co-creation: co-design and co-production, presents the main contribution. The paper closes with conclusions, limitations in the present research and projection of future work.

## 2  Related Work

This research crosses different knowledge areas, namely Service Science, Enterprise Engineering and Business Modelling. In this section we will briefly introduce relevant aspects of each and how they are related in addressing our problem.

### 2.1  Service Science

Service science focuses not merely on one aspect of service, but rather on service as a system of interacting parts that include people, technology, and business (Chesbrough and Spohrer 2006). This discipline has given a greater focus and attention toward intangible and dynamic aspects of exchange (Vargo et al. 2010), where its service-centred view is based on the idea that service – the application of competences for the benefit of another – is the basis of all exchange (Vargo and Akaka 2009).

In this understanding of service is important to note that in Service Dominant logic (S-D-logic) there are no "services" (intangible units of output), but only the service provision that occurs among service systems, and the nature of value co-creation among service systems (Vargo et al. 2010). Service provision can then be considered central to value creation and holistically, embedded in reciprocal systems of exchange, where service exchange and value co-creation need to be analysed as a complex phenomenon due to the fact that Actor relations characterize value co-creation as embedded in multi-agent systems with converging contributions (Wieland, Polese, Vargo & Lusch 2012).

In (Chathoth, P. et al. 2013), a fundamental distinction is made regarding multi-actor collaboration in different facets of service system development and operation:

- Co-production refers to the "interactive nature of services" (Yen et al. 2004). Yen et al. point out that "in service encounters characterised by high customer partici-pation (e.g., hairdressing, medical consultations, education) customers are usually physically present to receive the service and are often called on to provide critical information that is necessary for effective delivery of the service".
- Co-creation is described as involving a high level of customer participation in customising the product or service, which requires "collaboration with customers for the purpose of innovation" (Kristensson et al. 2008).

(Chathoth, P. et al. 2013) compares those two concepts according 6 criteria, namely, value creation, customer's role, customer participation and expectation, focus, innovation and communication. On co-production the customer is passive, rely on the physical environments provided and is perceived as resource, whereas, on co-creation customer is active, provide input to service provider before, during, and after service. Act as information provider or value creator. In fact, the authors already consider these two concepts as a continuum rather than a dichotomy. In this research, we propose a more objective definition of each through modelling.

## 2.2 The Discipline of Enterprise Engineering (EE)

The EE discipline addresses a set of methodological foundations for answering three generic goals: intellectual manageability, organisational concinnity, and social devotion (Dietz et al. 2013). Each of these goals are correlated with the design, governance, and management of an enterprise. In order to achieve these goals, Dietz (Dietz et al. 2013) has formulated seven fundamentals to be used as guidelines that are easier adopted than the class of EE theories.

**Enterprise Ontology (EO): Theory and Methodology.** The Ontological theory is one of the EE theory classes that addresses cause-effect relationships in systems. Its $\psi$-theory (Performance in Social Interaction theory) concern is towards the ontological essence of organizations. It clarifies and explains the construction and operation of organizations as social systems, where humans are given social roles, with a degree of authority and responsibility according to their role (Dietz et al. 2013). Hence, the ψ-theory provides an effective notion of EO, as the (constructional) essence of an organization depriving all of the realization and implementation understanding.

**DEMO.** Design and Engineering Methodology for Organizations (DEMO) includes a sound theory and a method for supporting EE. It goes beyond traditional function (black-box) perspective, aiming at changing organizations based on the construction (white-box) perspective. Organizations are considered as systems composed of social actors and their interactions in terms of social commitments regarding the production of business facts. From its Transaction Axiom, we find that actors perform two kinds of acts. By performing production acts (P-acts), the actors contribute to bringing about and delivering services to the environment. By performing coordination acts (C-acts), ac-tors enter into and comply with commitments. P-acts and C-acts occur in generic re-current patterns, called transactions. According to DEMO theory, every transaction process is some path through this complete pattern, and every business process in every organization is a connected collection of such transaction processes.

DEMO is able to produce concise, coherent and complete models (regarding its scope of application) with a significant reduction in model complexity, compared to traditional approaches like flowcharts and BPMN (J. L. G. Dietz 2008). This feature has a major role in intellectually managing complexity as it allows abstracting from information and data and to focus on business transactions specification.

DEMO does not aim at modelling the teleological aspects of a system, namely its purpose and development rationale. As such, while it excels at applying sound actor interaction theory to static configurations, its application to evaluating, deciding and executing change benefits from being used in conjunction with other approaches.

## 2.3    Value Modelling

**e3Value.** e3Value (Gordijn 2002) is an ontological approach for modelling networked value constellations. It is directed towards e-commerce and analyses the creation, exchange and consumption of economically valuable objects in a multi-actor network.

In e3Value, an Actor is perceived by his or her environment as an economically independent entity. Actors exchange Value Objects (VO) transferred through Value Ports, which are directional elements of Value Interfaces. Actors form an intercon-nected, value object-exchanging network. e3Value provides essential value mapping from a high-level perspective but, unlike DEMO, it lacks a holistic and formal framework for enterprise modelling, i.e., constructability.

In conjunction, the two approaches provide an integrated and complete conceptual coverage the 3 complementary perspectives of a system (Pombinho 2015): construction (white-box), function (black-box) and purpose (outside-box), as depicted in Fig. 1.

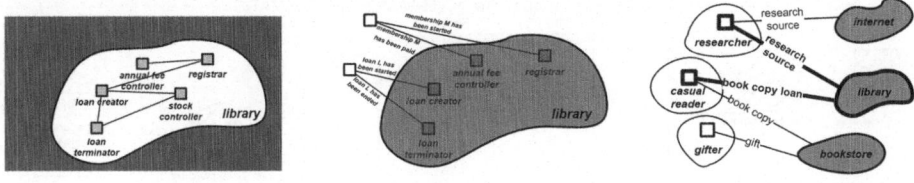

**Fig. 1.** Construction, function and purpose perspectives of a system – Library example

DEMO is adequate for construction and function perspectives and e3Value addresses the purpose perspective. As such, we chose to apply both approaches to shed light on different value co-creation modelling issues.

## 2.4 Value-Oriented System Development Process

In order to deal with model-supported change in enterprise settings (Pombinho 2015) defines an Enterprise Transformation Cycle. A formal specification of the process and the (sub) organization that implements it follows (Figs. 2, 3, and 5).

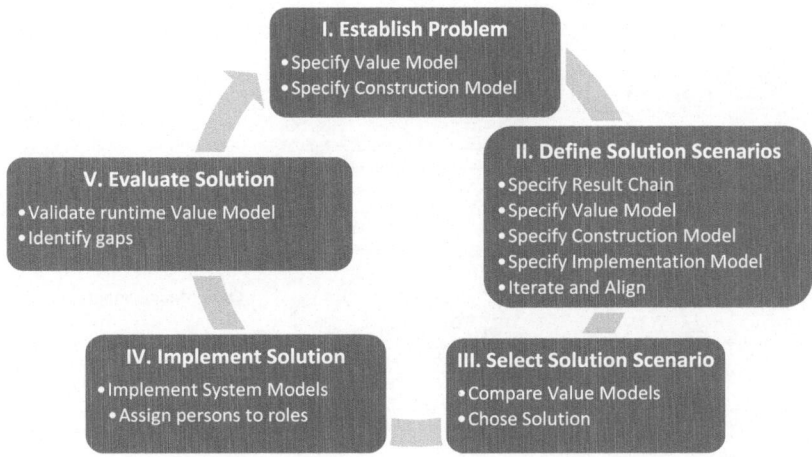

**Fig. 2.** Enterprise transformation cycle, adapted from (Pombinho 2015)

The cycle comprises 5 stages:

- **I. Establish Problem**. The process involves first establishing the problem in terms of a value model and ontological model of the Using System (US).
- **II. Define Solution Scenarios**. Beginning with the VO sought-after by the US, a number of solution scenarios is generated, followed by the corresponding value, construction and implementation models.

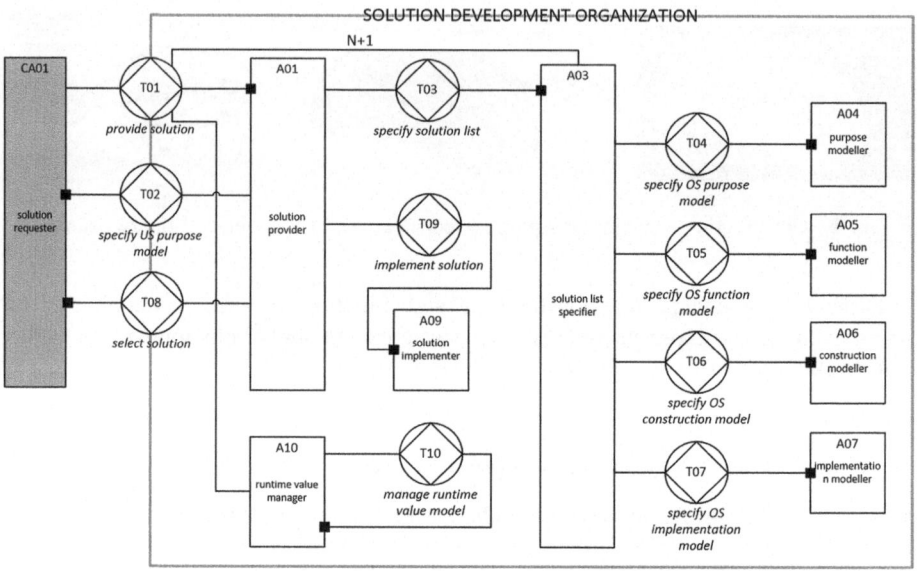

**Fig. 3.** Solution development organization (ATD), adapted from (Pombinho 2015)

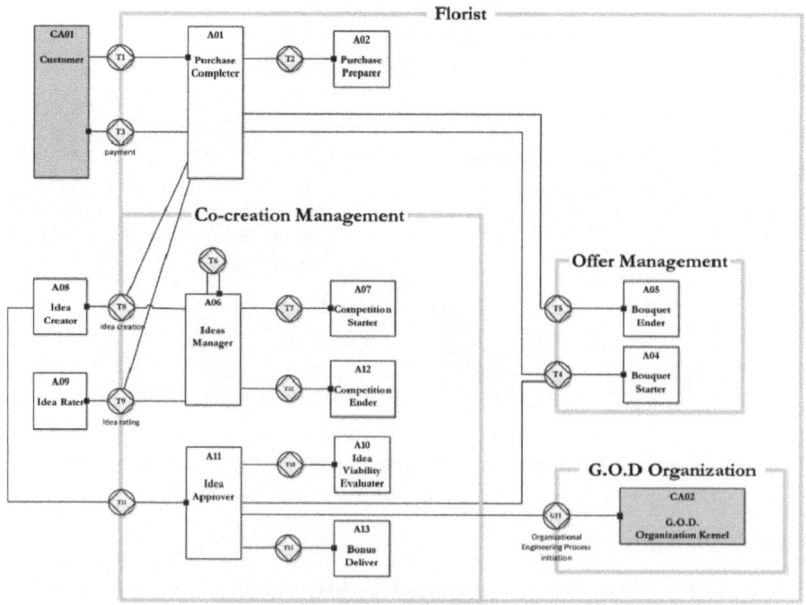

**Fig. 4.** Florist shop Actor Transaction Diagram (ATD)

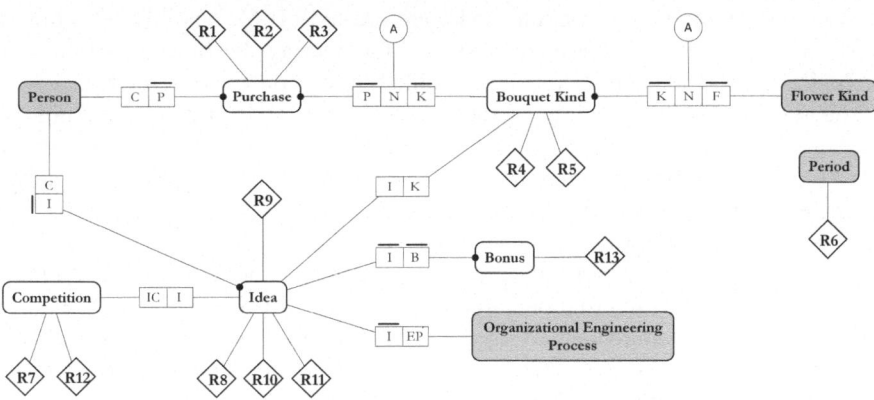

**Fig. 5.** Florist shop Object Fact Diagram (OFD)

- **III. Select Solution Scenario**. From the viable value models obtained in II, an estimated valuation of each implementation model is be propagated bottom-up in order to instantiate the corresponding value models.
- **IV. Implement Solution**. The selected solution is implemented using the specific technologies from the implementation models.
- **V. Evaluate Solution**. By using the value model of the implemented scenario, it is possible to evaluate operational reality versus estimated valuations and identify any gaps to address in a new iteration of the system development cycle.

Following, a specification of the (sub)organization that performs such method – the Solution Development Organization (SDO) – is presented.

The process begins with an external request to provide a solution (T01). The solution provider asks the solution requester to specify the Using System purpose model (T02), which is critical to identify rational solutions. Note that such model can be derived from the results of a process such as Design Thinking, by mapping a Value Proposition Canvas (Osterwalder et al. 2014) to the corresponding e3Value model as specified in (Caetano et al. 2016), for instance. This implies that, by construction of the SDO, every development decision is traceable and grounded on value specification. The solution provider then requests that the solution list specifier specifies a solution list (T03) to produce the requested result. A solution is a set of coherent models that include the purpose, function and construction perspectives of a (sub)system. The solution list manager actor role is responsible for setting and controlling available resources for specifying solutions, including time and effort, and negotiating with the requester whether to stop the analysis of a particular solution or expand solution search space.

The specify Object System purpose model transaction (T04) is the first creative step of this process, where different VOs that may provide a solution to the requester's demand are identified. This step can be based on a number of techniques, such as specialist input, brainstorming, research or knowledge bases.

Following, a set of function models that produce the transaction results that yield the required VOs identified in the purpose model are then specified (T05).

Next, one or more construction model are created (T06), possibly reflecting different ways of structuring the internal system for offering the function specification. Ontological transactions and actors are specified in the construction model.

The next step, creating an implementation model (T07), describes the technological means used to instantiate the construction model, particularly assigning operant and operand resources. Implementation models are needed as the costs can only be determined after assigning specific valuations and number of occurrence to the value transactions, both implementation technology specific.

If anytime during model specification a dependency comes about in producing the result, the current OS is repositioned, assuming the role of US in the new development cycle. Such a request would be made by the level N solution list manager to level N + 1 providers. For each crossing of these levels, a new system development cycle iteration takes place. Along each single thread of a solution chain, the alternation between each pair of levels is described by Dietz and Hoogervorst as function/construction alternation (J. L. G. Dietz 2006).

When the set of known solutions is considered satisfactory by the solution provider, it requires that the solution requester elects a solution from the presented alternatives (T08). The elected solution is then implemented (T09) and its value proposal is periodically monitored by the value manager (T10). If an inconsistency is found, the provide solution transaction is invoked to address the gap, presented as an economic viability problem.

The Solution Development Organization is a generic specification of the organization that runs the process of creating the set of aggregate models of each link in a value network. As we will see, the fact that the specification is actor independent is instrumental in objectifying co-design activities.

## 3 Objectifying Value Co-creation: Modelling Co-design and Co-production

In this section we begin by presenting the Flower Shop case built to include examples of co-design and co-production usually mentioned in the literature. Then, we model the case using DEMO and e3Value to bring about the relevant modelling issues. The resulting models are the basis for the next subsection, where we refine the co-creation, co-design and co-production definitions and principles.

### 3.1 Flower Shop Case Description

In this section we use a Flower Shop case considering the co-creation definitions in (Chathoth, P. et al. 2013):

- Value creation: creation of unique personalized experiences;
- Customers' role: active, providing input before, during and after service delivery;
- Customers' participation: repeated interactions and transactions across multiple channels. Co-create products and services;

- Focus: customer and experience centric;
- Innovation: co-innovate and co-design with customers;
- Communication: ongoing dialogue with customers.

Based on these topics we created a Flower Shop case with the following description[1]:

*Florist ACME is a company based in Lisbon. It < sells > bouquets of flowers in the shop and online. Each purchase may have several types of bouquets and each bouquet may have several types of flowers. In both cases, each purchase must < prepared > by the florist or by the client itself and it must be < paid > by the client. On some occasions the client needs are not represented in the bouquet types available. When that happens the florist may < create > a new bouquet type according to these needs and current available resources. In those situations and after the purchase is < completed >, the new bouquet type may be < discontinued >.*

*In order to continuously align the florist offer with clients' needs, the florist implemented co-creation techniques in which customers are active co-creators of the products they buy and use. The two essential activities in co-creation are: (1) the contribution of novel concepts and ideas, and (2) the selection of which specific concepts and ideas should be pursued. This florist decided to adopt a collaborating co-creation technique, meaning that customers have an active role in contributing with their own ideas and in selecting the components that should be incorporated into a new product offering.*

*Regarding the contribution of novel concepts and ideas, the florist decided to periodically < open > a competition for new ideas. To stimulate the participation, the florist < offers > a bonus (for instance a free bouquet) to the accountable of each chosen idea. The clients are (called) to participate in the competition and < create > new ideas when they visit the store and/or by email. In order to (submit) their ideas, the clients can do it physically in the store when they are buying products or submit it directly in a website used to store all the information regarding the competitions. In the first case, the florist enters the idea in the website afterwards.*

*Regarding the selection of which specific concepts and ideas should be pursued, the florist has the accountability for < approving > the ideas that should be implemented. However, the florist takes into consideration the clients' feedback when doing*

---

[1] The description was edited to identify the C-acts and P-acts, described by Enterprise Ontology (Dietz, J. 2006), with the following notation: brackets "(" and ")" to identify C-acts/facts and angled brackets "<" and ">" to identify P-acts/facts.

*so. The florist (invites) the clients (in the store and by email) to < rate > the ideas that are available in the website. When the competition period ends, the florist selects the ideas with most votes and for each one < makes > a viability evaluation in order to < approve > the ones that should be incorporated into a new product offering. Then the florist < rewards > the accountable for those ideas with the defined bonus, and informs all clients about the new offer.*

*The implementation of the ideas may have impact on the type of bouquets that are sold by the florist (new ones can be < added > and current ones can be < discontinued >) and even have impact on the construction of the florist itself (can be modelled using the G.O.D. theory[2]).*

### 3.2    Modelling the Case with DEMO and e3Value

As described in the related work, we chose to use DEMO and e3Value to model the Flower shop case to bring about the characteristics of the two perspectives we have elected for improving objectivity in value co-creation modelling. The next subsections present the respective models in DEMO and e3Value.

**DEMO.** After applying the method to the case description, the result was a DEMO white-box model composed by four models: Construction Model (CM), Process Model (PM), Action Model (AM), and State Model (SM). These models can be described using the diagrams and cross-model tables, such as the Transaction Result Table (TRT), Actor Transaction Diagram (ATD) and Object Fact Diagram (OFD) presented below (Table 1).

We identified 13 transactions: 3 concerning the usual transactions in the Florist Shop case (T01, T02, and T03), 2 transactions focusing on offer management (T04 and T05) and 8 transactions relating with co-designing of new business ideas (T06 through T13). The ATD represents these different environments more clearly.

We also modelled a connection with the G.O.D. theory (Aveiro, D. 2009), since the implementation of new ideas may involve changes in the ontological models of the florist and, therefore, the start of an organizational engineering process (OEP). Consequently, each idea may have one organizational engineering process as the OFD below illustrates.

This relation with the G.O.D theory contributes to the research subtopic presented in the introduction: aligning service design approaches with existing organizational structures. By connecting the creation of new designs (through ideas) with the G.O.D. theory we can establish a direct relation on how new service designs will impact the

---

[2] The G.O.D. Theory (Aveiro, D. 2009) explains ontological change events in organizations and specifies the sub(organization) that handles organizational artefact generation, operationalization and discontinuation according to EE principles.

**Table 1.** Florist shop Transaction Result Table (TRT)

| Transaction | Result | Executed by |
|---|---|---|
| T01 – Purchase Completion | R01 – Purchase P has been completed | Florist |
| T02 – Purchase Preparation | R02 – Purchase P has been prepared | Florist/Customer |
| T03 – Purchase Payment | R03 – Purchase P has been paid | Customer |
| T04 – Bouquet Type Start | R04 – Bouquet Type BT has been started | Florist |
| T05 – Bouquet Type End | R05 – Bouquet Type BT has been ended | Florist |
| T06 – Competition Management | R06 – Competition management for Period P has been done | Florist |
| T07 – Idea Competition Start | R07 – Idea Competition IC has been started | Florist |
| T08 – Idea Creation | R08 – Idea I has been created | Customer |
| T09 – Idea Rate | R09 – Idea I has been rated | Customer |
| T10 – Idea Viability Evaluation | R10 – Idea I viability has been evaluated | Florist |
| T11 – Idea Approval | R11 – Idea I has been approved | Florist |
| T12 – Idea Competition End | R12 – Idea Competition IC has been ended | Florist |
| T13 – Bonus Delivery | R13 – Bonus B has been delivered | Florist |

current ontological models of organizations. Nevertheless, the details the connection with the G.O.D. theory are still in development. For instance, we need to specify how the florist Process and Action Models relate with the G.O.D theory respective models, and if there are more categories from this theory related with the ones from this case.

**e3Value.** We will now present a value model to obtain a different perspective of the florist case, this time focused on content (i.e. the bouquet) creation instead of organizational design of its provider. Applying the methodology defined in (Pombinho 2015) we modelled this scenario as a series of successive solutions to a problem in the form of problem/solution pairs. In this case, we focus on making the "right" bouquet available to the customer and there are obvious many ways to make it happen. Particularly, this implies addressing both the creation of the bouquet value object and making sure it is made available to the customer (which can range from over-the-counter to scheduled delivery). We focused on the following value activities: create bouquet idea, compose bouquet, produce bouquet element, prepare bouquet, and deliver bouquet. Suchsuccession of value activities is the result of a system development process as the one presented in Sect. 2 and is one of many possible solutions for arriving at the desired end state.

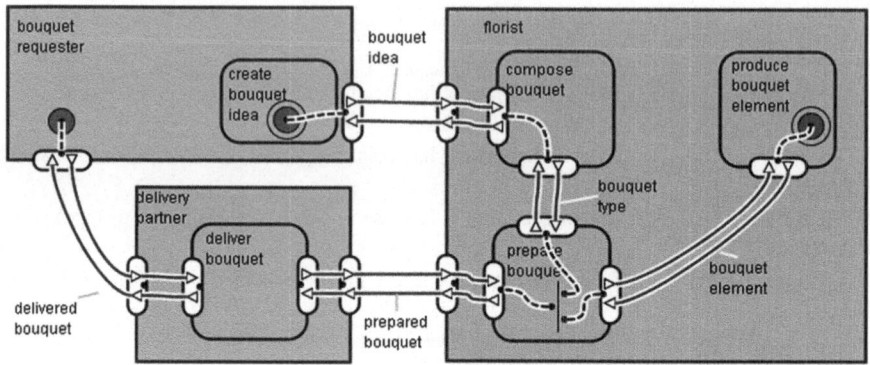

**Fig. 6.** Florist - bouquet creation and delivery (For clarity, only the value path of creating and delivering the bouquet is represented) value model

Furthermore, note there are many possible configurations of actors that can be assigned to execute these activities. For instance, it is very common that the bouquet is created by the florist taking a simple expression of intention by the buyer, e.g. a romantic occasion, as a starting point. In this case, we considered the bouquet creation was performed by the customer itself and derived the value model in Fig. 6.

The fact that the buyer can perform one or more value activities on behalf of the florist can create cycles in the value network, as it is apparent in this case by the start stimulus, end stimulus and the value paths between them.

## 3.3    (Re)defining Co-creation: Co-design and Co-production

Having set the goal of achieving a more objective value co-creation conceptualization we have defined it in terms of co-design and co-production. For each, we devised assertive actions that reflect our way of thinking:

1. Assert co-design support by checking compatibility of the white-box models of the organization with the generic co-design model;
2. Assert value co-production based on the corresponding value model.

We therefore consider value co-creation as a combination of co-design and co-production, each understood at follows.

**Co-design.** According to our observations of the Flower Shop case and other real examples (for instance Lego or Starbucks), we propose that **there is value co-design if there is one external actor role that participates in the creation of the design**. We define participation as fulfilling an actor role in the corresponding ontological trans-actions. This was the case on the Flower shop case, since there is an actor role that produces ideas and another actor role that rates ideas. These ideas, if approved, can be included by the organization in the future designs. We can, therefore, say that in the Flower shop case there is co-design since there are external actor roles that participate in the production and evaluation of new designs. Note that the co-designer customer

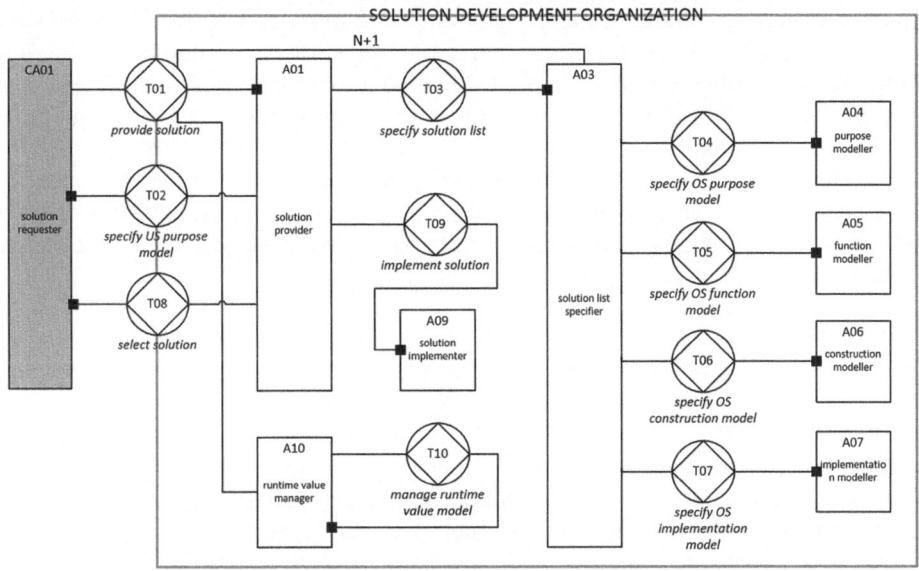

**Fig. 7.** Solution Development Organization (ATD), adapted from (Pombinho 2015)

may or not be a participant customer in runtime value production of the organization he co-designed.

Using this definition, we can find co-design examples in the industry, such as in Lego and Starbucks. Lego created the Digital Designer program[3] that allows customers to create their own toy designs and evaluate the designs that are eventually submitted online. Starbucks created the *mystarbucksidea* platform[4] that encourages the customers to share their ideas for new products/services.

This definition conforms to the implementation of the SDO (cf. Fig. 7) where the tester/evaluator impersonates the requester role. In this case, to support the scenario of an evaluator that is different from the solution requester, the solution requester actor role would have to be split to create an independent actor that implements the transaction T08 – select solution. Analogously, any of the modellers A04-A07 (respectively purpose, function, construction and implementation modellers) can be implemented by an actor that is external to the organization, thereby creating a coherent model instantiation of the co-design scenario.

By providing an accurate ontological specification in which to instantiate actors and perform validation, this definition objectifies co-design and contributes to the research topic on how to involve customers through participatory design and co-design to enhance service experience.

---

[3] Available at http://ldd.lego.com.
[4] Available at http://mystarbucksidea.force.com/.

**Co-production.** Co-production essentially differs from co-design since it focuses on can only be asserted during operation. Our definition is: **there is value co-production if the graph of value exchanges in the value model between 2 or more value actors is** *cyclic*. This definition applies to our bouquet creation scenario, presented in Fig. 6 (Sect. 3.2), where the customer performs the role of bouquet creator. Notice it could also perform the delivery role and any other, as long as the provider retained a value-generating activity. As it can be seen, both the degree of involvement of each participant and the number of participants can vary and by identifying the configuration of the cycle there can be specified a series of patterns.

The definition extends from the trivial configuration of a reciprocal value exchange between two actors – mutually dependent to generate value – to arbitrarily complex scenarios, for instance the case of ZON-FON in Fig. 8.

The ZON-FON case (Pombinho 2015) is a particular cyclic value production between 3 actors – a quite interesting one, as it is exponential due to network effect. FON[5] is a global network of hotspots that takes dramatic advantage of network effect by providing the means for users to share their third party internet access and, in return, get free access to hotspots made available by other users in the network. In the original

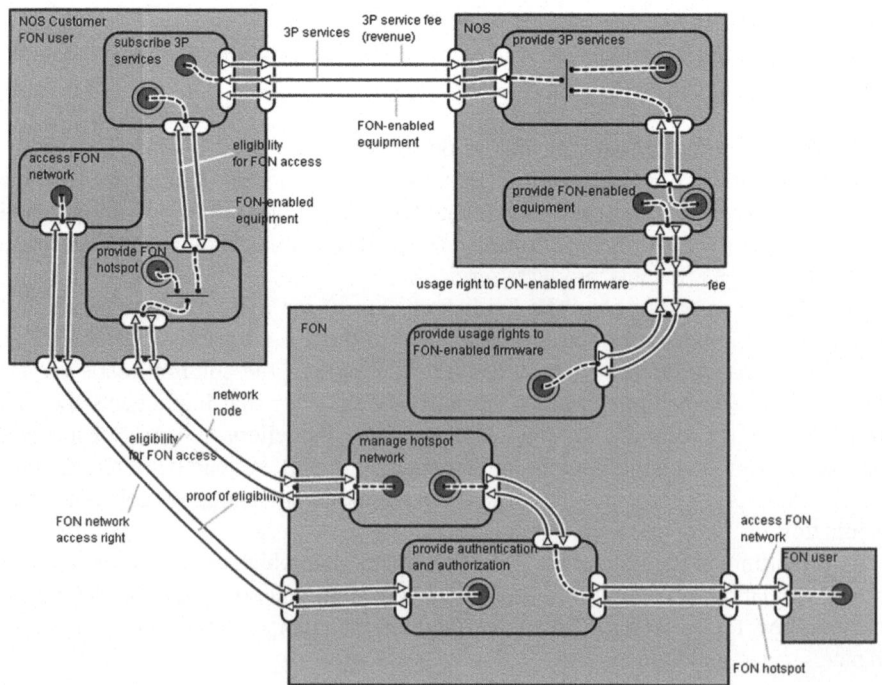

**Fig. 8.** ZON-FON case – mutual dependencies in value co-production with network effect.

---

[5] Institutional information available at https://corp.fon.com.

business model, these means implied having a standalone FON wireless router in addition to the third party internet access equipment such as a cable modem. In this particular scenario, ZON Multimédia has partnered with FON to bundle the FON firmware into the wireless cable modems provided by ZON to its customers. ZON offered its customers free access to FON's network in exchange for sharing fixed internet connection bandwidth. Since the ZON cable modem incorporated the firmware and was made available to the customer as part of the fixed internet service, i.e. at no additional cost, the customer did not need to acquire neither accommodate physical space or power supply to FON's equipment – an innovative scenario targeted at value co-creation for the three parties. This improved the value proposal towards ZON customers, consolidating fixed internet service attractivity and improving customer retention, increases as the coverage of the network expands. The benefits for each participant can be informally summarized as follows:

- FON increases customers and their network effect, while providing centralized authentication and governance;
- NOS increases customer value proposal and reuses the same logistics scenario of a regular internet service user;
- Customer receives access to Wi-Fi network outside, while keeping the same service fee and having no additional equipment costs; in turn, he provides premises and power to the FON router.

Regarding value co-creation, the business model can informally be viewed as a win/win/win situation. This is a special case of co-creation, the three actors are tied together by a cyclic value generation cycle that benefits from network effect – each time an actor joins the network and shares his access, every other user gets additional value due to increased network coverage. It is worth noticing the fact that the actors don't need to be directly included in the network design process order to benefit from value co-production. In this case, the customers were not involved in the design process and clearly benefit from it, as a sustainable component of the value generation network. Actually, customer input was later used in the ongoing phase of the business model, for instance to improve the registration process and pre-activation of the equipment.

## 4 Conclusion

In this research we addressed the goal of clarifying value co-creation by specifying co-design and co-production using sound theory and modelling techniques. Both Value Modelling (e3Value) and Enterprise Ontology (DEMO) were useful to analyse and refine the notions of co-creation, co-design and co-production of value.

First, we identified a co-creation (sub)organization that can be used as a template to assert the existence of white-box components that support the validation of the designer and evaluator roles in value co-design settings. Then, we differentiated (1) co-design - changes to structure resulting from incorporation of inputs from other participants in the value network and (2) co-production - operational, cyclic value generation between interdependent systems. Both contributions provide understanding of the ontological transactions and serve as a basis to address value co-creation in EE.

## 4.1  Limitations

This research is based on an exploratory study and the resulting artefacts are currently being developed. Consequently, a field study is necessary to evaluate the proposed artefacts. Additionally, there is an inherent limitation regarding DEMO modelling. Since DEMO models are implementation independent, these models do not include details concerning the subjects that implement the ontological transactions. That information is necessary to instantiate the value models and to understand value creation in multi-actor, network, and collaborative contexts.

## 4.2  Future Work

This research needs further development on the concepts presented in this paper, namely a deeper analysis of the five subtopics presented in the introduction. For instance, the relation with G.O.D. theory (Aveiro, D. 2009) be explored and integrated with the co-design DEMO white-box model (Fig. 4) in order to better align service design approaches with existing organizational structures. Furthermore, the proposed artefacts could be applied through field studies in real organizations and the value networks they take part in. This would allow evaluating if the preliminary proposal is generic enough to be applied to several contexts and also to validate its benefits. Nevertheless, we are convinced this contribution is a small but important step in evolving the research of value co-creation in organizations.

# References

Aveiro, D.: Towards a GOD-theory for organizational engineering: continuously modeling the (re)generation, operationalization and discontinuation of the enterprise. Ph.D. thesis, Instituto Superior Técnico (2009)

Caetano, A., Antunes, G., Pombinho, J., Bakhshandeh, M., Granjo, J., Borbinha, J., Mira da Silva, M.: Representation and analysis of enterprise models with semantic techniques: an application to Archimate, e3Value and business model canvas. Knowl. Inf. Syst., 1–32 (2016)

Chathoth, P., et al.: Co-production versus co-creation: a process based continuum in the hotel service context. Int. J. Hospitality Manage. **32**, 11–20 (2013)

Chesbrough, H., Spohrer, J.: A research manifesto for services science. Commun. ACM **49**(7), 35–40 (2006)

Dietz, J.: Enterprise Ontology: Theory and Methodology. Springer, Heidelberg (2006)

Gordijn, J.: Value-based Requirements Engineering: Exploring Innovatie e-commerce Ideas. Vrije Universiteit Amsterdam, Amsterdam (2002)

Osterwalder, A., Pigneur, Y., Bernarda, G., Smith, A., Papadakos, T.: Value Proposition Design: How to Create Products and Services Customers Want. Wiley, Hoboken (2014)

Ostrom, A., et al.: Service research priorities in a rapidly changing context. J. Serv. Res. **18**(2), 127–159 (2015)

Pombinho, J.: Value-oriented enterprise transformation - design and engineering of value networks. Ph.D. thesis, Instituto Superior Técnico, Universidade de Lisboa (2015)

Vargo, S., Maglio, P., Akaka, M.: On value and value co-creation: a service systems and service logic perspective. Eur. Manage. J. **26**, 145–152 (2008). Elsevier

Vargo, S.L., Akaka, M.A.: Service-dominant logic as a foundation for service science: clarifications. Serv. Sci. **1**(1), 32–41 (2009)

Vargo, S.L. et al.: Advancing service science with service dominant logic - clarifications and conceptual development (2010)

Wieland, H., Polese, F., Vargo, S.L., Lusch, R.F.: Toward a service (Eco) systems perspective on value creation. Int. J. Serv. Sci. Manage. Eng. Technol, 12–25, July–September 2012

# Towards Co-creation and Co-production in Production Chains Modeled in DEMO with REA Support

Frantisek Hunka[1]([✉]), Steven J.H. van Kervel[2], and Jiri Matula[1]

[1] Ostrava University, Ostrava, Czech Republic
{frantisek.hunka,jiri.matula}@osu.cz
[2] Formetis Consultants BV, Boxtel, The Netherlands
info@formetis.nl

**Abstract.** Co-creation and Co-production in production chains is the typical way of cooperation one observes in high value industrial production chains. The enterprises in these production chains constitute together also a sophisticated virtual enterprise. While many professional IT systems are operational within these enterprises, there are only IT technologies with a limited scope at a small scale available between these enterprises. The new technologies currently provided by enterprise engineering promise substantial operational improvements; operational control, compliance to business rules, optimization of efficiency and effectiveness. Another objective is support for the REA ontology for high quality financial information systems, which requires a conceptual mapping between REA and DEMO to be found. The first step, a generic DEMO model for co-creation and co-production, has been devised and subjected to early validation. This paper is also a positioning paper, defining future research, specifies two challenges for the DEMO theory and provides foundations for a professional production system.

**Keywords:** REA ontology · Enterprise ontology · DEMO · Co-creation · Co-production

## 1   Introduction

Co-creation and Co-production in production chains is the typical way of cooperation one observes in many high value industrial production chains such as finance, automotive etc. Instead of well-defined products directly available from stock, companies - contractors - that are part of virtual enterprise chains propose to develop custom-made products within a clearly defined domain of their competences and well-matching the specific needs of the customers - principals.

One sees [Sect. 3.1] that a whole production chain is composed of many specific 'virtual' 'co-creation and co-production enterprise pairs, triplets etc'. For each of these virtual enterprises the co-creation and co-production is so sophisticated that they are actually an independent virtual enterprise, composed of the independent enterprises, principal (DEMO initiator) and one or more contractor(s) (DEMO executor). There is a

© Springer International Publishing Switzerland 2016
D. Aveiro et al. (Eds.): EEWC 2016, LNBIP 252, pp. 54–68, 2016.
DOI: 10.1007/978-3-319-39567-8_4

great need to improve the operation of these virtual enterprises to meet the following objectives:

  (i)   Governance, defined here being the system and ways by which companies are directed and controlled. In virtual co-creation and co-production enterprises this is mostly defined by the contract(s) devised and signed by the constituting enterprises.
 (ii)   Risk, the application of methodologies through which parties identify, analyze, prioritize, define and mitigate risks that affect the interests of stakeholders.
(iii)   Compliance, defined being the overall approach through which an operation of the parties conform with stated requirements from outside the enterprise, such as legal regulations and moral rules. Notably the banking crisis resulted in extensive complex regulations such as Sarbanes-Oxley Act [22] that must be implemented by banks.
 (iv)   Efficiency, the careful use of precious resources to realize the desired results.
  (v)   Effectiveness, the degree of how well the requirements of the principal are met; a degree for quality.
 (vi)   Agility, the capability to adapt the operation of an enterprise at any time, driven by unpredictable changes in markets, imposed legislation and strategy.

There are many partial solutions for the co-creation and co-production domain in the professional world. Examples include Business-to-Business (B2B) and Business-to-Business-Customer (B2BC) electronic "e-invoicing" systems. Domain experts [7, 8] state that in general this domain is fragmented, captured by many stand-alone proprietary vendor-specific systems. The European Economic Community (EEC) estimates [21] annual savings of 65 billion euro if e-invoicing is widely adopted. This mass market is represented by 216 million households and 21.2 million SMEs in the European Uion-28 (EU-28).

No generic approaches that address the whole domain of co-creation, co-production and electronic invoicing and payments have been found today. The most serious limitations are: (i) they capture only a part of the important interactions between participating enterprises; (ii) they are not generic and not domain-independent; and (iii) they are proprietary, closed architectures, with vendor lock in mechanisms. Capturing the co-creation and the contract phase is mostly left out but is considered here of vital importance since the contract is the foundation of all interactions between participating enterprises, including electronic payments.

There is a lack of a generic, comprehensive approach to support production chains with high quality information systems. We define here high quality information systems as systems that either (i) provide some, one of several, *descriptive*, *truthful* and *functionally appropriate* perspective on the *operation* of an enterprise [12, 13]; or (ii) provide a *prescriptive control* [10–14] of the model-driven operation of the enterprise. An example of a descriptive information system is a financial information system that meets GAAP (Generally Accepted Accounting Principles) criteria. An example of a prescriptive information system is a workflow(-like) system that imposes actors in the enterprise to operate as defined by the workflow procedure.

## 1.1 Objectives of this Paper

The main objective of this paper is to provide a generic, application and business-independent foundation for IT systems, directly derived from enterprise models [13, 19], that support production chains and to identify future research topics to realize this further. The following derived objectives have to be met:

(i)   The need for a generic, application and industry-independent ontological DEMO enterprise model for co-creation and co-production chains [Sects. 3.1, and 3.2].
(ii)  The generic ontological DEMO model is/will be, the foundation for the many industry-specific implementations, extended with infological and datalogical transactions[1]. In this paper we limit ourselves to the ontological DEMO model.
(iii) The Resource-Event-Agent (REA) ontology [Sect. 2.1] aims to provide ontological foundations for descriptive financial information systems that must provide a truthful and appropriate perspective on the operation of the enterprise.
(iv)  Application of the available technologies of enterprise engineering [Sects. 2.3, and 2.4], needed to bring such a system in professional production.

## 1.2 Practical Objectives of the Approach

The various technologies needed to bring such a system in real world production are available with either proof of concept or already operating in professional production. It means that such a system may go into production when the objectives of this paper and the specified research [Sect. 4] have been realized. Specific benefits may be:

(i)   Reduction of costs for invoicing and payments, as described [7, 8]. If the whole of the co-creation and co-production domain is captured, the costs reductions may be even substantially higher.
(ii)  Reduction of risks of payments and related identity fraud since identities are already well-defined and cannot be falsified. If payments are controlled by such a system, essentially precisely defined payments only need to be (dis)approved but the payments cannot be tampered with.
(iii) Since total knowledge of all financial transactions of a specific enterprise is totally captured[2], a complete financial report, balance, profit and loss, can be rendered automatically, preferably using a REA based system.
(iv)  The "owner" of this data gains deep insight in all operations.

---

[1] DEMO theory [3] distinguishes (i) ontological transactions, those transactions that bring about changes in the world; (ii) so-called infological transactions where information is being produced; and (iii) datalogical transactions where data is transformed from one representation into another. Datalogical transactions support infological transactions and infological transactions support ontological transactions. A model comprised on only ontological transactions provides the highest, implementation-independent representation of such an enterprise.

[2] The Enterprise Operating System [Sect. 2.3] records each communicative act and fact for each actor, which provides 'total factual knowledge' of the enterprise in operation.

(v)  The complete history of all acts, facts and commitments is recorded. In a dispute the total truth is immediately available, which reduces/eliminates legal dispute costs.

This paper is mainly a position paper; it proposes an approach with an enterprise model, specifies further research topics but also reports on current progress. Several controversial stances are taken that will be refuted if proven wrong. In Sect. 1 the objectives and the potential of a system for co-creation and co-production have been described. In Sect. 2 an introduction to the REA and DEMO ontologies is provided with the supporting technologies for enterprise information systems engineering. In Sect. 3 an ontological DEMO model for co-creation and co-production is proposed. In Sect. 4 some topics for future research are described.

## 2   Introduction to REA, DEMO and Software Technologies

The REA ontology is very promising for so-called REA model driven financial information systems. We aim to enhance the REA ontology to a "high quality" ontology, meeting several very strict formal criteria. Once this has been realized, the Generic Systems Development Process for Model-Driven Information Systems (GSDP-MDE) [8, 13] provides a very clear and concise way to engineer (i) a suitable formal language for REA models (of financial information systems) and (ii) a matching model-executing REA software engine. Financial information systems are models expressed in the REA language, executed by the REA software engine. This constitutes a financial information system without programming and hence without software bugs. The costs in development of financial information systems can be reduced in a tremendous way. Further, adaptations to changing legal requirements, so-called GAAP's are most easily to implement and validate. The GSDP-MDE has been applied for the enterprise operating system [2.3] and proven strong enough for professional software [17]. However, this approach for REA is a long term goal.

### 2.1   REA Ontology

REA ontology originates from accountancy systems and provides a domain specific platform for value modeling business processes, see [20]. The term value modeling means that the REA modeling approach keeps track of primary and raw data about economic resource values. Economic resources can be exchanged for other economic resources within the scope of REA exchange process or they can be consumed, used or produced within the scope of the REA conversion process. REA model which describes the exchange or conversion process is composed of at least two transactions of economic resources, in which one transaction is in consideration for the other. Apart from economic resources, the REA approach to value modeling in its core pattern covers economic events, in which the corresponding economic resource changed its amount or feature, and the agents (actors) that participate in these events. The economic events are marked increment and decrement in relation to one of the economic agents which means the increasing or decreasing value of economic resources. The duality relationship that relates the economic events to each other holds the transactions together.

In REA, a commitment addresses the issue of modeling promises of future economic events and the issue of reservation of resources [6, 18]. The exchange reciprocity relationship between the increment and the decrement commitments identifies which resources are promised to be exchanged for which others. The claim entity is a temporary entity which reconciles time differences between economic events and can be materialized, for example as an invoice (Fig. 1).

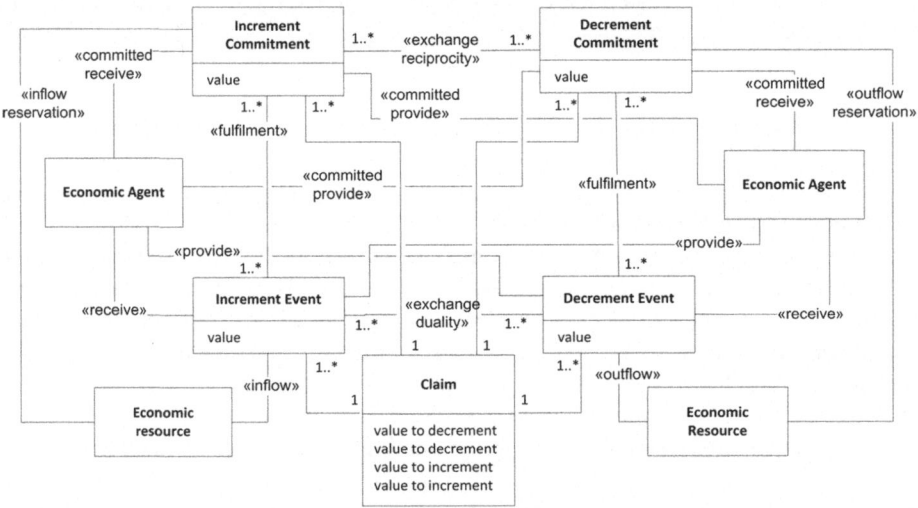

**Fig. 1.** REA model with commitments and claims entities. Adopted from [18]

The main benefit of the REA approach is that it facilitates the keeping track of primary and raw data about economic resources, thereby offering a wider, more precise, and more up-to-date range of reports, according to [18]. All accounting artifacts such as debit, credit, journals, ledgers, receivables, and account balances are derived from the data describing exchange and conversion REA processes. Reports based on accounting artifacts are always consistent, being derived from the same data [18]. The economic events provide the information on when, where, and how the exchanges of resources occurred. The economic agents provide the information on who controlled the economic resources during these exchanges. All this information is necessary for future generation of IT systems. In addition, REA models (business processes) can be arranged into REA value chains by which enterprise transaction cycles can be described.

REA ontology anomalies have its origin in absence of rigorous theoretical foundation. REA model itself does not have specific states from which a state machine can be derived. Instead, only the resource states are identified and frequently used as the states of the state machine. As a result of this, REA model does not provide revoking operations such as cancellation. In addition, REA model is predominantly design to capture events that are concerned with the resource value or resource feature. The other events such as business events or information events are difficult to capture and further processed. Consequently, REA has difficulty with so called information or knowledge entities such as contract or schedule because they are not resources. It is possible to create them because creation expresses some value. But the real problem comes to determine the state from which the contract is valid.

Core REA pattern which comes from double booking entry and covers resources, events and agents is a good and verified basis for further development. However, the other REA entities such as commitments, claims, contracts and schedule needs further elaboration and research. The high quality C4-ness criteria and the three cardinality laws must be met.

## 2.2 DEMO Ontology

DEMO, a methodology to derive conceptual models of enterprises, is based on an ontological theory, enterprise ontology [1–4] comprised of four axioms and a theorem. DEMO is part of the discipline of 'enterprise engineering' [4]. The emerging discipline of enterprise engineering is in fact founded on the same kind of theories as more mature engineering disciplines such as aviation and electronics. The quality of the applied methodology is guaranteed by the underlying theories, methodologies, formal methods [4, 13, 19] and a good body of empirical cases in many domains [17]. The DEMO methodology claims to provide models that meet the so-called C4-ness[3] quality criteria [9]. Specific results of C4-ness qualities are (i) that any enterprise that may exist in the real world, including virtual CC-CP enterprises, can be modeled correctly in one and only one way; and (ii) the DEMO model(s) for any such enterprise must provide concise and comprehensive factual knowledge about the operation of the enterprise. These two claimed results must be empirically tested for co-creation and co-production, as described in Sect. 3.

The generic pattern of DEMO transactions with clear phases of communication (actagenic, action execution, factagenic) provides analysts and participating enterprises with a powerful conceptual framework for reflection upon the trust foundations and risks between the initiator and the executor of the transaction.

An enterprise in operation is defined as a social system of actors who communicate about their productions [3]. The system is purposefully constructed to fulfill a specific function. Actors communicate about their productions by communication acts, which result in communication facts. All communication facts represent a shared understanding and a binding agreement of all actors about their production.

---

[3] C4-ness [3], an ontological quality criterion, is the abbreviation of Concise and Coherent and Consistent and Comprehensive. (i) Conciseness refers to the requirement that anything that is not in the domain of the ontology should not be represented in any model; (ii) Coherence refers to the 'semantic meaningfulness of the symbols and their relations from every perspective'; (iii) Consistency refers to the absence of anomalies; (iv) Comprehensiveness refers to the condition that the model encompasses "everything" that is part of the ontology.

## 2.3    Enterprise Operating System

In order to implement a working software engineering artifact, a number of technologies are available. The Enterprise Operating System (EOS) [8] is founded on (i) the DEMO methodology and theories [3, 4] to develop high quality DEMO enterprise models; (ii) the DEMO Engine [19], a software engine that executes DEMO models "as native source code"; and (iii) state of the art process mining tools. The enterprise operating system has been implemented precisely following the Generic Systems Development Process for Model-Driven Engineering (GSDP-MDE) [19].

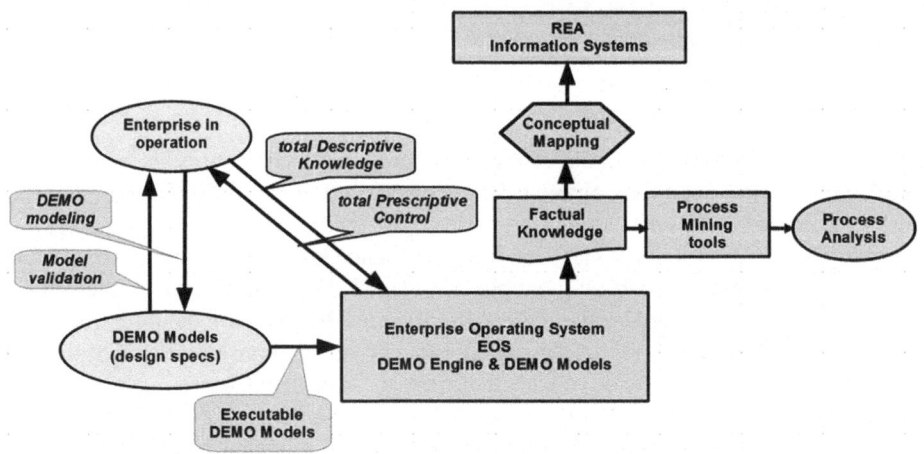

**Fig. 2.** Overview of the Enterprise Operating System (EOS) [13]

The EOS is analogous to an operating system for a computer, and represents the active abstraction layer between human actors of the organization, "enterprise in operation" and the enterprise information systems such as the intended REA based information systems and many more. The overview contains the following elements:

(i)   DEMO Modeling. The starting point of the process is some desired enterprise that must operate in the real world. Application of the DEMO modeling methodology provides the four DEMO aspect models, which are actually design specifications for an enterprise;

(ii)  Model Validation. The design science cycle [15, 16] of model validation by shared reasoning of stakeholders - designers may return a functionally 'better' design of that enterprise. This cycle is repeated until the stakeholder/designers accept a specific model as appropriate for the desired functional purpose;

(iii) Execution of DEMO models by the DEMO Engine. The DEMO engine that executes a DEMO model constitutes the enterprise operating system (EOS) [8]. Enterprise models in execution are dynamic discrete systems with a precisely defined state space and state transition space [10–12].

## 2.4    The Four Technologies of the Enterprise Operating System

The EOS provides four technologies to ensure that enterprises operate precisely according the defined DEMO models and that complete information is provided.

  (i)   Total Prescriptive control [10–12, 14], implying that the whole enterprise, including each actor - here the participating enterprises Principal and Contractor (Fig. 3), can act exclusively within the boundaries of the (DEMO) business process. More precisely stated: any actor can execute exclusively within the allowed discrete state space of the DEMO model. It is impossible [10, 11, 14] for an actor "doing things their own way", which guarantees operational compliance of each actor to the model. This approach provides all capabilities provided by contemporary BPMN-based workflow systems, offers new capabilities and eliminates the many flaws of BPMN-based workflow systems [21].
 (ii)   Total descriptive knowledge. Each communication act and resulting communication fact is captured and recorded [13, 19]. The completeness and correctness of all acts is guaranteed (within the scope of the EOS).
(iii)   Factual Knowledge. Based on (a) the recorded total descriptive knowledge; (b) the factual knowledge of the "outside world"; (c) specification of facts defined in the DEMO OFD (Object Fact Model) [3], the EOS renders Factual Knowledge about the operation of the enterprise with guaranteed completeness and correctness.
(iv)   Enterprise Operation Analysis (EOA). The factual knowledge can be analysed using state of the art process mining tools [5]. This provides deep insight in the quality of the operation in terms of governance, risk, compliance, effectiveness and efficiency. This insight may lead to a redesign of an improved DEMO model.

## 2.5    REA Ontology Support

The new technology to be investigated, defined in this paper [Sect. 4] as future research, is the provisioning of factual knowledge to REA based information systems. This demands some yet unknown conceptual mapping system to be devised. Factual knowledge for financial information systems may comprise items such as "invoice has been sent", "Payment has been made", "goods have been delivered", but also "invoice is disputed", "goods have been rejected", all items of relevance for financial information systems. The challenge is to map facts, defined by the DEMO Fact Model to REA defined facts for financial information systems, in such a way that correctness and completeness is guaranteed.

# 3    Ontological DEMO Model for Co-creation and Co-production

In this section the world of co-creation and co-production ("CC-CP") is investigated. The first version of a generic ontological CC-CP DEMO model is proposed and briefly validated.

## 3.1   The World of Co-creation and Co-production

Many highly specialized enterprises do not have a well-defined portfolio of products with fixed prices but offer their capabilities to meet the specific requirements of their Principals. We define as follows here: co-creation captures the principal and the con-tractor(s) working together on the engineering of an acceptable artifact; co-production captures the shared production of the engineering artifact by both principal and con-tractor(s), including matching financial transactions.

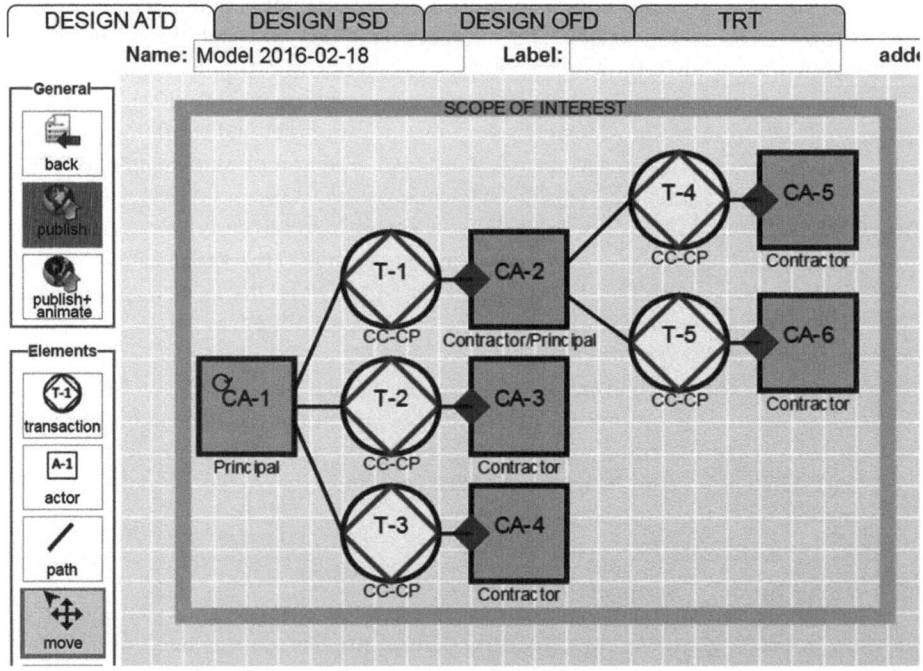

**Fig. 3.** Production chain example of virtual CC-CP enterprises. (Color figure online)

Typical examples are consulting firms, advertising companies and subcontractors in industries like the automotive industry. We observe, in line with the DEMO con-struction axiom, a hierarchical tree of enterprises, shown in Fig. 3, where ontological "red" transactions are shown. There is a parent enterprise, "Principal" CA-1, co-operating closely with "Contractor" enterprises, CA-2 to CA-6. A Principal with one or more Contractor enterprise constitute together a virtual co-creation and co-production "CC-CP" enterprise. In Fig. 3, CA-1 with CC-CP transaction T-1 and Contractor/Principal CA-2 constitute a CC-CP enterprise. Similarly CA-1 with CA-3, etc. CA-2 plays a dual role, within the CC-CP enterprise with CA-1, CA-2 executes the role of Contractor. Within the CC-CP enterprise between CA-2 and CA-5 CA-2 exe-cutes a Principal role. The difference with a "typical" enterprise is that a normal enterprise has boundaries defined by company status, has a management, has a business objective to be profitable etc. A virtual enterprise is only bound by the ad-hoc CC-CP agreements, captured by commitments based on communicative acts.

## 3.2    Proposed Ontological Co-creation and Co-production Model

The proposed CC-CP model is shown in Fig. 4, with two compound actors, Principal and Contractor. The Principal needs products from the Contractor of which the specifications and price are not yet well-defined. There are three different phases.

**The Co-creation Phase.** Transaction T-1 represents a production fact the definition of *what* the production to be delivered by the Contractor must be. Typically production specifications with quality criteria, materials used, testing procedures to be followed. The initiator of T-1 is the Principal who issues T-1.Request to the executor, Contractor, to provide appropriate production specifications. Usually this transaction encapsulates other transactions for engineering, product development etc. If T-1 is Stated and Accepted then there is a shared agreement, without any ambiguity, between Principal and Contractor about *what* the co-production must be.

Transaction T-2 represents as production fact the definition of the price, including specific payment terms and conditions, etc. precisely applied to the production defined by the transaction result of T-1. The Principal is the initiator who issues a T-2.Request to the Contractor for a price for the production defined in T-1. This implies the condition that T-1.Accepted must be true before T-2.Request can be issued by the Principal. T-2.Accepted means that the two actors agree that there is a well-defined price for the production. It does not mean yet that the two actors have decided to commit to a delivery and payment. However, price negotiations may occur here; a T-2. Stated is a quotation that can be accepted or rejected. One option is that there is no agreement, for example the production in this way is too expensive. This is a common situation, leading to the possibility to revoke T-1.Accepted and T-1.Stated and redesign the production in T-1 via a renewed T1.Request and T-1.Promise.

**The Contract Phase.** At this stage, with T-1.Accepted and T-2.Accepted, represent the situation that there is a well-defined but yet unsigned contract on the table. The contract is composed of two directly related mutually binding obligations; defined by the two transaction results of T-1 and T-2. It is important to realize that a contract is *not the delivery* of goods/services itself, a contract is a *binding commitment to deliver* goods/services/payments in both directions, depending on certain defined conditions. The Principal requests the Contractor a commitment to deliver the production, T-3, by issuing T-3.Request. The Contractor requests the Principal a commitment to pay the price, T-4, by issuing T-4.Request. The two signatures on the contract are represented by T-3.Promised and T-4.Promised. Transaction T-3 represents the commitment, an *obligation* that the production has to be delivered by the Contractor, executor, to the Principal, initiator. This obligation is not identical to the actual delivery of productions, which are represented by multiple transaction instances of transaction T-5.

At some moment the Contractor may issue T-3.State, meaning that the Contractor thinks that the contractual agreement to deliver the product has been fulfilled.

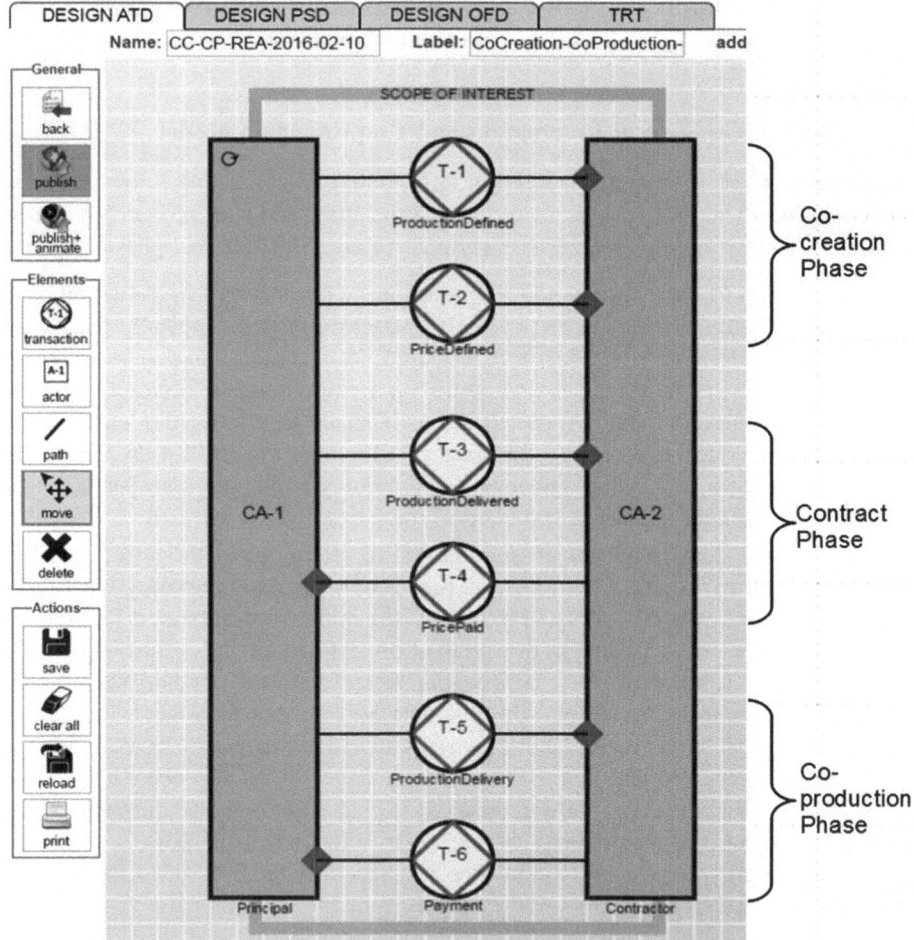

**Fig. 4.** The proposed ontological CC-CP DEMO model.

If the Principal agrees then the Contractor may issue T-3.Accept, the contractual obligation for the production has been fulfilled. Similarly, transaction T-4 represents the obligation to pay the price to be paid by the Principal, executor, to the Contractor, initiator. Multiple instances of T-6, separate payment(s) may constitute the fulfillment of the obligation of T-4. If both actors agree, they will issue T-4.State and T-4.Accept, the contractual obligation to pay the correct price has been fulfilled. Contract disputes are very common and may involve either the payment, or the production or both. Parties may reach agreement that the contract has been fulfilled partially, only correct payment of the price (T4.Accepted) or correct delivery of the production (T-3. Accepted). The communicative act T-3.Promised by the Contractor binds the Contractor to its obligation. This obligation can be fulfilled by one or more deliveries of "things" to the Principal, each delivery represented by an instance of T-5. When the whole of all delivered "things" may constitute the fulfillment of the contract, the Contractor may issue T-3.State. If the Principal agrees he issues a T-3.Accept and parties agree that the contract has been fulfilled by the Contractor. Parties may disagree about the delivery by a T-3.Reject etc.

Similarly, the Contractor may request for partial payments, each represented by an instance of T-6.Request, implemented by sending an invoice. These payments may or may not be directly linked to accepted deliveries, depending on the contract. An invoice may be rejected by issuing a T6.Decline. A payment (by bank) by the Principal, executor, represents an implicit T6.Promise followed by a T6.State. The Contractor, initiator may however reject this payment, typically if the payment does not comply with the amount specified by the invoice. This an important legal figure, a partial payment that is either going to be accepted or rejected.

**The Co-Production Phase.** The actual co-production is captured by one or more instances of transaction T-5 and T-6. Since the Contractor signed the contract, he has the obligation to issue T-5.Promise for multiple deliveries of productions, as long as the T-5.Request fits within the contract. The co-production phase encompasses also multiple payments, instances of T-6. Often an instance of T-6 is directly related to an instance of T5, as stipulated in the contract. The co-production phase ends when the Principal and the Contractor have fulfilled their obligations defined in T-3 and T-4. The fulfilment of the obligation of goods/services delivered by instances of T-5 will result in T-3 being Stated and Accepted. Similarly, the fulfilment of the obligation of PricePaid delivered by instances of T-6 will result in T-4 being Stated and Accepted. The contract has been fulfilled by both parties.

### 3.3 Discussion of the Model Duality

There is a strong duality in this model; the specification of the products versus the price to be paid in T-1 and T-2; the two sides of the contract in T-3 and T-4 and the deliveries of products and price being paid in T-5 and T-6. The notions product and price are commonly used in daily language. However, in the CC-CP model there is no real difference between products and price. A transfer of goods/services in T-5 is balanced by a matching transfer of something else, also goods/services in T-6. In daily life the goods of T-6 are concrete (or abstract titles to) certain round pieces of metal, also known as "coins". In other economic systems this might be potatoes or shoes. A bank transfer is the delivery of a number of abstract coins from one account to another. So, the Principal and the Contractor agree finally in T-3 and T-4 that the goods/services defined in T-1 are well-balanced by the coins/potatoes/shoes defined in T-2.

### 3.4 Avoiding the Notion of Value in DEMO Models

The notion of 'value' is relevant in society. In most cases we observe there is not a one sided transaction with only a transfer of goods/services from the executor to the initiator. The matching exchange is usually called value, price or payment. Also in production environments some value has to be assigned to products in the inventory.

However, there are deep-rooted problems with the stance that "value" should be part of DEMO models. The most important is the recognition that value is a (inter)subjective "concept", "in the eye of the beholder(s)". Value is not an abstract or concrete thing that exists within the theory of enterprise ontology. Adding such a notion to enterprise ontology would give rise to unacceptable flaws. Value is certainly a concept that drives actors' behaviour or the design of DEMO models. Another problem is that there is no objective way to assign a well-defined value to some objects in the real world. Shared definitions formulated in an objective way can be devised for the calculation of some value, but these definitions are also intersubjectively created. In the REA ontology the notion of value exists, and this is one of the major problems to solve. It is recognized that this stance is controversial. If it is flawed this stance will be refuted and other approaches will be investigated.

## 4   Future Research Topics

### 4.1   Extensive Ontological CC-CP Model Validation

The CC-CP model validation should provide sufficient confidence that any imaginable Co-creation and Co-production cooperation is well captured. This means that the ontological model is generic, application-independent and suitable for real life application. Analysis of a sufficient number of business cases is needed.

### 4.2   Extension of the CC-CP Model with Implementation Specific Transactions

The ontological CC-CP model is implementation-independent, which means that the model is absolutely generic. Validation using real life cases should also lead to extension of the ontological model into an implementation specific DEMO models. So-called infological and datalogical transactions are defined. The extended CC-CP models should align well with the delivered business cases. Of great importance is the requirement that any imaginable CC-CP enterprise must be implemented with perfect correctness, meaning that the model reflects precisely the business case.

   Notably extensions include transactions that implement:

  (i)   electronic invoicing with matching payments (implemented, fit for a production);
 (ii)   verification of authorized actors following company specific procedures, for example, a payment must be approved by at least two different authorized actors;
(iii)   transactions that handle legal Value Added Tax obligations, and ensure that these are followed correctly, implementation of other fiscal laws;
(iv)   for the Contract Phase the (bitcoin) blockchain technology may provide trustless truth, guaranteed correctness about authenticity of the contract.

### 4.3 Conceptual Mapping of DEMO to REA

The result is an executable specification how factual knowledge rendered by the EOS can be mapped to the REA (Fig. 2, "Conceptual Mapping") in such a way that a REA-based information system can operate directly. This is considered a major task.

### 4.4 REA Value Chain Analysis

Value chains as proposed by the REA ontology seem to be, or must be, well represented by DEMO CC-CP models. The mapping of concepts must be elaborated. An REA value chain is represented by a network of REA models that are linked together by resource stockflow creating thus so called transaction cycle that is continually repeated. The purpose of REA value chain is to directly or indirectly contribute to the creation of the desired features of the final product or service. An REA value chain defines interfaces between individual REA models. In REA value chain analysis "conceptual mapping" will be utilized, in which a resource is represented by a production fact in DEMO methodology. Apart from conceptual mapping between DEMO primitives and REA concepts, synchronization mechanism between individual business processes has to be identified and described. By utilizing value chain one can get an overview of the whole enterprise model.

**Acknowledgements.** The paper was supported by the grant provided by Ministry of Education, Youth and Sports Czech Republic, reference no. SGS15/PRF/2016. We thank Dr. Jorge Sanz who identified the challenges of the CC-CP domain to us.

**Reflection.** The representation of the real world, populated with humans, based on the limited set of concepts of an ontology and control their actions, is a reductionist approach. On one side it may be very useful, on the other side it may turn out later to be inhumane. If it is found to be inhumane then it must be refuted.

# References

1. Ciao! Consortium; Cooperation & Interoperability - Architecture & Ontology. www.ciaonetwork.org
2. DEMO Knowledge Centre, Design and Engineering Methodology for Organizations (2012). www.demo.nl
3. Dietz, J.L.G.: Enterprise Ontology: Theory and Methodology. Springer, Heidelberg (2006)
4. Dietz, J.L.G., Hoogervorst, J.A.P.: The discipline of enterprise engineering. Int. J. Organisational Des. Eng. 3(1), 86–114 (2013)
5. Dudok, E., Guerreiro, S., Babkin, E., Pergl, R., van Kervel, S.J.: Enterprise operational analysis using DEMO and the enterprise operating system. In: Aveiro, D., Pergl, R., Valenta, M. (eds.) EEWC 2015. LNBIP, vol. 211, pp. 3–18. Springer, Heidelberg (2015)
6. Dunn, C.L., Cherrington, O.J., Hollander, A.S.: Enterprise Information Systems: A Pattern Based Approach. McGraw-Hill/Irwin, New York (2004)
7. e-Invoicing/e-Billing – Key stakeholders as game changers - Bruno Koch, Billentis, August 2014

8. European Multi-Stakeholder Forum on e-invoicing. Electronic invoicing for small and medium enterprises: Activity 2 – Experience and Good practice (2013)
9. Gómez-Pérez, A., Rojas-Amaya, D.: Ontological reengineering for reuse. In: Fensel, D., Studer, R. (eds.) EKAW 1999. LNCS (LNAI), vol. 1621, pp. 139–156. Springer, Heidelberg (1999)
10. Guerreiro, S.: Enterprise governance enforcement in the operation of the runtime transactions using DEMO and ACM. In: Enterprise Engineering Working Conference
11. Guerreiro, S., Vasconcelos, A., Tribolet, J.: Adaptive access control modes enforcement in organizations. In: Quintela Varajão, J.E., Cruz-Cunha, M.M., Putnik, G.D., Trigo, A. (eds.) CENTERIS 2010. CCIS, vol. 110, pp. 283–294. Springer, Heidelberg (2010)
12. Guerreiro, S., van Kervel, S.J., Vasconcelos, A., Tribolet, J.: Executing enterprise dynamic systems control with the demo processor: the business transactions transition space validation. In: Rahman, H., Mesquita, A., Ramos, I., Pernici, B. (eds.) MCIS 2012. LNBIP, vol. 129, pp. 97–112. Springer, Heidelberg (2012)
13. Guerreiro, S., Kervel, S., Babkin, E.: Towards devising an architectural framework for enterprise operating systems. In: Proceedings of the 8th International Conference on Software Paradigm Trends (2013)
14. Guerreiro, S., Tribolet, J.: Conceptualizing enterprise dynamic systems control for run-time business transactions. In Proceedings of the 21st European Conference on Information Systems, paper 56 (2013)
15. Hevner, A.R., March, S.T., Park, J., Ram, S.: Design science in information systems research. MIS Q. 28(1), 75–105 (2004)
16. Hevner, A.R.: A three cycle view of design science research. Scandinavian J. Inf. Syst. 19 (2), 87–92 (2007). Information systems and Decision Sciences
17. Hintzen, J., van Kervel, S.J.H., van Meeuwen, T., Vermolen, J.A.J., Zijlstra, B.: A professional case management system in production, modeled and implemented using DEMO. In: Proceedings of the 16th IEEE Conference on Business Informatics (2014)
18. Hruby, P.: Model-Driven Design Using Business Patterns. Springer, Heidelberg (2006)
19. van Kervel, S.J.H., Dietz, J.L.G., Hintzen, J., van Meeuwen, T., Zijlstra, B.: Enterprise ontology driven software engineering. In: Proceedings of the International Conference on Software Paradigm Trends (2012)
20. McCarthy, W.E.: The REA accounting model: a generalized framework for accounting systems in a shared data environment. Account. Rev. 57, 554–578 (1982)
21. Van Nuffel, D., Mulder, H., Van Kervel, S.: Enhancing the formal foundations of BPMN by enterprise ontology. In: Albani, A., Barjis, J., Dietz, J.L. (eds.) CIAO! 2009. LNBIP, vol. 34, pp. 115–129. Springer, Heidelberg (2009)
22. Sarbanes-Oxley act, "SoX", 107th Congress Public Law 204, United States of America, 30 July 2002. http://www.gpo.gov/fdsys/pkg/PLAW-107publ204/html/PLAW-107publ204.htm

# Evolvability

# Building an Evolvable Prototype for a Multiple GAAP Accounting Information System

Els Vanhoof[1(✉)], Peter De Bruyn[1], Walter Aerts[1,2], and Jan Verelst[1]

[1] University of Antwerp, Antwerp, Belgium
{Els.Vanhoof,Peter.DeBruyn,Walter.Aerts,Jan.Verelst}@uantwerp.be
[2] Tilburg University, Tilburg, The Netherlands

**Abstract.** In this paper we build a prototype of an evolvable Accounting Information System (AIS) that supports multiple Generally Accepted Accounting Standards (GAAP) reporting. Reporting in multiple GAAP can have different origins: differences in local and tax GAAP, belonging to an economic group or additional regulations. Regulations change frequently: additional GAAP are imposed on companies and GAAP themselves are updated to changing economic conditions. AIS need to support multiple GAAP and evolvability is important because of the changing nature of these GAAP. Normalized Systems Theory (NST) proposes theorems for building evolvable information systems, but lacks specific guidance in business domains (e.g. accounting). Therefore we contribute to literature by showing the feasibility of using NST to design and build an AIS. We use design principles from literature to start building our prototype. The resulting prototype shows into more detail how the design principles are used into an actual software design.

**Keywords:** Multiple GAAP · Normalized Systems Theory · Design science · Mixed methods · Prototyping

## 1 Introduction

Companies need to report financial information to different stakeholders like the regulating and supervisory (government) bodies, investors/shareholders, customers and suppliers. However, the different regulators use different GAAP (generally accepted accounting principles) that prescribe how companies need to record and process events, which financial information they need to report, how this information needs to be presented and so on [1]. A company might be obliged to simultaneously record and process events in reports using different GAAP.

Moreover, GAAP are not a static given: they change frequently. For example, recent events like the credit crisis and corporate fraud scandals have increased the demand for transparency (and an increased quality and relevance) of financial information. Other changes might include more guidance on specific issues that were not addressed before.

To support recording and processing of events, companies use accounting information systems (AIS). Therefore, such information systems need a design

© Springer International Publishing Switzerland 2016
D. Aveiro et al. (Eds.): EEWC 2016, LNBIP 252, pp. 71–85, 2016.
DOI: 10.1007/978-3-319-39567-8_5

which supports reporting in multiple GAAP (each subject to change). While the implementation of different and multiple GAAP typically requires customizations and changes to an AIS over time, research indicates that performing changes to software packages becomes more difficult over time [2]. AIS are usually not designed to cope with multiple GAAP, although this is not a new issue [3]. Moreover, whenever changes occur in these GAAP or a change of GAAP is necessary, this results in difficulties in changing and maintaining the AIS [4]. In the AIS literature, evolvability is not studied and no guidance on how to handle multiple GAAP is provided. Although multiple authors acknowledge the need to study the multiple GAAP issue [3,5,6].

Normalized Systems Theory (NST) [7] prescribes principles and design theorems to design an evolvable information system so that a set of predefined anticipated changes can be applied easily. This theory is aimed towards information systems in general and hence does not formulate specific guidelines for the design of AIS that are able to report in multiple GAAP.

Previous research on this matter is conducted by [8,9]. [8] identifies combinatorial effects in existing multiple GAAP AIS by the use of case studies. Combinatorial effects are used within NST to operationalize instances of lack of evolvability (see Sect. 4). [9] uses these combinatorial effects to formulate a set of design guidelines (or design principles). We contribute to literature by building a prototype that adheres to three of the design principles of [9], which have been only theoretically evaluated up to now. The prototype will serve as a proof-of-concept for the first three design principles of [9]. Moreover, the prototype has practical relevance by investigating the relevance and feasibility of the design principles of [9] in a realistic setting. In this paper we ask ourselves the following research question: can we implement an AIS for multiple GAAP using NST? This general research question can be refined into the following questions:

1. Can we use the design principles of [9]?
2. If not, how can we redefine them?
3. What do we need in addition to these design principles?
4. How feasible is it to build an evolvable multiple GAAP AIS?

We frame our work within design science methodology work in Sect. 2. In Sect. 3, we elaborate on the multiple GAAP reporting problem within AIS. Normalized Systems Theory, our theoretical framework, is the subject of Sect. 4. Next, we describe how we built our prototype in Sect. 5. In Sect. 6, we evaluate the prototype. We conclude this paper in Sect. 7.

## 2   Design Science Methodology

The use of design science can be motivated by the perceived lack of professional relevance of IS research [10,11]. Design science addresses this relevance problem by designing artifacts (such as software systems) that solve real-world problems or improve upon existing solutions [12,13]. Hevner [14] proposes three cycles to conduct design science research: relevance, rigor and design. We address the relevance of our research (which addresses both professional as academic relevance) by electing the real-world problem of designing an evolvable AIS that supports multiple GAAP reporting. The motivation for this problem is described in Sects. 1 and 3. Rigor in this paper is ensured by using NST (described in Sect. 4). The results of this paper, described in Sect. 7, contribute to literature (and hence also to the rigor) because the evolvability criterion is an improvement (positioned in the DSR knowledge contribution framework of [15]) upon existing solutions. In Sects. 5 and 6, we describe the design cycle: the actual building and evaluation of our artifact, the prototype. The prototype itself is a level 1 contribution (classified as in [15]): a situated implementation of an artifact. Additional design principles we develop, based on the prototype are a level 2 contribution [15]: nacent design theory, which is prescriptive in nature.

Lastly we want to relate our paper to the research project it is part of. In order to describe the overall methodology, we can use the framework presented by [16]. The entire research project consists of four design science research activities: identify problem, design, construct and use. After each of these activities, an evaluation of the activity needs to take place. Applied to our research project, the first activity (identify problem) and its evaluation are described in [8] and the design activity and its evaluation in [9]. The current paper is the third activity, being the construct in the form of a prototype and its evaluation. If our prototype would be further developed into a working AIS that can be used in practice, the actual implementation by a real company could be the fourth activity.

The evaluation we conduct in Sect. 6 adheres to the evaluation framework presented by [17] in the following ways. First, we explicate the goals of the evaluation. We want to know whether the prototype we have built adheres to the principles of the NST and in which way. Moreover, we want to evaluate to which extent the design principles of [9] are applicable in a prototype and to which extent they provide a sufficient degree of guidance. Second, we discuss the why, when and how of our evaluation. We use a formative (why) ex-post (when) evaluation, because our prototype is not a finished product yet and will only provide us with insights to further develop a working AIS. The how of our evaluation is performed by imposing changes to the prototype and evaluating whether they cause combinatorial effects or not. Thirdly, the main property we want to evaluate is whether the prototype is evolvable or not. Fourth, the individual evaluation episodes are described in Sect. 6.

To be able to build the prototype, we first describe the basic modular structure of the accounting domain as shown in Fig. 1 in terms of the NST elements. This includes the identification of data elements, their relationships and their attributes. Next, we use the design principles of [9] to guide us during the extension of this initial design with additional functionality (to provide for instance the multiple GAAP possibility). Then we impose two changes as mentioned in [8,9] on the prototype and evaluate their impact. We conclude how we should implement the design principles and what additional implementing principles we need, by relating our conclusions to NST theorems.

# 3    Problem Statement and Earlier Research

## 3.1    Problem Statement

Multiple GAAP reporting affects most companies, even though some of them are not aware of this. Several situations force companies to deal with multiple reporting standards concurrently and/or over time. First, all companies need to report their statutory annual financial statements to the local filing office (in Belgium for example the National Bank, in the USA the SEC) and an adjusted report to the tax authorities. Tax legislation is usually only seen as an additional burden and never considered as a separate GAAP. Often, companies adjust their chosen accounting methods to limit the differences between local GAAP and tax GAAP. Second, an additional reporting burden is put on a company when it is part of an international group, as it usually needs to report in the standard of the parent company or an international standard like International Financial Reporting Standards (IFRS) or US GAAP. Third, in case of mergers or acquisitions the GAAP might change: being sold to another parent company might result in the need to report in yet another GAAP. Finally, many companies get additional questions from authorities to provide complementary information for statistical purposes or get requests from suppliers, customers or the bank to provide certain information. Although these additional reporting requirements become only apparent on an ad-hoc basis, they might require a vast effort from the person preparing the reports by re-collecting the information from scratch in case the AIS is not adequately designed to cope with it.

Next to the fact that companies have to handle the different GAAP in which they need to report, changes related to these GAAP occur as well. This concerns both changes regarding the GAAP in which they need to report (like in case of mergers and acquisitions) as well as changes authorities make to the GAAP themselves. GAAP can differ from each other in five different ways [18]: definition of concepts, recognition, measurement, presentation and disclosure and the two additional issues of alternatives and lack of requirements.

## 3.2    Earlier Research

Some explicit research efforts to design multiple GAAP handling AIS are [8,9]. [8] uses case studies to study how companies design their AIS to be able to report in multiple GAAP. Next they describe combinatorial effects (violations of NST principles) present in those designs. These combinatorial effects are used by [9] to propose a set of design principles to prevent combinatorial effects. These design principles are the following [9]:

- "Postings to different GAAP should be made in separate ledgers;
- All GAAP should use the same chart of accounts;
- Postings to different GAAP should be made independently of each other;
- Every transaction that could have an accounting impact should pass through at least five tasks (versions of the following tasks: definitions of concepts,

recognition, measurement, presentation and disclosure) before any posting is made;
- Every measurement method, definition of a concept, recognition criterion, presentation requirement and disclosure requirement that has a separate change driver should be separated in a distinct task, independent of the GAAP."

Although the design principles already provide some specific guidance on how a more evolvable multiple GAAP AIS should be built, the principles were merely proposed on a theoretical basis. Also their impact was merely tested conceptually by assessing the impact of the following three changes on a hypothetical design [8,9]: (1) Creating a new account (2) New version of an entry processing task for one GAAP (3) New version of an entry processing task for all GAAP. This means that neither the actual effectiveness, nor the feasibility of the above mentioned design principles to actually build an AIS in practice have been tested up to now. Therefore, in order to perform this validation in practice, this paper reports on the construction of an AIS prototype based on the first three design principles.

## 4   Normalized Systems Theory

NST uses the concepts of stability (from systems theory) and entropy (from thermodynamics) to prove a set of theorems for the design of information systems [7,19]. It is aimed towards the elimination of combinatorial effects. Combinatorial effects occur when a functional change to a system has a constructional impact that is not only proportional to the change itself, but is also proportional to the size of the system to which the change is proposed [7,20,21]. The theory proposes a set of theorems which should be adhered to in order to avoid combinatorial effects. NST is originally applied in software design [7,20], but has shown its relevance in the context of business process design [22] and enterprise architectures [23]. [21] generalizes the theory so it becomes applicable for the design of modular structures in general. This causes the study of combinatorial effects and the application of NST theorems to become relevant in domains outside software design as well. The NST theorems can therefore be considered as ways to design modular structures so that they exhibit a higher degree of evolvability.

Applying the theory in the context of accounting, we could consider a multinational company with a considerable number of subsidiaries (which we consider to be its modules), each having their own AIS. We assume that all subsidiaries report to the parent using US GAAP. Suppose the parent wants to change the internal reporting standard from US GAAP to IFRS. The impact of this change is now proportional to the number of subsidiaries: every subsidiary needs to change their AIS. Since the change is proportional to the size of the system (here: organization), it can be considered as a combinatorial effect. Another way to modularize (a part of) the accounting domain was proposed by [8]. Figure 1 provides a visual representation of these primitives (modular building blocks). In this paper, we therefore use a modularity viewpoint to analyze the accounting

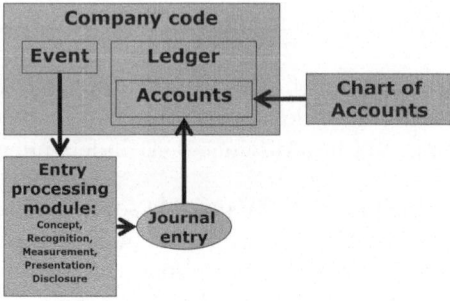

**Fig. 1.** Modular structure

domain and the NST theorems [7, 19, 21] to design a modular (accounting) structure which meets the evolvability criterion we put forward. That is, a modular
structure that adheres to the theorems will be able to change more easily over
time (with respect to a set of predefined anticipated changes), as it will not be
subject to combinatorial effects.

As adhering to NST theorems has proven to be challenging, a set of design
patterns have been proposed in certain domains [21]. These patterns are called
elements and facilitate the application of the theorems in that particular domain.
They are the recurring building blocks used to construct the envisioned modular structure. Five elements have been proposed at the software level by [24]:
data element, action element, workflow element, connector element and trigger
element. As a consequence, the development of a working software application
prototype requires the identification of the different instances of each of these
elements for the considered domain. Based on the instantiation of these elements,
major parts of the actual software code can be generated (each element instance
is expanded into a predefined recurring software structure) providing basic out-
of-the-box functionalities such as CRUD screens, waterfall screens, data import,
document upload/download, basic user management, basic reporting, etcetera.
Customizations (additional required functionality which is not offered by the
code expansion in a standard way) can afterwards be added in a structured way
by software developers, if necessary.

## 5    Prototype

### 5.1    Creating Prototypes

Our prototype was built by using the Prime Radiant, a software tool developed
by the Normalized Systems Institute (NSI) and Normalized Systems eXpanders
factory (NSX). Among other things, this tool provides a graphical user interface (GUI) for the formulation of NST software elements. It therefore allows a
business analyst to insert the specification of data elements, action elements and
flow elements into the Prime Radiant. The analyst can subsequently also expand

(generate) and build (compile) software code into a working software prototype. In this way, the analyst (1) has a more concrete representation of the envisioned application (a real working application vs. an abstract UML diagram) to validate the completeness, consistency, accuracy, etcetera of his own analysis model, (2) can use this prototype to communicate and refine the functional requirements in consultation with potential end users (a real working application vs. an abstract UML diagram or set of use cases), (3) prove the actual feasibility of the development of a NST compatible application of the considered model and domain, and (4) use this prototype as a starting point to interact with software developers adding custom code into the generated application to provide non-generated functionality [25]. Moreover, it allows an iterative way of working in which a first version of a prototype is built, feedback is given and incorporated in an updated model, after which a new version of the prototype is developed, and so on.

## 5.2   Building an Initial Data Model and Prototype

We stated before that the first step of building a NST software prototype should consist out of the identification of instances of the different NST software elements. As our prototype aims to assess the feasibility of the design principles of [8], they should be taken into account. Moreover, NST analysis best practices suggest the identification of these elements on an anthropomorphic (i.e., concurring with meaningful real-world entities) basis [25]. In doing so, we identify the following core *data elements* within a typical AIS as our starting point, based on the modular structure which is visualized in Fig. 1: Event, JournalEntry, Gaap, CompanyCode, Ledger, ChartOfAccounts and Account. Several remarks regarding this first set of data elements can be made. First, we currently leave out the entry processing module and entry processing tasks for reasons of simplicity. Second, it can be noticed that a many-to-one relationship exists between Account–ChartOfAccounts, Ledger–JournalEntry, Ledger–Gaap, Ledger–CompanyCode and Event–JournalEntry. A many-to-many relationship exists between JournalEntry–Account, which should be avoided [25]. This leads to the creation of an additional data element JournalEntryLine and a many-to-one relationship between Account–JournalEntryLine and JournalEntryLine–JournalEntry. Third, we cannot use the data element Event, as it is too general: we need to identify different events that occur and should be recorded in an AIS. For example, we identify a SalesInvoice, a SalesDelivery, a SalesOrder and a Payment as events in a standard order-to-cash process and therefore additional data elements. Lastly, the data element CompanyCode is artificial and non-anthropomorphic (in the sense that it does not concur with an actual real-world concept) in nature. As a consequence, we replace this data element with the data element Company.

Next, *attributes (fields)* for the different data elements can be identified. First, all data elements have an attribute "name", which acts as a unique identifier. Next, for all many-to-one relationships, the data element at the many side of the relationship needs to have an attribute that links the data element to one particular instance of the other data element. For ChartOfAccounts, Company,

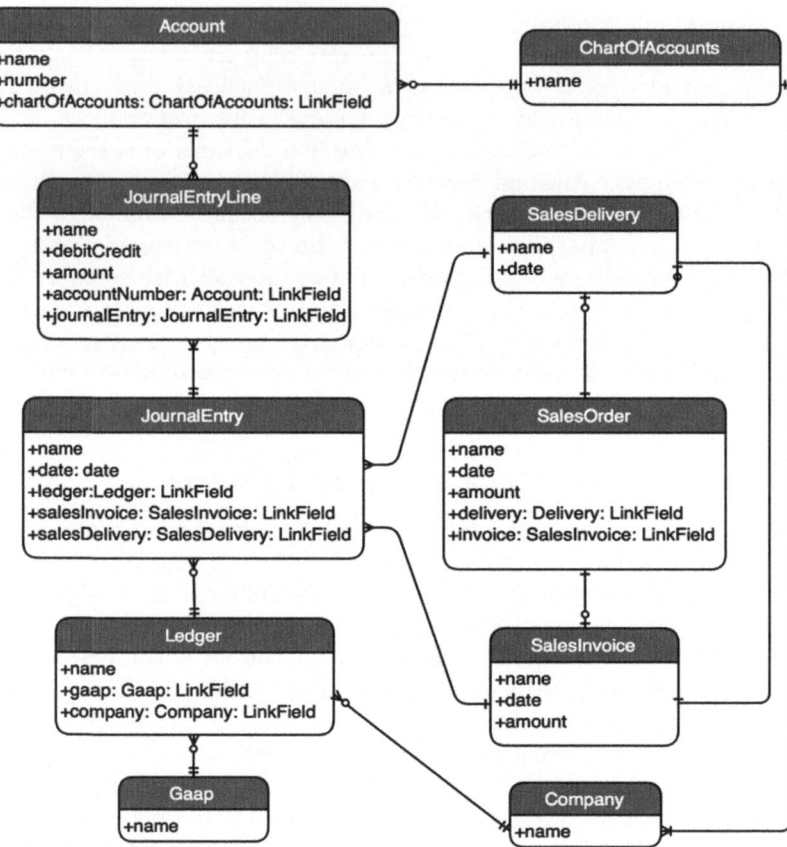

**Fig. 2.** Entity relationship diagram of the prototype

Ledger and Gaap no additional attributes are needed, at this point in time. For Account we use both a name and a number as attributes. A JournalEntry has a date, a JournalEntryLine has an amount and a debit/credit attribute. The determination of data value types (such as String or Integer) is currently left out of scope. In Fig. 2, we represent the final model in an entity relationship diagram.

Based on the data model as described above, we can generate a **first version of a prototype**. As explained earlier, a set of out-of-box functionalities such as CRUD screens is provided by the code generation as triggered by the Prime Radiant. We can therefore immediately start to create instantiations of the data elements in the model. Stated otherwise: we can start with inserting data of the company for which we want to use this AIS.

## 5.3   A Second Version of the Prototype

In the first version of the prototype, the design principles of [9] are not yet used. Therefore, in this section we propose additional functionality that helps to enforce the first two design principles. For the first design principle, "separate ledgers", we add functionality that automatically creates the needed ledgers when a new GAAP or a new company is added to the system. For the second design principle, "use the same chart of accounts", an additional restriction should be added to the data model: a many-to-one relation between Company and ChartOfAccounts. Further, the prototype should make sure only Accounts from the right ChartOfAccounts can be selected in a JournalEntryLine. Updating the model (for the second adaptation), implementing some small customizations (for the first and third adaptation), and regenerating the application then results in **a second version of the prototype**.

### 5.4 Adding Posting Functionality to the Prototype

Now that we have set up an AIS, we want it to be capable to allow the actual posting of journal entries based on events. We will use an example in which Revenue needs to be posted after a *SalesInvoice* event. Hence, we create a data element SalesInvoice with a date and amount attribute. For example, the date of a particular SalesInvoice is 15/08/2016 and the amount is 20,000. The SalesInvoice is related to the data element JournalEntry with a one-to-many relationship.

Furthermore, some processing functionality needs to be added to the prototype as an accounting context requires the processing of a SalesInvoice resulting in journal entries for all GAAP. We therefore create a *SalesInvoiceProcessor* action element which is triggered after a SalesInvoice is created, therefore representing an elementary flow element operating on the SalesInvoice data element. This action element is responsible for processing each individual SalesInvoice which is created by instantiating the appropriate JournalEntries and JournalEntryLines. In a situation with two GAAP (for example, Belgian GAAP and IFRS) having identical recognition criteria, the SalesInvoiceProcessor would therefore create two identical JournalEntries, with linked JournalEntryLines. Adding this processing functionality results in a **third version of our prototype**.

Table 1 provides an overview of the exemplary booking in this context. For every data element (indicated in bold), the attributes are indicated in the left column and their specific values in the right column.

## 6  Evaluation

### 6.1  Evaluation Regarding the Design Principles

The initial data model (described in Sect. 5.2) is rather general and does not yet incorporate the design principles as proposed by [9]. It is also not straightforward to actually impose these principles on the system. For instance, the first design principle requires to separate ledgers for different GAAP in the system: however, this is not enforced by this data model, this is a choice that needs to be made when preparing the system for operational use (by setting up the configuration such as the creation of actual ledgers, accounts, GAAPs, etcetera).

**Table 1.** Resulting journal entries from SalesInvoiceProcessor

| SalesInvoiceProcessor | | | |
|---|---|---|---|
| **JournalEntry 1** | | **JournalEntry 2** | |
| ledger | ledger for Belgian GAAP | ledger | ledger for IFRS |
| date | 15/08/2016 | date | 15/08/2016 |
| journalEntryLine | link to: JournalEntryLine 1 JournalEntryLine 2 | journalEntryLine | link to: JournalEntryLine 3 JournalEntryLine 4 |
| **JournalEntryLine 1** | | **JournalEntryLine 3** | |
| debit/credit | debit | debit/credit | debit |
| amount | 20,000 | amount | 20,000 |
| account | Trade Receivables | account | Trade Receivables |
| **JournalEntryLine 2** | | **JournalEntryLine 4** | |
| debit/credit | credit | debit/credit | credit |
| amount | 20,000 | amount | 20,000 |
| account | Revenue | account | Revenue |

Stated otherwise: this prototype allows but does not enforce the adherence of the considered design principles. Accurate documentation could assist in this matter. For example, such documentation would describe that the data element Ledger is the collection of JournalEntries according to one GAAP. The second design principle, to use only one chart of accounts, is also not enforced by the current data model and again a configuration setting. Hence, documentation should clarify that all Ledgers should use the same ChartOfAccounts.

Also in the second version of the prototype, there are some additional constraints added, but they do not prevent misuse of the system. For example, it is still possible to create multiple Companies for the different GAAP and in that way avoid the constraint to use the same ChartOfAccounts. Therefore, we believe these design principles cannot be enforced by the data model, but documentation for the use of the prototype is necessary.

The third design principle is proposed in the third version of the prototype. Although, it depends on the implementation of the SalesInvoiceProcessor, which is a choice made at design time.

## 6.2 Configuration of Prototype

Now we start to configure our prototype for use. First, we create an instance of the data element Company for which we want to set up the AIS (we will call this company "AntwerpComp"). Second, we instantiate "IFRS" and "Belgian Gaap" from the data element Gaap, assuming that our company needs to report in multiple GAAP. Third, we create a separate *Ledger* for each GAAP (following the design principle "separate ledgers"). Next, we create a *ChartOfAccounts* in which all needed accounts can be contained (following the design principle "use the same chart of accounts for all GAAP"). Finally, we create some *Accounts* that belong to the created ChartOfAccounts (for example, 7000000 Revenue product X and 7100000 Revenue product Y).

## 6.3   Evaluating the Impact of Change 1

To further demonstrate the practical value of the design principles, we impose changes to the prototype incorporating the design principles of [9] and analyze whether they result in a combinatorial effect. This allows us to further evaluate the effectiveness of the design principles and the prototype.

As a first change, we consider the creation of a new account in the ChartOfAccounts that is used by all GAAP. For example, a company starts selling a new product and wants a separate account to record the revenue of the product: account number 7200000 with description "Revenue product Z". This requires the creation of that one Account and the definition to which ChartOfAccounts that Account belongs. Since we are enforced to use the same ChartOfAccounts for all Ledgers of the same Company, the Account should only be created once within the same Company. This impact is located at only one place and is not related to the number of GAAP, the amount of entries in the system or any other variable reflecting the size of the system.

By using our prototype, we can therefore conclude that the creation of a new account can be incorporated without a combinatorial effect. The prototype furthermore illustrates the feasibility of the first two design principles of [9]. We can also clearly define the boundary of our current design: the combinatorial effect that arises when adding a new account is prevented as long as the new account is only used by one company. If a new Account needs to be added to all ChartOfAccounts of all Companies (for example, a new kind of tax on labor is introduced by the government and this new kind of tax needs to be recorded separately in the statement of profit or loss), this change causes a combinatorial effect.

## 6.4   Evaluating the Impact of Change 2

As a second change, we study the creation of a new version of an entry processing task for one GAAP. We consider the situation in which some revenue recognition criteria are changed [8,9]: from recognition when the invoice is drafted to recognition when the goods are delivered. For this purpose, we first need to add some data element instances to our prototype to represent this additional complexity. Next to the event SalesInvoice, also the event *SalesDelivery* becomes relevant now, which we add. Date is the only relevant attribute for SalesDelivery. For example: the date of a particular SalesDelivery is 03/08/2016.

Having created these data and action element (instances), we can analyze the impact of changing one entry processing task. If we change the considered revenue recognition criterion, a SalesDelivery will from that moment also be related to a JournalEntry with a one-to-many relationship. Moreover, SalesDelivery and

**Table 2.** Resulting journal entries from SalesDeliveryProcessor and SalesInvoice-Processor

| SalesDeliveryProcessor | | | |
|---|---|---|---|
| **JournalEntry 1** | | | |
| ledger | IFRS ledger | | |
| date | 03/08/2016 | | |
| journalEntryLine | link to nr 1 and 2 | | |
| **JournalEntryLine 1** | | **JournalEntryLine 2** | |
| debit/credit | debit | debit/credit | credit |
| amount | 20,000 | amount | 20,000 |
| account | Invoices to be prepared | account | Revenue |
| **SalesInvoiceProcessor** | | | |
| **JournalEntry 2** | | **JournalEntry 3** | |
| ledger | Belgian GAAP ledger | ledger | IFRS ledger |
| date | 15/08/2016 | date | 15/08/2016 |
| journalEntryLine | link to nr 3 and 4 | journalEntryLine | link to nr 5 and 6 |
| **JournalEntryLine 3** | | **JournalEntryLine 5** | |
| debit/credit | debit | debit/credit | debit |
| amount | 20,000 | amount | 20,000 |
| account | Trade Receivables | account | Trade Receivables |
| **JournalEntryLine 4** | | **JournalEntryLine 6** | |
| debit/credit | credit | debit/credit | credit |
| amount | 20,000 | amount | 20,000 |
| account | Revenue | account | Invoices to be prepared |

SalesInvoice have a one-to-one relationship. To process the SalesDelivery in an accounting context we need a task, *SalesDeliveryProcessor*, to be executed after the SalesDelivery is created. For IFRS, revenue should from now on be recognized on delivery, so we need to adjust the IFRS journal entries. The entries for Belgian GAAP remain unchanged. The result of the SalesDeliveryProcessor cannot yet be depicted, because at delivery date no instance of SalesInvoice is created yet and since the SalesDelivery has no amount, the amount of Revenue is not yet known. Therefore we introduce another event, *SalesOrder*, having the attributes date and amount. In our example we assume an order with date 01/08/2016 and amount 20,000. SalesOrder also has a one-to-one relationship with SalesDelivery. The amount of the SalesOrder will be used as the amount of revenue we recognize. In Table 2 we show the resulting JournalEntries and JournalEntryLines for the SalesDeliveryProcessor and the SalesInvoiceProcessor. We also show the result in JournalEntries and JournalEntryLines in the graphical user interface of the prototype in Fig. 3.

The impact of the change is a change of the JournalEntry for the changing GAAP (IFRS), the creation of a SalesDeliveryProcessor and the additional JournalEntry for the IFRS. All these changes are dependent on the change itself

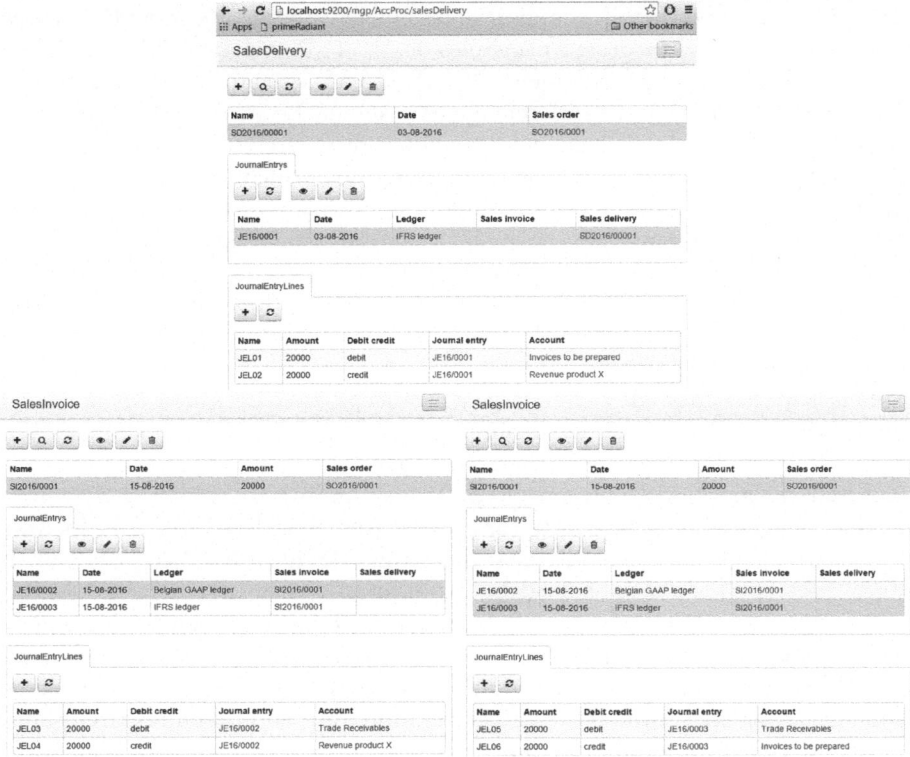

**Fig. 3.** Three screenshots of the JournalEntries and JournalEntryLines in the prototype

and not on the number of GAAP, the amount of entries in the system or any other variable reflecting the size of the system.

By using our prototype, we can therefore conclude that changing an entry processing task for one GAAP can be performed without combinatorial effects. The prototype furthermore illustrates the feasibility of the third design principle of [9]. We can even note that ideally, the principle should be applied in a more strict way: the processor tasks should be separated for each GAAP. Moreover, where we considered the entire entry processing module as one atomic (processor) task for illustrative reasons, the module might consist out of different tasks in reality. Some more guidance on how to design this inner structure of an entry processing module is provided by design principles 4 and 5 of [9], of which we stated before that they are out of scope for this paper.

## 7  Conclusion

In this paper, we test the first three design principles of [9] to build a prototype AIS that supports multiple GAAP reporting. With this prototype we contribute to the literature by providing evidence that building an evolvable

AIS (with respect to certain changes) is feasible. Moreover, we provide practical evidence for three of the design principles of [9]: (1) Postings to different GAAP should be made in separate ledgers (2) All GAAP should use the same chart of accounts (3) Postings to different GAAP should be made independently of each other. In this process, some additional insights were obtained regarding the limitations and required additions of these design principles in the context of building an actual software system. The design principles have implications at both the design time and run time of the prototype: whereas some principles can be enforced during the definition of the model of the prototype, others (like using the same chart of accounts) have to be configured at run time. This configuration phase is the phase before actually starting the posting of individual JournalEntries to Ledgers of a company.

This paper is limited to building a prototype that does not cover enough functionality to be regarded as a comprehensible AIS, testable by companies in practice. Moreover, since the design principles do not cover all possible combinatorial effects of AIS, our prototype is also limited to providing a solution to avoid the combinatorial effects targeted by the considered design principles. That also implies that several design issues in AIS have not been covered. In future research this can be solved by extending the scope: searching for additional combinatorial effects in AIS by studying more case companies and by studying other aspects of AIS like for example XBRL and cash flow statements using the direct method. Next, there are research opportunities in other business domains like logistics, production, etcetera. Moreover, additional research efforts will be made to develop additional general design principles at the business (like [22]) and the enterprise level (like [21,23]) based on NST.

# References

1. Sinnett, W.M., Willis, M.: The time is right for standard business reporting. Financ. Executive **25**(9), 23–27 (2009)
2. Lehman, M.: Programs, life cycles, and laws of software evolution. Proc. IEEE **68**(9), 1060–1076 (1980)
3. Grabski, S.V., Leech, S.A., Schmidt, P.J.: A review of ERP research: a future agenda for accounting information systems. J. Inf. Syst. **25**(1), 37–78 (2011)
4. Meall, L.: Can you comply? Accountancy **133**(1329), 73–74 (2004)
5. Guan, J., Levitan, A.S., Kuhn, J.R.: How AIS can progress along with ontology research in IS. Int. J. Acc. Inf. Syst. **14**(1), 21–38 (2013)
6. Geerts, G.L., Graham, L.E., Mauldin, E.G., McCarthy, W.E., Richardson, V.J.: Integrating information technology into accounting research and practice. Acc. Horiz. **27**(4), 815–840 (2013)
7. Mannaert, H., Verelst, J.: Normalized Systems: Re-creating Information Technology Based on Laws for Software Evolvability. Koppa (2009)
8. Vanhoof, E., Huysmans, P., Aerts, W., Verelst, J.: Evaluating accounting information systems that support multiple GAAP reporting using normalized systems theory. In: Aveiro, D., Tribolet, J., Gouveia, D. (eds.) EEWC 2014. LNBIP, vol. 174, pp. 76–90. Springer, Heidelberg (2014)

9. Vanhoof, E., Aerts, W.: Guidelines to design evolvable multiple GAAP accounting information systems. In: Proceedings of the Twentieth Americas Conference on Information Systems (AMCIS 2014), Savannah, 7–9 August 2014
10. Benbasat, I., Zmud, R.W.: Empirical research in information systems: the practice of relevance. MIS Q. **23**(1), 3–16 (1999)
11. Hirschheim, R., Klein, H.K.: Crisis in the is field? a critical reflection on the state of the discipline. J. Assoc. Inf. Syst. **4**, 237–293 (2003)
12. March, S.T., Smith, G.F.: Design and natural science research on information technology. Decis. Support Syst. **15**(4), 251–266 (1995)
13. Hevner, A.R., March, S.T., Park, J., Ram, S.: Design science in information systems research. MIS Q. **28**(1), 75–105 (2004)
14. Hevner, A.R.: A three cycle view of design science research. Scand. J. Inf. Syst. **19**, 87–92 (2007)
15. Gregor, S., Hevner, A.R.: Positioning and presenting design science research for maximum impact. MIS Q. **37**(2), 337 (2013)
16. Sonnenberg, C., vom Brocke, J.: Evaluations in the science of the artificial – reconsidering the build-evaluate pattern in design science research. In: Peffers, K., Rothenberger, M., Kuechler, B. (eds.) DESRIST 2012. LNCS, vol. 7286, pp. 381–397. Springer, Heidelberg (2012)
17. Venable, J., Pries-Heje, J., Baskerville, R.: A framework for evaluation in design science research. Eur. J. Inf. Syst. **25**(1), 77–89 (2014)
18. Fischer, M., Marsh, T.: Accounting and reporting convergence. Int. J. Acad. Bus. World **6**(1), 1–10 (2012)
19. Mannaert, H., De Bruyn, P., Verelst, J.: Exploring entropy in software systems - towards a precise definition and design rules. In: Proceedings of the Seventh International Conference on Systems, Saint Gilles, Reunion, pp. 93–99 (2012)
20. Mannaert, H., Verelst, J., Ven, K.: The transformation of requirements into software primitives: studying evolvability based on systems theoretic stability. Sci. Comput. Program. **76**(12), 1210–1222 (2011)
21. De Bruyn, P.: Generalizing normalized systems theory: towards a foundational theory for enterprise engineering, Antwerp. Ph.D. dissertation - AES faculty, MIS department, University of Antwerp, Antwerp (2014)
22. Van Nuffel, D.: Towards Designing Modular and Evolvable Business Processes. Ph.D. dissertation - AES faculty, MIS department, University of Antwerp (2011)
23. Huysmans, P.: On the Feasibility of Normalized Enterprises: Applying Normalized Systems Theory to the High-Level Design of Enterprises. Ph.D. dissertation - AES faculty, MIS department, University of Antwerp (2011)
24. Mannaert, H., Verelst, J., Ven, K.: Towards evolvable software architectures based on systems theoretic stability. Softw. Pract. Experience **42**(1), 89–116 (2012)
25. Mannaert, H., Verelst, J., De Bruyn, P.: Normalized Systems Theory: Towards a Foundational Theory for Evolvable Design (2016)

# On the Evolvable and Traceable Design of (Under)graduate Education Programs

Gilles Oorts[1](✉), Herwig Mannaert[1,2], Peter De Bruyn[1], and Ilke Franquet[2]

[1] Normalized Systems Institute, University of Antwerp, Antwerp, Belgium
gilles.oorts@uantwerp.be
[2] Unit for Innovation and Quality Assurance in Education of the Faculty of Applied Economics, University of Antwerp, Antwerp, Belgium

**Abstract.** Over the past decades, universities have been required to offer increasingly flexible study programs. Furthermore, study program designs exhibit by their nature large amounts of dependencies due to constraints of prerequisite courses, courses being taught in several study programs, etcetera. These characteristics make managing and changing study programs very complex, on occasion even preventing study program changes. In this paper we present solutions to these challenges based on the concept of modular and evolvable system design. Basic engineering concepts such as modularity, coupling and cohesion are used to explain and illustrate the evolvability and traceability of study programs.

**Keywords:** Normalized systems theory · Pedagogic · Case study · System engineering · Modularity · Evolvability

## 1 Introduction

Over the past decades, several educational challenges have emerged with which universities have to cope. The global financial crisis has put a strain on budgets, the internationalization of education has made coordinating with other universities ever more important. Furthermore, higher demands for accountability mean there are ever more increasing quality requirements that need to be monitored and satisfied [1]. The integration of sustainability concerns in academic curricula is getting essential in the search of long term solutions to the current societal issues.

Another immanent challenge universities have to tackle is the need for greater flexibility. This is fueled by amongst others things the marketization of higher education, students increasingly assuming the role of consumers (i.e., demanding new ways of educational provision) and the need for customization by offering an ever growing variety of study programs [2]. These trends are strongly related to the massification and widening access of higher education [1]. Traditionally, study programs define the prescribed composition and succession of courses for a student to take in order to graduate. As such, every subject or degree has

D. Aveiro et al. (Eds.): EEWC 2016, LNBIP 252, pp. 86–100, 2016.
DOI: 10.1007/978-3-319-39567-8_6

one corresponding study program. Yet, when students are free to select courses within a subject, several variants of the study program will emerge. Nowadays, students are often required to choose a major and/or minor discipline in which to graduate, several optional courses, etcetera. As students are offered an increasing amount of customization options within a study program, the amount of potential study program variants will grow exponentially. Any potential combination of these customization options represents one version of a study program. This poses serious complications for managing study programs.

As a result of these trends and characteristics, the concept of study programs has been subjected to great pressure to become ever more flexible. For example, some study programs at Belgian universities allow students to compose up to 70 % of their study programs from courses off an eligible course list [3]. As a consequence, very few students have the same variant of a study program. This results in a drastic increase in the possible variations of a study program. All these effects have resulted in the design, management and updating of study programs to become ever more complex endeavors.

One obvious tool that has been proposed to satisfy the study programs flexibility requirements is digitalization [1]. In this paper however, we will propose a solution that addresses the root of the problem (i.e., the study program architecture) using of Normalized Systems theory. This theory specifies the design of modular and evolvable (i.e., flexible) software [4]. In this paper, we will discuss how Normalized Systems thinking can be used as guiding principles to structure study program design and improve its flexibility.

As the principles of Normalized System theory are the underpinning of the solutions proposed in this paper, the theory will first be discussed in the next section. Next, we will discuss our vision of a study program design as a modular system in Sect. 3. Based on this proposition, Sect. 4 will include solutions on how to improve the evolvability and traceability of a study program design. We will conclude the paper by illustrating how these solutions are implemented in two cases in Sect. 5.

## 2   Normalized System Theory

In contemporary advanced and agile (economic) environments, all sorts of systems need to cope with changes in their structure and functionality. The way in which systems can assimilate these changes, determines their evolvability. Furthermore, current systems are more complex than they have ever been in both their structure and functionality. To handle these challenges, *modularity* has been repeatedly proposed as a way to divide complex system in easier to handle subsystems. Additionally, modularity also allows system engineers to cope with the flexibility or evolvability requirement by allowing the modules to change independently [5,6].

Based on the modularity concept, *Normalized Systems (NS) theory* was proposed to achieve such modular evolvability. Although originally defined for software architectures, its applicability and value in other domains (e.g., organizational design, business processes, accountancy) quickly became clear [7–9].

To obtain flexible systems that can easily evolvable over time, NS theory states that so-called *combinatorial effects* should be eliminated. These effects occur when changes to a modular structure are dependent on the size of the system they are applied to [10]. This means the impact of the change does not solely depend on the nature of change itself. Assuming systems become more complex over time, combinatorial effects would therefore become ever bigger barriers to change. As such, it is clear how combinatorial effects should be avoided if systems need to be changed easily (i.e., be evolvable).

To eliminate combinatorial effects, NS theory proposes four *theorems*, two of which are of importance in this paper [10]:

- *Separation of Concerns*, stating that each change driver (concern) should be separated from other concerns. This closely relates to the concept of cohesion, which will be discussed later on;
- *Version Transparency*, stating that modules should be updatable without impacting any linked modules;

In practice, the consistent application of these theorems results in a very fine-grained modular structure.

The theory also defines *cross-cutting concerns*. This concept is often used in information technology and refers to functionality or concerns that cut right across the functional structure of a system. These cross-cutting concerns should also be encapsulated to exhibit any form of evolvability. As we will illustrate in this paper, this is not self-evident as the functionality of these concerns are embedded deep down within systems.

## 3   Study Program Design as a Modular System

As we demonstrated in previous work (i.e., the work mentioned earlier), several systems (such as accountancy, business processes and enterprises) can be regarded as modular systems. Applying this view of the systems also entails important benefits in the design, maintenance and support to the system. In the next sections, we will illustrate this modular view of a study program design by discussing some basic principles of a modular system.

### 3.1   Modularity

Over the last decades, the concept of modularity has proven to be a very popular and useful as a design principle in various settings. Areas it has been applied to include product, system and organizational design [11].

We will argue a study program can be considered a modular system as well. In our approach, we define a module as a part of the system that is used or activated separately. Once a part of the system cannot be used or activated as such, it is considered to be on a sub-modular level.

Looking at the study programs, it is generally accepted they consist of at least one level of modules: courses. In most educational institutions this still is the only level of hierarchy in study programs. We however advocate the use of intermediate and sub-levels of hierarchy for several reasons. The advantages of these additional levels of modules will be discussed later on.

Specifically, we suggest the use of two intermediate levels of modules: learning-teaching tracks and sub-tracks. Each study program should consist of several learning-teaching tracks. These tracks are defined as collections of simultaneous or sequential courses within a study domain. Learning-teaching sub-tracks are related to more specific sub-study domains. An example of such track and sub-track are respectively 'Business economics' and 'Accountancy'. More extensive examples of this modules will be discussed in Sect. 5.

A second level of modules that would offer significant benefits is the addition of course parts as the lowest level of modularity. These course parts can vary significantly in size. As such, a lecture can consist of several course parts, or a course part can be the subject of several lectures. Currently, courses are the most modular level within study program hierarchies in practice. This because they are the most basic module that can be used or activated (i.e., it can be taken by students). Therefore, course parts are currently considered to be on a sub-modular level, as they cannot be taken as such by students and therefore cannot be included in a study program.

## 3.2   Cohesion

When structuring a system into modules, an essential question becomes how exactly to split a system into modules. A specific division for a study program design has already been proposed in the previous section. Why we proposed this specific division has a lot to do with the principle of cohesion.

The cohesion of a module is defined as the coherence of its content. General design principles advise to pursue high cohesion within modules [12]. This means the module exhibits internal content that is highly connected and related.

There are several reasons for which one would pursue to design modules with a high degree of cohesion. First, having related content bundled into modules benefits the management and maintenance. This can be done by people with the best skills and expertise for the specific content. Second, bundling related content improves reusability of a module. And when unrelated content is included into a module that is reused, it needs to be needlessly duplicated which can cause negative effects. Either this leads to additional effort to update this unnecessary content, or the outdated content could cause troubles.

A study program design can be structured in several ways. We will discuss three solutions that are situated on a spectrum of possible implementations.

One extreme implementation would be to have a single module for an entire study program. This means a study program would be considered as one single monolithic module. There would be one single version of the study program without any breakdown into courses. This implementation is however purely theoretical, as it clearly is unrealistic in practice.

A second possible implementation would mean having customized study programs for every combination of courses in every order, including uncommon courses such as preparatory and optional courses. Even with a small amount of courses offered, this would result in an enormous amount of study programs. Of course, not all combinations of courses need to be defined as a study program. Conditions such as ineligible courses and prerequisite courses somewhat limit the amount of combinations that constitute a study program. Still, courses are included and unnecessarily duplicated in many study programs. This is detrimental to the cohesion of the proposed architecture. Additionally, the development and maintenance costs of this implementation are high as well. Although the knowledge required to manage a study program is extensively smaller than the previous implementation, every study program still needs to be managed individually. This entails extensive overhead costs.

Finally, a third possible implementation is the solution presented in the previous section. In this implementation every course is considered a module, which consist of course parts that are on a sub-modular level. This allows every study program to exist of a set of courses without having to unnecessarily duplicate this courses. This implementation constitutes the highest level of cohesion. There is a separate module (i.e., course) for every collection of related subject material. As such, the development and maintenance of the modules enables a wide set of possible compositions of study programs.

As advocated in the previous section, splitting the courses even further (into 'course parts') would even further improve the modular composition of a study program design. According of the Separation of Concerns principle, this would allow the course parts to evolve freely, independent of other course parts. Additionally, it would increase the level of cohesion within the course part modules.

To illustrate this, we will look for example at a course which is taught to students in several study programs. Although the course is instructed by the same teacher, the course needs to differ partially because of the different foreknowledge and skills of students from the different study programs. In this case, one is placed in the dilemma to define these courses either as two different courses or as two variants of the same course. Arguments can be made for either solution. On the one hand, the courses are named identically and have the same instructor so they should be defined as two variants of the same course. On the other hand, they are part of other study programs and have (slightly) different contents and should therefore be different courses. If course parts were to be included as a new lower modular level however, this dilemma would disappear. This additional level would enable the course parts to be taught and examined. As such, two variants of the course can be defined without the duplication of course parts, each included within a specific study program. It is however important to bear in mind the increased coupling of such a solution, as changes in a common course part could have an impact within several study programs. Therefore a careful implementation of version transparency is necessary. This kind of coupling that is a result of this additional level in hierarchy will be discussed in the next section.

## 3.3   Coupling

One of the other consequences of having a modular system architecture, is that modules will be coupled. Coupling refers to the amount of dependencies and interactions one module has with other modules in order to function properly. It is generally accepted that one should strive for lowly coupled modules. There are several reasons for this pursuit. First of all, dependencies from other modules will negatively impact reliability. Any dependency that is added, brings along a possibility to disturb the proper functioning of a module. The module becomes prone to any faulty behavior from the linked modules in addition to its own possible errors. A second advantage of low coupling is the opportunity it creates for reusing modules. Modules that are independent of other parts of a system can be more easily reused to provide the same functionality in other use cases. As reuse decreases the need for duplicate modules, this reduces the amount of impact locations affected by changes to the system, thus improving evolvability. Finally, low coupling also reduces the probability that changes should be made when adjacent (but not coupled) modules undergo modifications.

Study program designs are traditionally susceptible to large amounts of coupling. This is because coupling manifests itself in several ways. A study program is carefully designed to support the learning process of students. This means the succession of courses is planned so all students have the necessary foreknowledge to start a course. This is mostly achieved by defining prerequisite courses that need to be completed before one is allowed to start a course. When we now look at courses as being modules in the system of a study program, we can see how courses are naturally highly coupled. Additionally, some courses are taught in several study programs. As such, these courses are inextricably bound with pre-requisite and follow-up courses from different study programs. These ties can in fact be defined on the underlying level of course parts. Take for example a single change in the content of a course that is taught in several study programs. This change will have ripple effects in several other courses. Because of the change in content, follow-up courses –and potentially even prerequisite courses– might need to be adapted. Furthermore, second-degree or even higher-degree ripple effects will extend the amount of changes needed to courses or course parts. Similar to ripple effects that result from a stone dropped in water, ripple effects in study programs affect larger areas further away from the initial impact area. As such, higher-degree ripple effects symbolize the potential for ever-increasing impact locations due to the initial change in a course part. This example clearly shows the negative impact of high coupling on the evolvability of a system.

## 4    Evolvability and Traceability of a Study Program Design

Based on the fundamental principles of Normalized System theory, we believe a flexible design of study programs can be achieved. As such, the study program design becomes less prone to ripple effects caused by changes to a system with a high level of dependencies. In the next sections, we will show how exactly a flexible design of study programs can be achieved through the use of several engineering practices defined in Normalized System theory.

## 4.1   Evolvability

Study program are very susceptible to ripple effects due to changes in courses and course parts. Looking at higher level modules of study programs, this problem becomes even more complex. Changing the composition, sequence or prerequisite requirements of courses in a study program leads to ripple effects. These effects occur as a result of what seem to be trivial changes. Take for example moving a course to a different semester or year, replacing a course by a new one or adding the requirement for a prerequisite course. Although these changes might seem easy to implement, the range of dependencies and cohesion prevents such straightforward changes, making it in some instances even impossible to perform these changes.

One other challenge that hinders study program changes are *transition effects*. It is both financially and practically impossible for a university to support both the old and new version of a study program when this is changed. Instructors cannot be expected to teach both old and new versions of courses or change a course for specific students if they do not have the foreknowledge specified in new prerequisite courses. Traditionally this problem is solved by phasing out the old version of the study program one year at a time, starting at the first bachelor year. The emergence of increased flexibility in study programs (i.e., optional courses, taking a course for a second time, etc.) and interrelated study programs (i.e., courses taught in several study programs) have made this solution less suitable. This means phasing out a study program equally for every student is no longer possible. Therefore a university needs to cope with transition effects. These are measures that need to be taken for students for whom the phasing out implementation cannot be applied because of the flexibility complexity. For these students, individual solutions need to conceived in which courses are moved to a different year, they receive an exceptional exemption for a course, they need to take a part of a course of the new study program, etc. These transition effect are very labor-intensive to plan and execute and should therefore be avoided at all costs. To demonstrate how this can be done, consider the following numerical example.

A bachelor study program change requires a transition for every student that has started the study program. This change needs to occur in a bachelor study program consisting of 30 courses. To simplify the calculation, we will abstract from the definition of prerequisite courses. Considering a student can have either taken or not taken each of these 30 courses, there are $2^{30}$ states to indicate the study program progress of students. This equals to more than 1 billion permutations. Although the exact amount of study progress cases also depends on the number of students and will therefore not be as high as this number, the calculation shows the potential amount of labor-intensive transition effects. If the university were to add the learning-teaching track and sub-track levels of modularity, the amount of permutations would drastically decrease. Consider a bachelor study program which consist of 6 sub-tracks, each filled with 5 courses. This would result in $6 * 2^5 = 192$ possible states of study progress in the study program. Handling transition effects for study programs that not comply with the phasing out solutions clearly becomes much more feasible with this remarkably smaller amount of variants to deal with. One could argue that this problem requires the definition of even more variants of study programs, in addition to the ones needed due to the customization options within study programs. The state of study progress of a specific student could be included as an additional dimension in which study program variants can be defined. This would in turn drastically increase the complexity of managing study programs.

This example clearly shows the practical impact of adding hierarchical structure to the study program design. By implementing intermediary levels of modules (i.e., learning-teaching tracks and sub-tracks), the design is much less resistant to change. The amount of transition effects that need to be drawn up for students is far lower, meaning that the effort to facilitate a study program change is drastically lower. As such, study program that would otherwise have been postponed or canceled due to required effort can efficiently be implemented.

## 4.2   Traceability

As mentioned before, there are ever more quality and environmental requirements that need to be monitored and satisfied in education. Such requirements include achieving course and teaching quality requirements, the realization of a number of student competences (both domain specific and knowledge related), and more generic competences like for instance skills related to international and multicultural environments, or various teaching and evaluation methods like papers, presentations, and assignments. These requirements may also include the realization of competences and skills related to certain societal issues, like sustainability and/or ethical awareness.

Many of these requirements are specified or articulated at a general study program level, while they need to be realized and implemented at the level of individual courses and assignments. Like in all system consisting of many parts and/or modules, this gives rise to a problem of traceability: how to ensure that overall requirements articulated at a general level are realized throughout the individual parts or modules. In other words, the realization of the requirements needs to be traced all the way down to the individual course modules.

**Traceability and Cross-Cutting Concerns.** The realization of global requirements throughout the individual functional modules is in fact quite similar to the concept of *cross-cutting concerns* in information technology. The introduction or modification of such concerns may yield a significant impact – or combinatorial effect – through the many modules that are affected.

The concept of cross-cutting concerns is an intrinsic part of Normalized Systems theory. Its name however might suggest otherwise, as it seems to insinuate this functionality is somewhat less important. We argue that this is not the case, and one should consider cross-cutting concerns as often occurring functionality that manifests itself in a second dimension. This functionality has always existed, but is simply from a different nature due to its frequent recurrence.

One can think of several cross-cutting concerns related to the courses offered in study programs. Potential cross-cutting concerns include e-learning, planned learning, case studies, internationalization, assignments, teaching methods, ethical awareness, sustainability, etc. It is import to realize that although this is an extensive enumeration of cross-cutting concerns, it is far from an exhaustive list. Cross-cutting concerns may also appear in a limited amount of courses and are therefore more difficult to define. An important requirement to manage cross-cutting concerns is to provide traceability of the concerns. As mentioned earlier, it is imperative to trace the courses in which cross-cutting concerns are present. One way of representing the presence of cross-cutting concerns is using a matrix, of which an example is included later on in Fig. 2.

**Embedding the Cross-Cutting Concerns.** There are several ways of structuring cross-cutting concerns in study program designs. In the next paragraphs, we will propose three potential implementations. These will be discussed using the example in which the cross-cutting concern of case studies is required to be added to several courses.

One possible implementation is to have lecturers provide the cross-cutting concern for the courses it is required for. This means every lecturer has to make the effort to search for applicable case studies and convert them into usable pedagogic material for every single course he would like to use cases in. From a modularity standpoint, this entails the duplication of functionality and effort in the organization of a study program. This implementation can generically be presented as separate case study modules that are located within the course they relate to. This is shown by the smaller modules in the upper left panel of Fig. 1. Traditionally, cross-cutting concerns are implemented in this way in study programs. There are however some disadvantages to this implementation. Consistent with the discussed additional effort, this implementation does not allow benefits of economies of scale. Every instance of the implementation needs to be applied from scratch. Second, when a change is required in the way case studies are used in courses, this would require a change by every instructor in every course where case studies are used. This clearly constitutes combinatorial effects as defined in Normalized System theory.

A second way of implementing the cross-cutting concerns is through the use of a centralized entity. Some cross-cutting concerns are so widespread that many systems need to deal with them. As a result, it is viable for centralized providers of this cross-cutting concern to exist. The university could for example set up a centralized entity specialized in providing educational case studies. They would provide turnkey case studies composed according to the wishes of lecturers. The upper right panel of Fig. 1 shows how this centralized entity in linked to all courses with case studies. This also shows how this entity is located in a different functional dimension (shown as a plane) on top of the course dimension. One limitation of this implementation is that lecturers become dependent on this centralized entity. Because of its specialization in delivering case studies, the provider can however achieve economies of scale and leverage its knowledge in the matter to provide better quality cases.

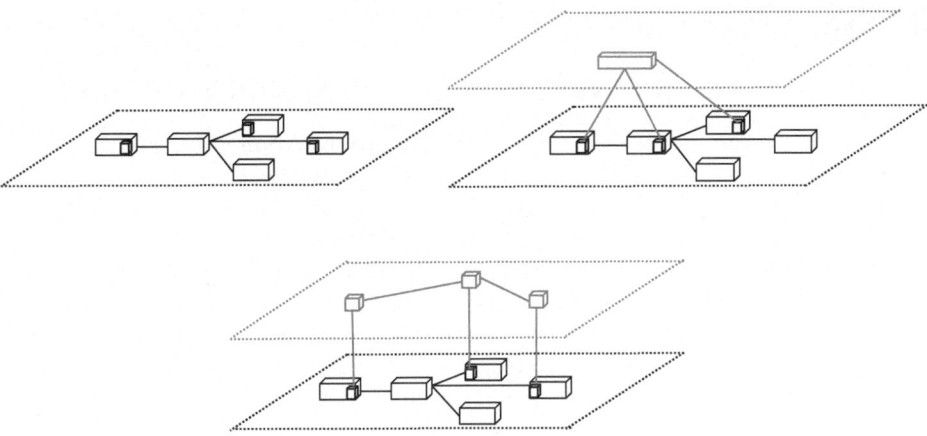

**Fig. 1.** Overview of three implementations of cross-cutting concerns in a study program

A third and final option we suggest for implementing cross-cutting concerns is to clearly separate modules with different functionalities. As such, the main modules can be shielded from changes in the case studies, thereby providing loose coupling. This setup is presented in the lower panel of Fig. 1. The case study modules are also positioned in a different functional dimension. Within the study program setting, this could be implemented by having working groups that provide case studies for each course in which they are needed. Such a working group could be a single person (such as a teaching assistant) or a group of university employees. Every entity however coordinates the case studies with other entities in a way that the organization of the case studies is similar. For this reason there are links shown between the case study modules. In this system, changes can be made more easily to the way case studies are organized because of the cooperation and coordination between the case study working groups.

It is important to remark that the implementation of cross-cutting concerns can pose a hurdle for the evolvability of study programs. The three implementation types will each have an impact on the cohesion of the modules, as the cross-cutting concerns will be spread over one, several or even all modules. It is clear from the unconnected cross-cutting modules (represented as small boxes within courses) in the upper left panel of Fig. 1 how making a change will require more effort in this implementation. Every lecturer has to be informed of the change, and needs to individually implement it without the help of a centralized or specialized unit. In the upper right implementation, the cross-cutting concerns are centrally managed and changes can be applied in one location by experts in case studies. In the third solution (presented in the lower panel), changes need to be done by several people. There is however coordination and cooperation in managing the change in the cross-cutting concern.

# 5   Study Program Cases

## 5.1   Study Program Design at a Faculty of Applied Economics

Recently, the study program design of the Faculty of Applied Economics at the University of Antwerp was modified to include learning-teaching tracks and sub-tracks. In this section, we will discuss how this new study program design was updated to include the solutions presented in this paper.

To its 3,250 students, the faculty offers five distinct bachelor study programs and seven study programs at a master level. The bachelor programs are 'Applied Economic Sciences - Business Economics' (BE), 'Applied Economic Sciences - Economic Policy' (EP), 'Business Engineering' (BE), 'Business Engineering in Management Information Systems' (MIS) and 'Social and Economic Sciences'. At the master level, two additional study programs are offered by the faculty: 'Culture Management' and 'Organization and Management'. The Social and Economic Sciences and the two master study programs are quite different from the other study programs, and will therefore not be included in this case study.

Across the study programs, a total of 258 courses are offered. As proposed in this paper, these courses are incorporated into nine learning-teaching tracks consisting of 27 sub-tracks, shown in Table 1. Each course belongs to one main (sub)track, but can be connected to other (sub)tracks. This because a course can contain subject matters belonging to several (sub)tracks. The collection of tracks is used to define the four well composed, balanced and comprehensive study programs. The premise of these learning-teaching tracks is that the knowledge and skills of students start out small at the beginning of their studies, but grow as they progress and take the courses defined within a track.

Take for example the learning-teaching track 'Quantitative methods'. This track consists of the sub-tracks 'Mathematics' and 'Statistics'. Within the 'Business Engineering' study program, this track holds the courses 'Statistics 1', 'Statistics 2' and 'Mathematics 1' in the first year of the bachelor degree. During the second year, the course 'Mathematics 2' and seminar 'Applied mathematics' continue to expand the knowledge and hone the skills of the students according to the 'Quantitative methods' learning-teaching track. The mandatory part of the track is finalized with the courses 'Econometrics and multivariate statistics' and 'Advanced data sciences' during the third bachelor and first master year.

How courses within a sub-track can be linked to study programs is shown in Table 2. This table contains all courses that are part of the bachelor sub-track 'General economics - Fundamentals'. Each course has its unique course code, course name and amount of ECTS credits listed. The next columns show whether the course is included in the particular study programs offered by the faculty. As such, this table shows a clear overview of which year and study program the courses are a part of.

As we proposed in this paper, considerable attention was also paid to defining cross-cutting concerns that manifest themselves in the courses taught in the faculty. In Fig. 2, some of these cross-cutting concerns are presented on the vertical axis. On the horizontal axis, the learning-teaching tracks and sub-tracks

**Table 1.** Overview of the learning-teaching tracks and sub-tracks

| Learning-teaching track | Sub-track |
|---|---|
| General economics | Fundamentals |
| | Policy |
| Business economics | Accountancy |
| | European and international business |
| | Finance |
| | Marketing |
| | Strategy and organization |
| | Transport and logistics |
| Engineering | Fundamentals |
| | Sustainable technology |
| | Supply chains and operations |
| Information systems | Fundamentals |
| | Engineering and architecture |
| | Governance and audit |
| Quantitative methods | Mathematics |
| | Statistics |
| Practice | Apprenticeship and internship |
| | Summer school |
| Broadening areas of study | Social sciences |
| | Jurisprudence |
| Business communication | English |
| | French |
| | German |
| | Spanish |
| Projects and dissertations | Bachelor project |
| | Master dissertation |
| | Master integration project |

**Table 2.** Courses in the bachelor sub-track 'General economics - Fundamentals'

| Course code | Course name | Cr. | BE | EP | BE | MIS |
|---|---|---|---|---|---|---|
| 1101TEWAEC | Introduction to general economics | 6 | B1 | B1 | B1 | B1 |
| 1103TEWVSG | European and international law | 6 | B1 | B1 | | |
| 1201TEWAEC | Micro economics | 6 | B2 | B2 | B2 | B2 |
| 1201TEWKOO | History of economic thought | 6 | B3 | B3 | B3 | B3 |
| 1202TEWAEC | Macro economics | 6 | B2 | B2 | B2 | B2 |
| 1301TEWECB | Contemporary economic and political history | 6 | | B3 | | |

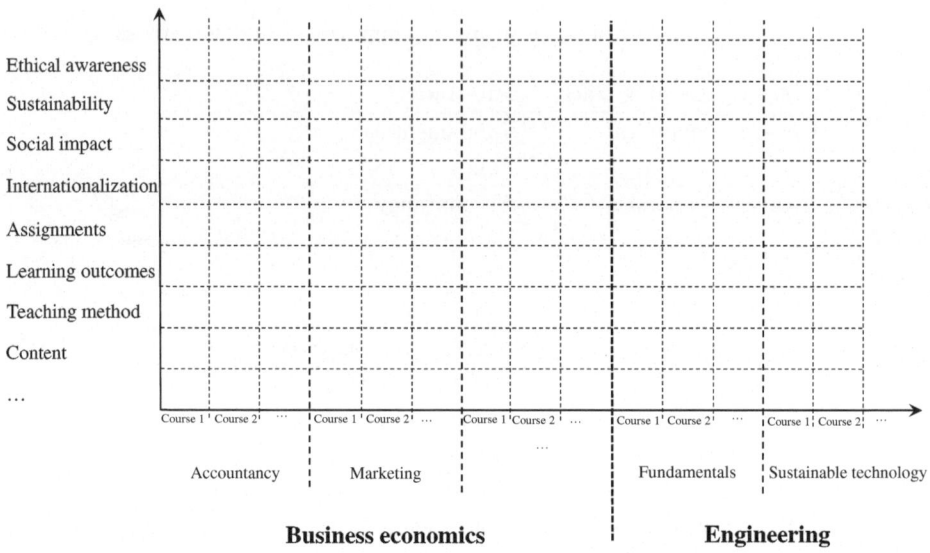

**Fig. 2.** The cross-cutting concern presence in learning-teaching tracks and courses

are listed, each with the included courses. This matrix facilitates the design of well-balanced study programs. It allows for example to check that there is at least one course in each learning-teaching sub-track that includes assignments by marking cells in the matrix. At this moment, the faculty has made a mapping of all learning outcomes, teaching methods and assignments. The mapping of internationalization, sustainability and ethical awareness are still in progress.

### 5.2   Study Program Design at a NGO

As a second case, we consider a set of training programs offered by some NGOs (non-governmental organizations) in Antwerp. These organizations have as their goal to assist people during their quest for fixed employment in the labor market. Although the considered NGOs are different from the previous case organization in several aspects (types of courses, number of students, target audience, etcetera), several similarities can be noticed. We now discuss how a similar modularity assessment and design can be applied for this case in terms of learning-teaching tracks, coupling and cross-cutting concerns.

To start with, learning-teaching tracks can be discerned. Typically, however different the profile of coached people in the NGOs may be, three major learning-teaching tracks are present (Table 3). First, people are screened for their general Dutch and mathematical knowledge. If their level on these subjects is insufficient for their envisioned job, they are signed up for a course in these domains. Sharpening their general knowledge therefore constitutes a first learning-teaching track. Next to that, people follow one or more courses to sharpen their technical knowledge. Finally, an important third learning-teaching track consists of courses for increasing the job application skills of the participants.

Next, it is clear that coupling between the several organized courses is present. This holds for both the courses within one learning-teaching track and between different learning-teaching (sub)tracks. Within tracks, as several consecutive courses of Dutch, electronics etcetera exist of which the end competences of a preceding course are considered as the starting competences of the follow-up course(s). And between tracks, as the "general knowledge" needs to be sufficient before the courses within the technical knowledge track can be initiated and the job application courses can only be initiated as soon as the profile of the coached person is more or less determined.

Finally, some similar types of cross-cutting concerns as in the previous case are relevant here. That is, the need for ethical awareness, content and end competence tracking, as well as a vision on what types of assignments have been fulfilled are present in this context as well. Some dimensions are new, such as the need to show that each course contributes to more mature job compliant attitudes. Others seem less relevant in the context of the considered NGOs, such as the need for internationalization. As stated before, this shows that the concept of cross-cutting concerns is relevant and useful in the context of study programs, although the specific filling-in might differ from case to case.

**Table 3.** Overview of all learning-teaching tracks and sub-tracks of the NGOs

| Learning-teaching track | Sub-track |
|---|---|
| General knowledge | Dutch |
| | Mathematics |
| Technical knowledge | Metal |
| | Electronics |
| | Cleaning |
| | Administration |
| Job application | |

# 6   Conclusion and Future Research

In this paper, we demonstrated that managing and changing study programs is far more complex than one might think. Study program designs exhibit by their nature a large amount of dependencies. These may result in ripple effects that spread across the whole system when changes need to be made to a study program. This may hamper or even prevent changes being made in study programs.

To offer a solution to these problems, we illustrated how study program designs can be regarded as modular systems. As Normalized Systems theory offers a well-founded solution to design evolvable modular systems, we have shown how study programs can be shielded from detrimental combinatorial and ripple effects. By adding modular layers to the hierarchical architecture, one can also reduce the impact and added complexity of study program changes. Furthermore, these additional layers help managing the expansion of study program variants that occur with transition effects when changing a study program.

An interesting avenue for future research is the document management related to study programs. Naturally, an evolvable study program design requires all related documents to be adaptable as well. Additionally, the well-defined modular structure of the study programs allows for new possibilities in generating related supporting documents. Just imagine being able to generate on the fly the entire collection of course materials of all courses in a specific learning-teaching track of a specific study program.

# References

1. D'Andrea, V., Gosling, D.: Improving Teaching And Learning in Higher Education: A Whole Institution Approach. McGraw-Hill Education, Maidenhead (2005)
2. Barnett, R.: Conditions of Flexibility: Securing a More Responsive Higher Education System. The Higher Education Academy, York (2014)
3. University of Antwerp. Study program: Bachelor of social and economic sciences (2016). https://www.uantwerpen.be/en/education/education-and-training/e-bachelor-in-de-socia/study-programme/
4. Huysmans, P., Oorts, G., De Bruyn, P., Mannaert, H., Verelst, J.: Positioning the normalized systems theory in a design theory framework. In: Shishkov, B. (ed.) BMSD 2012. LNBIP, vol. 142, pp. 43–63. Springer, Heidelberg (2013)
5. Baldwin, C.Y., Clark, K.B.: Design Rules: The Power of Modularity, vol. 1. MIT Press, Cambridge (1999)
6. MacCormack, A., Lagerstrom, R., Dreyfus, D., Baldwin, C.Y.: A methodology for operationalizing enterprise architecture and evaluating enterprise it flexibility. Harvard Business School Working Paper, vol. 15–060, January 2015
7. Van Nuffel, D.: Towards designing modular and evolvable business processes. Ph.D. dissertation, University of Antwerp (2011)
8. Huysmans, P.: On the feasibility of normalized enterprises: Applying normalized systems theory to the high-level design of enterprises. Ph.D. dissertation, University of Antwerp (2011)
9. Vanhoof, E., Huysmans, P., Aerts, W., Verelst, J.: Evaluating accounting information systems that support multiple GAAP reporting using normalized systems theory. In: Aveiro, D., Tribolet, J., Gouveia, D. (eds.) EEWC 2014. LNBIP, vol. 174, pp. 76–90. Springer, Heidelberg (2014)
10. Mannaert, H., Verelst, J., Ven, K.: Towards evolvable software architectures based on systems theoretic stability. Softw. Pract. Experience $42(1)$, 89–116 (2012)
11. Campagnolo, D., Camuffo, A.: The concept of modularity in management studies: a literature review. Int. J. Manage. Rev. $12(3)$, 259–283 (2010)
12. Ethiraj, S.K., Levinthal, D.: Modularity and innovation in complex systems. Manage. Sci. $50(2)$, 159–173 (2004)

# Modelling, Patterns and Viability

# Perceptual Discriminability in Conceptual Modeling

Jeannette Stark[✉]

Chair of Wirtschaftsinformatik, esp. Systems Development, Technische
Universität Dresden, Dresden, Germany
jeannette.stark@tu-dresden.de

**Abstract.** Perceptual discriminability can be used to help distinguishing
modeling constructs in conceptual models. It can further be used to produce
parallel processing of modeling constructs that make these constructs virtually
pop-out from the model. Moody has described a condition which is necessary to
produce a pop-out effect in his principle of perceptual discriminability. This
work extends the principle of perceptual discriminability for further conditions
to produce a pop-out. Extended perceptual discriminability is exemplarily
applied to a modeling grammar.

**Keywords:** Conceptual modeling · Parallel processing · Pop-out · Perceptual
discriminability · Visual attention

## 1 Introduction

Using conceptual models for communication can reveal advantages over textual representations as information of these models can visually be perceived within a short
time and is rapidly available for further cognitive processing in working memory
(WM) [1]. Yet, not every conceptual model does better than text. Several empirical
studies show that conceptual models may be poorly understood if the visual notation of
the modeling grammar used to create the model is defined on the soul basis of instinct
and imitation [2]. To exploit advantages of conceptual models for understanding, prior
research has developed several design principles (see [1, 3–5] for example). In particular, the principles described within the 'Physics of Notation' (PoN) have extensively been used to assess and improve visual notations of modeling grammars [6, 7].
PoN "defines a theory of how visual notations communicate" [1], p. 759 and further
succeeds in providing "the foundations for a science of visual notation" [1], p. 759. In
this work MOODY proposes nine design principles that are based on several cognitive
theories and models such as Human graphical information processing. This process is
divided into two stages: Perceptual processing and cognitive processing (see Fig. 1). In
perceptual processing elementary visual variables used to encode information such as
colour and shape [8] are visually perceived and distinguished from the background
(perceptual discrimination) as well as structure and relationships among them are
detected (perceptual configuration) [9, 10]. In this stage visual variables are perceived
in parallel and without any attention [10]. A part of the information perceived is then
transferred into WM and integrated into a mental model that now enables reasoning by

© Springer International Publishing Switzerland 2016
D. Aveiro et al. (Eds.): EEWC 2016, LNBIP 252, pp. 103–117, 2016.
DOI: 10.1007/978-3-319-39567-8_7

using thinking operations as well as enrichment from long-term memory (LTM) in the stage of cognitive processing [11]. PoN design principles aim at effecting perceptual processing or cognitive processing. For example, the principle of perceptual discriminability relates to perceptual processing. Perceptual discriminability is defined as 'the ease and accuracy with which graphical elements can be differentiated from each other' [1], p. 763 and depends on the extent of visual variables in which the symbols differ [7]. While perceptual discriminability mainly impacts on perceptual processing other principles such as cognitive fit have an effect on cognitive processing. Cognitive fit is reached when a suitable representation is selected for a certain task or for a certain audience and allows a construction of an appropriate mental model that rather reflects the solutions than a mental model built on representations that do not fit task or audience [12]. That way, design principles help deriving conceptual models that are cognitive effective for perceptual and cognitive processing.

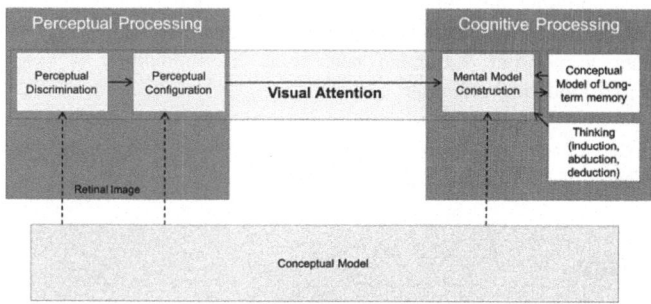

**Fig. 1.** Human graphical information processing based on [1]

Yet, perceptual and cognitive processes do not cover the whole process of human graphical information processing. The two stages do not explain how information is selected for being transferred into WM. Therefor attention is required. Only the part of perceived information that is seen with attention can further be used for cognitive processing and can hence be understood. Attention is studied within Theories of Visual Attention [13] and is dependent on goals and objectives (influence from top down) [14] as well as on how visual variables are used (influence from bottom up) [15].

The principle of perceptual discriminability is related to the stage of perceptual discrimination of human graphical information processing but does already touch the stage of visual attention between perceptual and cognitive processing. In this principle Moody proposes that if a modeling construct has a unique value for at least one visual variable it appears to 'pop-out' from the rest of the model [1]. Yet, there are further conditions for such a 'pop-out' effect that are discussed within the theories of Visual Attention [13]. Furthermore, not every modeling construct needs to pop-out to increase model understanding. We have to decide for the most important constructs of a model to pop-out.

This work extends the principle of perceptual discriminability for further conditions to produce a pop-out and discusses several opportunities how to find the most important constructs for a pop-out. The contribution is twofold. For theory, the fundament of cognitive theories is increased with those of Visual Attention. Furthermore, a procedure how perceptual discriminability can be expanded for different modeling grammars is provided. For practice, a framework which can be used to apply a pop-out for modeling constructs is described.

This paper is structured as follows: After having motivated the research, Sect. 2 introduces the principle of perceptual discriminability. Theories of Visual attention are used to extend this principle for a bottom-up as well as top-down perspective in Sect. 3. Section 4 deals with further operationalizing the top-down perspective by specifying the basis for a pop-out and exemplarily shows how this can be done for an Entity Relationship Diagram (ERD) in Sect. 5. The outcome of the paper will be discussed and future research ideas are presented in Sect. 6.


## 2   Perceptual Discriminability

Perceptual Discriminability determines how easy it is for a model user to visually distinguish between different modeling constructs [7]. Perceptual discriminability is principally improved when the visual distance of modeling constructs increases. This can be achieved (a) with an increasing number of visual variables on which the constructs differ and (b) with an increasing extent of these differences [1, 10]. Bertin has defined horizontal and vertical position, shape, size, colour, brightness, orientation and texture as visual variables that are used to encode information [8]. Out of these variables shape has a significant impact on object recognition [16]. Humans mainly distinguish objects on the basis of shape which is why Moody suggests shape to be the primary visual variable to distinguish between modeling constructs [1]. For producing a high visual distance he further proposes that modeling constructs should be differentiated in multiple visual variables. Some variables are necessary to encode semantic information in modeling constructs. For example, in BPMN 2.0 shape and texture is used to derive the majority of modeling constructs [6]. While shape and texture are required to distinguish between constructs, the variables colour, brightness, orientation, position and size are free to redundantly encode modeling constructs for an increase of visual distance. That way, Genon et al. propose to use colour in an additive manner to distinguish between BPMN constructs [6].

Perceptual discriminability can also be used to allow parallel processing of modeling constructs which leads these constructs to virtually pop-out from the rest of the model [1]. Reijers et al. have assessed this effect by highlighting matching operators in business process models (BPM) with the use of colour [17]. To achieve parallel processing for a certain modeling construct, this construct needs to have a unique value for at least one visual variable [18, 19]. There are, however, further conditions that are discussed in theories of Visual Attention. If these conditions are met, modelers and notation designers can use parallel processing effectively to guide attention to relevant aspects of a model.

# 3  Visual Attention

TREISMAN was the first who made an attempt to determine those variables that can be detected preattentively and can hence be processed in parallel in experiments such as the one depicted in Fig. 2 [20, 21]. In Fig. 2a) only one visual variable of the elements is discriminated: Shape of the objects. In such a display the target item, circle, can be easily detected preattentively within less than 200–250 ms, in less than a fixation. The target value has a unique value for at least one visual variable and virtually pops-out of the display regardless of the number of distractor elements [13, 22]. In Fig. 2b) the target is defined by two visual variables: Colour and shape with the target values red and circular. In this case the target does not have a unique value since red and circular do also appear in distractor elements. This is why probands must perform a serial search to confirm the presence of the red circle. This task is called conjunction search and can in general not be performed within a single fixation [13].

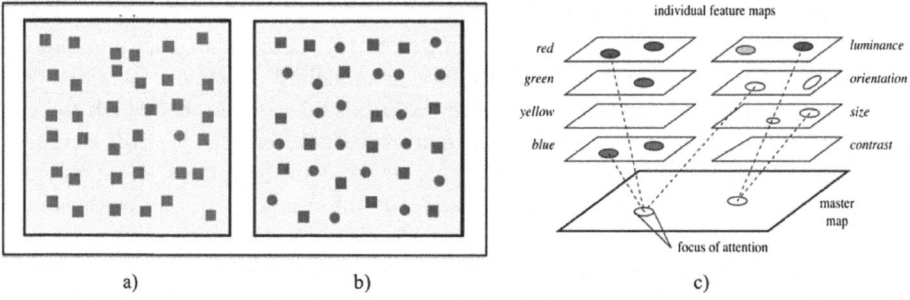

**Fig. 2.** Target detection: a) target: circle; b) target: red circle [13] and c) Feature integration theory from [13, 19] (Color figure online)

TREISMAN further gave an explanation of how the visual system performs preattentive processing in her Feature Integration Theory (FIT) [19]: When an individual views an image, visual variables are encoded into individual feature maps. These maps only record activity for a particular variable such as colour or size (see Fig. 2c). Feature maps do not contain information about spatial arrangements, locations and relationships to those variables of other maps. This information is collected within a master map. While individual maps can be assessed in parallel, information that is depicted within the master map is mainly assessed in serial (conjunction search) [13]. A target element that has a unique value for at least one visual variable can be found on an individual target map and can according to FIT be processed in parallel. In her early research Treisman supposed a strict dichotomy of processing visual variables in parallel or in serial which was expanded within her later work, where parallel and serial processing represent two pols of a spectrum. Healey and Enns have reviewed theories of Visual Attention that try to explain the continuum of parallel and serial processing [13].

## 3.1 Similarity Theory

Founders of Similarity Theory supposed that the time to identify a target is influenced by target-nontarget similarity (T-N-similarity) and nontarget-nontarget similarity (N-N-similarity) [15, 23]. Figure 3 demonstrates the effect of N-N-similarity when searching an L-shaped target: While search efficiency for target-detection in a) is relatively high it decreases in b) with decreasing N-N-similarity. Duncan and Humphreys have also assessed the influence of T-N-similarity: Individuals have templates of the target's properties available during search. While searching, an image is structured into structural units that show some common variables such as color or shape. The more similar a structural unit is to the individual's target-template, the more attention it receives in respect to other units. If only little similarity between template and structural unit exists, the individual rejects the structural unit. Other units that are similar to the rejected unit can also efficiently be rejected [15]. That way, a structural unit that closely matches the target-template has the highest probability to access WM [13].

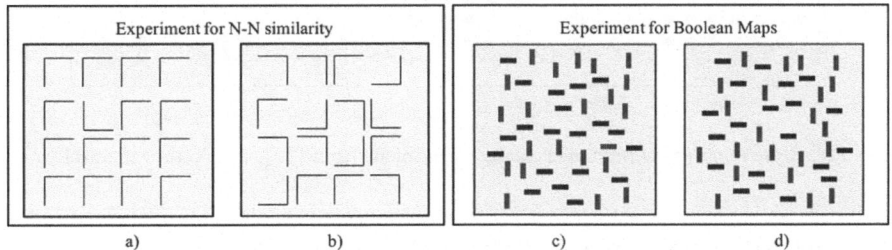

**Fig. 3.** a) and b): N-N similarity effects for an L-shaped target based on [15]; c) and d) Boolean map search for a blue horizontal target: present in c), absent in d) [13] (Color figure online)

## 3.2 Boolean Map Theory

According to Boolean Map Theory the visual system is capable to divide elements into selected and excluded elements (boolean map). Selected elements can then be processed within a more detailed analysis [24]. Boolean maps can be created in two different ways: First, a map can be created based on elements located within a spatial location. Second, a viewer can select all elements that contain a specific value for a visual variable (for example blue items for a search of a blue horizontal item as depicted in Fig. 3c and d). The selected items can now be subject for a further operation (in this case the viewer can assess all blue items for a horizontal arrangement). A viewer can only cognitively process a single boolean map. The processing outcome immediately replaces the current map. According to this theory the time to finish search depends on how many boolean maps are required [13].

### 3.3    Feature Hierarchy

Researchers of Feature Hierarchy (FH) discovered that a hierarchy for visual variables appears to exist in the visual system [13]. Callaghan for example showed that the visual system favors colour over shape [25]. As presented in Fig. 4a) background variations in colour can slow the ability to identify the presence of spatial patterns formed by different shapes. On the contrary, if the background varies in shape as in Fig. 4b) spatial patterns formed by different colours are immediately visible [13]. Further dominances have been found for brightness over colour [26], colour over texture [27] and colour plus depth over orientation [22] (see Fig. 4c).

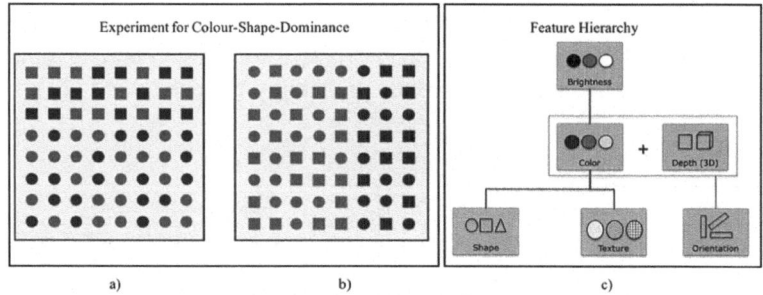

**Fig. 4.** (a) and (b) colour over shape experiment from [13]; (c) Feature hierarchy

### 3.4    Implications for Conceptual Modeling

Based on presented theories parallel and serial processing present two ends of a continuum (Fig. 5). A construct can be arranged within this continuum based on (a) its unique values for one or several visual variables (according to FIT), (b) similarities between the construct and non-targets (T-N) as well as similarity between the non-targets (N-N) in the model (according to Similarity Theory) and (c) the number of boolean maps required to reach the construct (according to Boolean Map Theory).

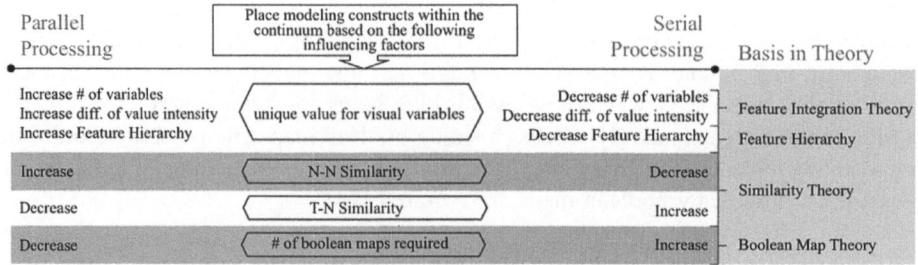

**Fig. 5.** Influencing factors of parallel and serial processing of modeling constructs

The unique value for visual variables is already mentioned as influencing factor for parallel processing within the principle of perceptual discriminability [1]. Yet, this factor should be extended for implications from FH. A unique value for the visual variable texture would not have the same effect than a unique value for brightness. According to FH brightness dominates texture. While a search for a construct with a unique variable in brightness would not be affected by the presence of constructs having a unique value in texture, a search for a construct with a unique value in texture might be influenced by the presence of constructs with a unique value for brightness. That way, the influence of the unique value for a visual variable depends on the position within FH. Influencing factors from FIT and FH effect parallel processing from bottom up as these factors focus on how to use visual variables without focusing on possible objectives and targets of the model user. On the contrary, influencing factors from Similarity Theory and Boolean Map Theory effect from bottom-up as well as from top-down since both theories comprise goals and targets and can be used to align visual variables based on these targets. Before applying influencing factors, possible objectives and targets of a model user need to be integrated which is why the top-down perspective is further elaborated in Sect. 4.

## 4    Central Constructs of Modeling Grammars

Several items can be placed among the continuum between parallel and serial processing that comprise modeling constructs, elements that belong together or even elements that are perceived as a chunk in WM. Reijers et al. have shown in [17] that parallel processing of matching operators in BPMs reveal advantages for model understanding. That way, elements that belong together pop-out from the model and allow model users to easier understand the structure of the model. Zugal et al. have discussed chunks as an integration of elements that belong together and have proposed optional activities as a chunk in BPMs. If a schema for chunks like optional activities has already been learned and does this way exist in LTM, it can be used as only one information item in WM. Those who have integrated the optional activity chunk into LTM can increase their WM capacity, while those who have not integrated this chunk into LTM might need more items for the same amount of information [28]. Yet, capacity for WM is limited to around seven information items [29] and recent research estimates its capacity even lower to 3, 4 items [30]. Using chunks can help model users to increase the number of elements that can be processed in WM. In [31] further chunks such as parallel and alternative activities are discussed. Placing these chunks on the parallel side of the continuum would also help model users to easier understand the model. Besides parallel processing of matching operators and chunks, also parallel processing of single constructs might reveal advantages for model understanding. Notation designers usually not distinguish semantic constructs on a systematic basis. Sometimes constructs are even treated equally. But some studies have already questioned equality for modeling constructs. For example Zur Muehlen and Recker have analyzed 120 BPMN diagrams and found that less than 20 % of its constructs are used regularly [32]. Based on the theories of Semantic Network [33] and Spreading Activation [34] Weber has shown that entities dominate attributes [35]. This is why notation designers should decide which constructs are most important for model understanding. Not every modeling construct can be processed in parallel as (a) free visual variables are limited and can therefore not be used to highlight any modeling construct and (b) visual variables influence according to the FH. If a unique value for brightness is used to highlight a certain construct, it would slow the processing for another construct, even if that construct has a unique value for another visual variable. That way, only few modeling constructs can be placed on the parallel side of the continuum. Notation designers need to decide which constructs should be placed there. Based on their decision they influence parallel processing from top-down.

This work focusses on single constructs and tries to determine those constructs that are central for model understanding (hereafter called central constructs) by searching for questions that can be answered with conceptual models. Based on a content analysis according to Krippendorff [36], typical questions and ERDs investigated. ERDs were used for the following reasons: First, results of this research are broadly accessible as the modeling grammar is easily comprehensible and widespread. Second, ERDs that contain complex domain information tend to be relatively large and that way show a relevant effect when central constructs are processed in parallel. Third, results of this study of this relatively low complex grammar, which comprises only few different semantic constructs, can also be applied to other grammars that focus on data modeling. To assure a high quality for questions and models we have based our analysis on laboratory experiments that have been published in IS-centric-journals summarized in [37], (Appendix c). Out of obtained articles the following data is assessed: Type and content of questions (Table 1), searches based on the conceptual model(s) necessary to answer the questions and the visual variables used within the models. Out of identified 169 studies 163 could be rejected because no experiment was conducted, the experiment did not match the right scenario or no models and questions were provided. Six articles are left for further evaluations.

**Table 1.** Relevant experiments of IS-Centric-Journals

| IS-Journal | Lit. | Semantic comprehension | Syntactic comprehension | Problem solving |
|---|---|---|---|---|
| Data and Knowledge Eng. | [38] | schema-based | schema-based | recall |
| | [39] | schema-based | schema-based | - |
| Inf. Systems Research | [40] | schema-based | schema-based | schema-based |
| | [41] | schema-based, recall | schema-based | recall |
| J. of Database Manag. | [42] | schema-based, recall | - | recall |
| J. of Man.. Inf. Systems | [43] | schema-based | schema-based | - |

Across the articles either schema-based or recall-questions were found. While in schema-based questions the model is still provided to find the answer, recall-questions have to be solved without the model. In this work schema-based semantic comprehension and problem-solving tasks are included. Recall-tasks are excluded as no visual search occurs. Moreover, syntactic comprehension questions are not used, as these questions aim on focusing on model grammar comprehension instead of domain understanding. Out of the six relevant experiments 76 relevant questions were extracted. Only three questions were problem-solving tasks as most problem-solving experiments consisted of recall-tasks. 83 visual search processes were required to solve these 76 questions. One problem-solving question consisted of two sub-questions [40] and in six questions the searches differed due to variations of the independent variable (mandatory vs. optional attributes) [38, 41].

Ten search-types could be identified (see Fig. 6a) out of the search processes taken into consideration. In these search-types ERD users generally proceed their searches in two different steps. They first search the whole model for one or more construct(s) and than process searching the area around the(se) construct(s) they previously identified. This is why in this paper the first step is called global search because the whole model is scanned for relevant constructs and the second step local search as search occurs locally around previously identified constructs. In global search ERD users generally search for one or more entity-types that fit their problem, which is why for global search entity-types can be identified as central constructs. For local search, diversity of constructs that ERD users search for is much higher than for global search (see Fig. 6b). In local search ERD users mainly focused on cardinalities, relationship-types, attributes and paths. Within the conceptual models, semantic constructs were distinguished in shape. Furthermore, texture is used to differentiate attributes [40] and cardinalities [39]. Those studies that discriminate between optional and mandatory attributes have used the visual variable brightness [39, 41].

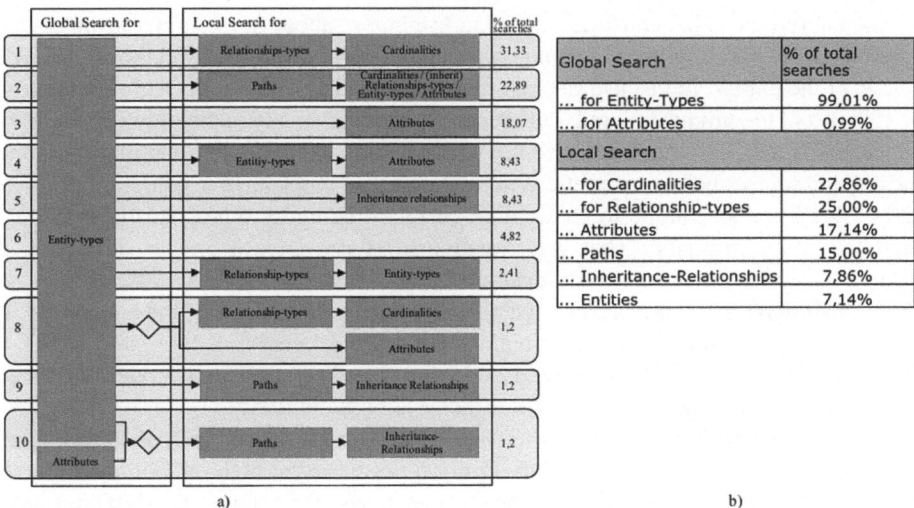

**Fig. 6.** a) search types; b) rank of constructs for global and local search

# 5   Applying (Extended) Perceptual Discriminability to ERD

ERD users generally process global search for entity-types and local search for a wide range of constructs (see Sect. 4), which is why entity-types are treated as central constructs. This section shows how entity-types can be placed on the parallel side of the continuum between serial and parallel processing. For local search cardinalities, relationship-types and attributes are identified as constructs ERD users were mostly searching for and are further placed along the continuum (Fig. 7). Original and changed variables of these constructs are shown in Fig. 8.

**Unique values** exist for entity-types, relationship-types, attributes as well as cardinalities. For Entity-types, relationship-types and attributes the number of variables is increased (for colour and brightness). Furthermore, these constructs have at least two variables with a unique value (shape, colour) whereas shape is necessary to encode the semantic construct. Colour as well as brightness are used redundantly to allow ERD users to better distinguish between the constructs. In Fig. 8a) cardinalities are so far not visually encoded whereas in Fig. 8b) the crow foot notation is used to encode the semantic constructs with a unique value for shape. That way, the number of visual variables for entity-types, relationship-types, attributes as well as cardinalities could be increased. For the entity-type a further unique value for brightness is created. That way, this construct is characterized with three unique values in brightness, colour and shape. Since brightness is the variable in highest FH and the entity-type is the only construct with a unique value for this variable, this construct is processed in parallel and pops-out from the rest of the model. Also attributes and relationship-types have a unique value for colour and shape. Yet, these constructs should not interfere a search for entity-types since their variables with unique values are lower in FH. The differences of value intensity vary among the constructs. The greatest differences of value intensity exists for the entity-type. This construct differs in brightness about 30 % from attributes and relationships while brightness is hold constant among attributes and relationships. The colour of the entity-type is also the most intense colour of those used with a saturation of 100 % and the unique hue red. Differences in value intensity is the only dissimilarity between relationship-types and attributes and was used to create different places among the continuum for these constructs. While relationship-types have a saturation of 62 % and a blue hue (not unique to create differences to the entity-types) attributes are not saturated and achromatic. That way, relationship-types have a greater difference in value intensity to other constructs than attributes.

**N-N similarity** is influenced by the unique value for brightness of the entity-type. If relationship-types, attributes or cardinalities would be a target in local search in Fig. 8 than N-N similarity in Fig. 8a) would be higher than in Fig. 8b) since we introduced more variables. That way, we could not increase N-N similarity.

**T-N similarity** has been increased for all constructs placed into the continuum between parallel and serial processing. Entity-types have the highest T-N similarity as this construct has a unique value for three different visual variables. Cardinalities have the lowest T-N similarity since this construct has only one unique value for shape. T-N similarity of relationship-types and attributes is arranged between those of entity-types and cardinalities.

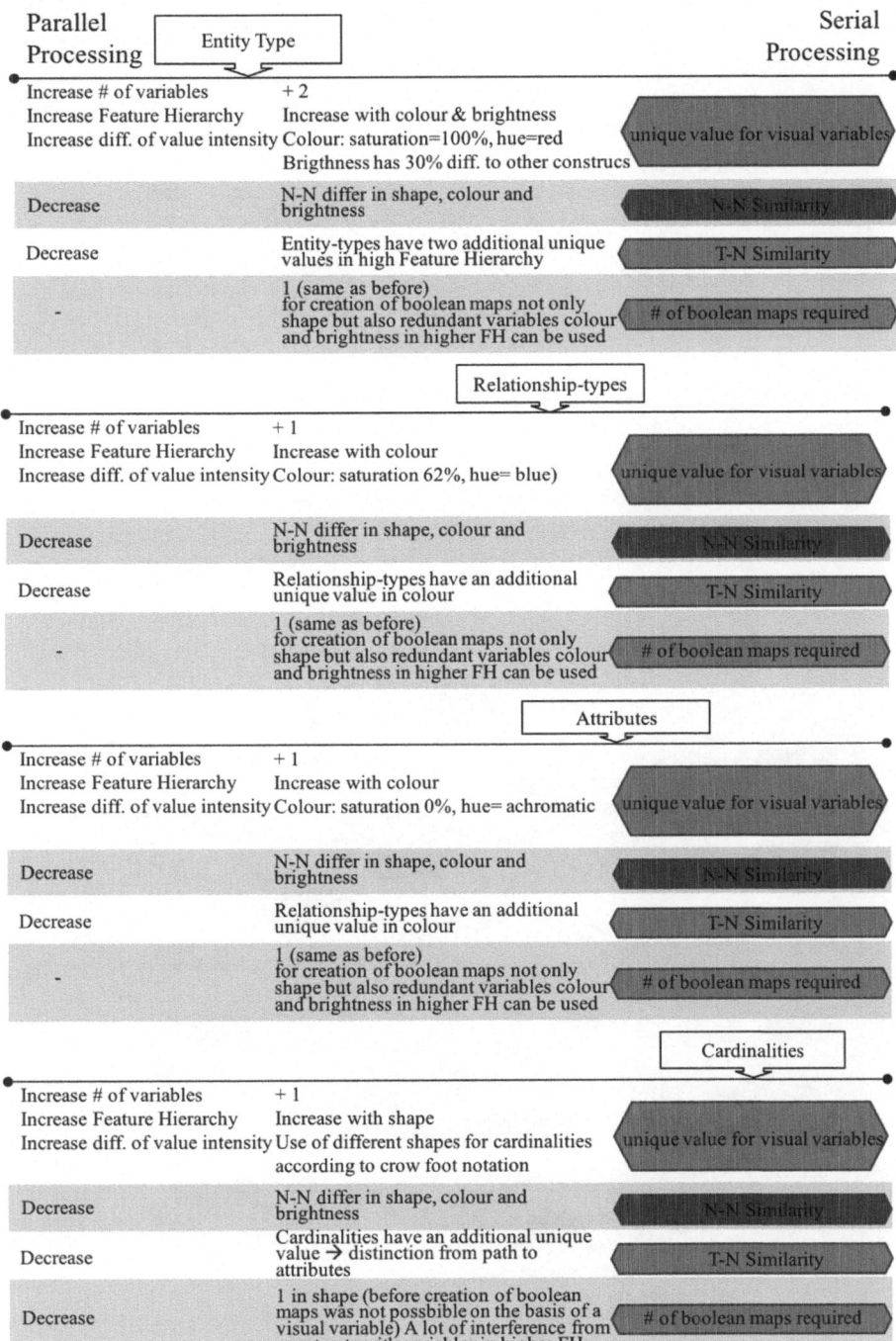

**Fig. 7.** Placing ERD constructs within continuum of parallel and serial processing

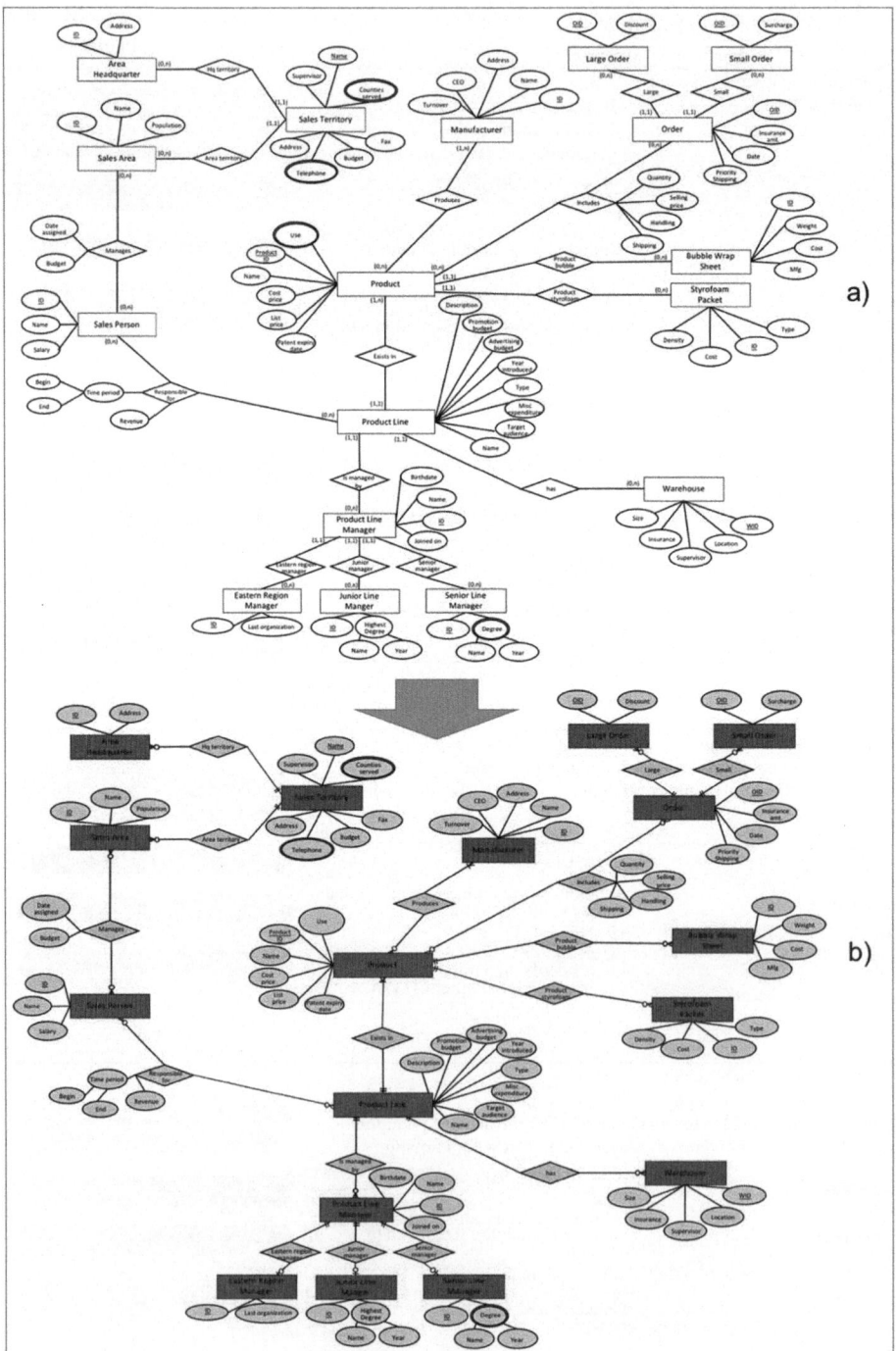

**Fig. 8.** a) original ER-model (on the basis of [40]) and b) optimized ERD (Color figure online)

As only one **boolean map** is required to identify entity-types, attributes and relationship-types in Fig. 8a) no reduction of Boolean maps could be achieved for those constructs. Nevertheless, creating a boolean map is enhanced based on visual variables since redundant coding is used for all three constructs. For cardinalities the construction of Boolean maps on the basis of shape is allowed. In Fig. 8a) a construction of boolean maps is prevented since cardinalities were so far not visually encoded.

## 6 Discussion

With this paper the PoN principle of perceptual discriminability has been extended for further conditions and its application to produce parallel processing for central constructs of a modeling grammar. While reviewing theories of Visual Attention this work describes how visual variables can be used to allow parallel processing and could thereby describe further conditions for a pop-out effect (extension from bottom-up). To effectively use parallel processing for conceptual modeling, notation designers need to decide which constructs are important for model understanding. The focus of this work lays on those constructs that are central to answer typical questions. Additionally, it is exemplarily shown how this can be done for ERDs (extension from top-down).

For both perspectives further research is required. For the top-down perspective this work has only focussed on central constructs. Yet, parallel processing might further reveal advantages for compositions of constructs that can be used as a single chunk or a combination of model elements that belong together. Parallel processing can also be used to highlight a certain story within the model or as a filter on a tool-level to help answering different types of questions. Furthermore, advantages of this research for ERDs have only been shown exemplarily for a low complex modeling grammar. Results from this work still need to be applied to more complex grammars such as BPMN. For the bottom-up perspective more research is needed to effectively combine visual variables such as colour and brightness. Researching in detail only one or few of those variables might lead to further extensions of perceptual discriminability since these variables interrelate. Finally, an evaluation is still required to confirm advantages of extended perceptual discriminability.

## References

1. Moody, D.: The "physics" of notations: toward a scientific basis for constructing visual notations in software engineering. IEEE Trans. Softw. Eng. **35**(6), 756–779 (2009)
2. Caire, P., Genon, N., Heymans, P., Moody, D.: Visual notation design 2.0: towards user comprehensible requirements engineering notations. In: 21st Requirements Engineering Conference, pp. 115–124 (2013)
3. Mendling, J., Reijers, H.A., van der Aalst, W.M.: Seven process modeling guidelines (7PMG). Inf. Softw. Technol. **52**(2), 127–136 (2010)

4. Blackwell, A.F., Britton, C., Cox, A., et al.: Cognitive dimensions of notations: design tools for cognitive technology. In: Beynon, M., Nehaniv, C.L., Dautenhahn, K. (eds.) CT 2001. LNCS (LNAI), vol. 2117, pp. 325–341. Springer, Heidelberg (2001)
5. Green, T.R., Petre, M.: Usability analysis of visual programming environments: a 'cognitive dimensions' framework. J. Vis. Lang. Comput. **7**(2), 131–174 (1996)
6. Genon, N., Heymans, P., Amyot, D.: Analysing the cognitive effectiveness of the BPMN 2.0 visual notation. In: Malloy, B., Staab, S., van den Brand, M. (eds.) SLE 2010. LNCS, vol. 6563, pp. 377–396. Springer, Heidelberg (2011)
7. Figl, K., Mendling, J., Strembeck, M.: The influence of notational deficiencies on process model comprehension. J. Assoc. Inf. Syst. **14**(6), 312 (2013)
8. Bertin, J.: Semiology of Graphics: Diagrams, Networks, Maps. Univ. of Wisconsin Press, Madison (1983)
9. Palmer, S., Rock, I.: Rethinking perceptual organization: the role of uniform connectedness. Psychon. Bull. Rev. **1**(1), 29–55 (1994)
10. Winn, W.: An account of how readers search for information in diagrams. Contemp. Educ. Psychol. **18**(2), 162–185 (1993)
11. Wade, N., Swanston, M.: An Introduction to Visual Perception. Routledge, London (1991)
12. Agarwal, R., Sinha, A.P., Tanniru, M.: Cognitive fit in requirements modeling: a study of object and process methodologies. J. Manag. Inf. Syst. **13**, 137–162 (1996)
13. Healey, C.G., Enns, J.T.: Attention and visual memory in visualization and computer graphics. IEEE Trans. Vis. Comput. Graph. **18**(7), 1170–1188 (2012)
14. Wolfe, J.M., Cave, K.R., Franzel, S.L.: Guided search: an alternative to the feature integration model for visual search. J. Exp. Psychol. Hum. Percept. Perform. **15**(3), 419 (1989)
15. Duncan, J., Humphreys, G.W.: Visual search and stimulus similarity. Psychol. Rev. **96**(3), 433 (1989)
16. Biederman, I.: Recognition-by-components: a theory of human image understanding. Psychol. Rev. **94**(2), 115 (1987)
17. Reijers, H.A., Freytag, T., Mendling, J., Eckleder, A.: Syntax highlighting in business process models. Decis. Support Syst. **51**(3), 339–349 (2011)
18. Quinlan, P.T.: Visual feature integration theory: past, present, and future. Psychol. Bull. **129**(5), 643–673 (2003)
19. Treisman, A.M., Gelade, G.: A feature-integration theory of attention. Cognit. Psychol. **12**(1), 97–136 (1980)
20. Treisman, A., Gormican, S.: Feature analysis in early vision: evidence from search asymmetries. Psychol. Rev. **95**(1), 15 (1988)
21. Treisman, A.: Search, similarity, and integration of features between and within dimensions. J. Exp. Psychol. Hum. Percept. Perform. **17**(3), 652 (1991)
22. Snowden, R.J.: Texture segregation and visual search: a comparison of the effects of random variations along irrelevant dimensions. J. Exp. Psychol. Hum. Percept. Perform. **24**(5), 1354–1367 (1998)
23. Duncan, J.: Boundary conditions on parallel processing in human vision. Perception **18**(4), 457–469 (1989)
24. Huang, L., Pashler, H.: A Boolean map theory of visual attention. Psychol. Rev. **114**(3), 599 (2007)
25. Callaghan, T.C.: Interference and dominance in texture segregation: hue, geometric form, and line orientation. Percept. Psychophys. **46**(4), 299–311 (1989)
26. Calloghan, T.C.: Dimensional interaction of hue and brightness in preattentive field segregation. Percept. Psychophys. **36**(1), 25–34 (1984)

27. Healey, C.G., Enns, J.T.: Large datasets at a glance: combining textures and colors in scientific visualization. IEEE Trans. Vis. Comput. Graph. **5**(2), 145–167 (1999)
28. Zugal, S., Pinggera, J., Weber, B.: Assessing process models with cognitive psychology. In: EMISA 2011, vol. 190, pp. 177–182 (2011)
29. Miller, G.A.: The magical number seven, plus or minus two: some limits on our capacity for processing information. Psychol. Rev. **63**(2), 81 (1956)
30. Cowan, N.: The magical mystery four how is working memory capacity limited, and why? Curr. Dir. Psychol. Sci. **19**(1), 51–57 (2010)
31. Natschläger, C.: Deontic BPMN. In: Hameurlain, A., Liddle, S.W., Schewe, K.-D., Zhou, X. (eds.) DEXA 2011, Part II. LNCS, vol. 6861, pp. 264–278. Springer, Heidelberg (2011)
32. Zur Muehlen, M., Recker, J.: How much language is enough? Theoretical and practical use of the business process modeling notation. In: Advanced Information Systems Engineerin, pp. 465–479 (2008)
33. Collins, A.M., Quillian, M.R.: Experiments on semantic memory and language comprehension. In: Gregg, L.W. (ed.) Cognition in Learning and Memory. Wiley, New York (1972)
34. Anderson, J.R., Pirolli, P.L.: Spread of activation. J. Exp. Psychol. Learn. Mem. Cogn. **10** (4), 791 (1984)
35. Weber, R.: Are attributes entities? A study of database designers' memory structures. Inf. Syst. Res. **7**(2), 137–162 (1996)
36. Krippendorff, K.: Content Analysis: An Introduction to its Methodology. Sage, Thousand Oaks (2012)
37. Lowry, P.B., Moody, D., Gaskin, J., Galletta, D.F., Humphreys, S., Barlow, J.B., Wilson, D.: Evaluating journal quality and the association for information systems (AIS) senior scholars' journal basket via bibliometric measures: do expert journal assessments add value? MIS Q. **37**(4), 993–1012 (2013)
38. Gemino, A., Wand, Y.: Complexity and clarity in conceptual modeling: comparison of mandatory and optional properties. Data Knowl. Eng. **55**(3), 301–326 (2005)
39. Genero, M., Poels, G., Piattini, M.: Defining and validating metrics for assessing the understandability of entity–relationship diagrams. Data Knowl. Eng. **64**(3), 534–557 (2008)
40. Khatri, V., Vessey, I., Ramesh, V., Clay, P., Park, J.-S.: Understanding conceptual schemas: exploring the role of application and IS domain knowledge. Inf. Syst. Res. **17**(1), 81–99 (2006)
41. Bodart, R., Patel, A., Sim, M., Weber, R.: Should optional properties be used in conceptual modelling? A theory and three empirical tests. Inf. Syst. Res. **12**(4), 384–405 (2001)
42. Masri, K., Parker, D., Gemino, A.: Using iconic graphics in entity-relationship diagrams: the impact on understanding. J. Database Manag. **19**(3), 22 (2008)
43. Parsons, J.: Effects of local versus global schema diagrams on verification and communication in conceptual data modeling. J. Manag. Inf. Syst. **19**(3), 155–183 (2002)

# From the Essence of an Enterprise Towards Enterprise Ontology Patterns

Tanja Poletaeva[1](✉), Habib Abdulrab[1], and Eduard Babkin[2]

[1] INSA de Rouen, LITIS Lab, Rouen, France
ta.poletaeva@gmail.com, abdulrab@insa-rouen.fr
[2] National Research University Higher School of Economics,
Nizhny Novgorod, Russia
eababkin@hse.ru

**Abstract.** In this paper we partially present an initial version of a Formal Enterprise Ontology Pattern Language, which has been developed to support conceptual enterprise modeling and a subsequent construction of different design and implementation artifacts. The proposed enterprise ontology patterns address problems related to the correlated modeling of both the intersubjective world and the production world of an enterprise, as well as the effective conjunction of the domain knowledge and the operational knowledge of an enterprise. The proposed language builds on a synthesis of the Unified Foundational Ontology (UFO) and the DEMO Enterprise Ontology. We also demonstrate how the pattern language was applied to the domain-specific enterprise modeling.

**Keywords:** Conceptual modeling · Enterprise ontology · Foundational ontology · Ontology pattern · Ontology pattern language

## 1 Introduction

In recent years, ontologies have been recognized as a powerful instrument for an explicit and formal representation of conceptualizations of reality, providing theoretical foundations for conceptual modeling languages [1]. Particularly, an enterprise ontology is essential for a deep understanding of the construction and operation of an enterprise via its coherent, comprehensive, consistent, and concise conceptual models [2]. However, while being provided with the proper expressive modeling language preserving the enterprise-world semantics, one can experience ambiguous choices when expressing knowledge additional to the modeled enterprise essence [3–5] or when constructing design and implementation artifacts upon the created conceptual models [4, 6]. There is a lack of languages that have enough expressivity for enterprise knowledge, while preserving a formal semantics.

In [7], the authors proposed the Enterprise Ontology Pattern Language (E-OPL) aimed at facilitating enterprise conceptual modeling. According to [8], "an ontology pattern describes a particular recurring modeling problem that arises in specific ontology development context and presents a well-proven solution for the problem". The patterns of E-OPL were extracted from different enterprise ontologies addressing five aspects: Organization Arrangement, Team Definition, Institutional Roles,

© Springer International Publishing Switzerland 2016
D. Aveiro et al. (Eds.): EEWC 2016, LNBIP 252, pp. 118–131, 2016.
DOI: 10.1007/978-3-319-39567-8_8

Institutional Goals, and Human Resource Management. Moreover, the E-OPL patterns in [7] are represented in OntoUML [1], a UML profile that preserves the ontological distinctions put forth by the Unified Foundational Ontology (UFO) [1].

In this paper, we propose an initial version of alternative enterprise ontology patterns which comprise the elements and the axiomatization derived from a synthesis of (i) the Unified Foundational Ontology (UFO) [1] and (ii) the enterprise ontology DEMO – the Design and Engineering Methodology for Organizations [2]. We have obtained our synthesis by (i) applying UFO and its well-founded conceptual modeling language OntoUML to articulate the theory of enterprise ontology in a system of general categories; (ii) and adding some additional ontological categories based on their relevance for the theory of enterprise ontology.

The most important property of the DEMO modeling language is that conceptual models represented in this language are essential, i.e., they show the core enterprise knowledge. In contrast, the ontology patterns presented in this work are aimed at expressing the core knowledge in the form that facilitates its extension and integration. Particularly, the authors focus on the correlated modeling of both the intersubjective world and the production world of an enterprise. The patterns founded on both the upper level ontology and the enterprise ontology preserve a formal semantics together with a real-world semantics in a broad sense. Therefore, this work would hopefully contribute to the integration of the domain knowledge and the operational knowledge of an enterprise.

The outline of this paper is organized as follows. First, the theoretical background of our work is summarized in Sect. 2. In Sect. 3, we elaborate on the proposed enterprise ontology patterns. Then, Sect. 4 illustrates the application of the enterprise ontology patterns for a domain-specific enterprise conceptual modeling. Finally, Sect. 5 presents the final considerations and directions for further research.

## 2    Ontological Foundations of Enterprise Ontology Patterns

In this section, we focus on some important aspects of the underlying ontologies UFO [1] and DEMO [2] of the proposed enterprise ontology patterns.

### 2.1    The Unified Foundational Ontology (UFO)

The philosophically, linguistically and cognitively well-founded foundational ontology UFO was first proposed by Guizzardi in [1] and has been developed in many works afterwards [9–15]. UFO consists of four main parts: an ontology of endurants (objects, continuants) – UFO-A [1], an ontology of perdurants (events, occurrents) – UFO-B [11], an ontology of social entities – UFO-C [12], and an ontology of services – UFO-S [13]. Hereafter, we briefly summarize the formal and ontological meta-properties of some types elaborated in the first three parts of UFO. These types are represented by stereotypes in the OntoUML metamodel.

UFO-A explains a number of distinctions among object types. Whilst all types carry a principle of application, only sortal types either provide or carry a uniform principle of identity for their instances. In this research, we exploit the following sortal types: *Kind*, *Subkind*, *Role*, *Phase*. While Kinds provide a principle of identity for their instances, Subkinds carry the principle of identity supplied by Kinds. Moreover, Kinds and Subkinds carry out a meta-property of rigidity being necessarily applied to their instances in every possible world. In contrast, anti-rigidity characterizes a type whose instance(s) can cease to be an instance of that type without ceasing to exist and without altering its identity. For example, a particular individual, which is an instance of type *Student* in one world, can cease to instantiate this type in another world without ceasing to exist as the same individual of type *Person* [1]. Thus, Roles and Phases are distinguished as anti-rigid sortals. A Phase is a relationally independent type whose instantiation is characterized by a change of an intrinsic property of an individual. A Role is a relationally dependent type whose instantiation is obligatory related to other entities.

Non-sortals represent an abstraction of properties that are common to multiple disjoint kinds and, therefore, do not carry a unique principle of identity for their instances. *Category* represents a rigid and relationally-independent non-sortal type that aggregates essential properties common to different kinds. *Role Mixin*, in turn, represents an anti-rigid and relationally dependent non-sortal type that aggregates properties common to different roles.

Another important distinction in the UFO ontology is within the categories of relations. It recognizes two broad categories of relations, namely, *formal relations* and *material relations*. Formal relations hold between two or more entities because of very nature of these entities, without any further intervening individual. Conversely, material relations have a material structure of their own, which mediates the connected entities and inheres in the mereological sum of them [14]. Such mediating entities constitute the extension of *Relators*. For example, a *medical treatment* connects a patient with a medical unit; a *marriage* connects a wife and a husband [1]. The formal relation of mediation between a relator and the entities it connects is a sort of inherence and, hence, a special type of existential dependence relation. Relators can only exist while connecting the relata, i.e. they exhibit mutual dependency patterns involving all arguments, as well as dependencies on external entities besides the arguments [14].

Axiomatization of *situations*, *events*, and *dispositions* was summarized in UFO-B. Situations are special type of endurants. They are complex entities that are constituted by possibly many endurants (including other situations). In other words, situation is a portion of reality that can be comprehended as a whole. A relation of "being present at" is defined between endurants and the situations they constitute [12]. Situations can be factual or counterfactual. Factual situations (or Facts) are said to obtain at particular time points.

Events are perdurants composed by temporal parts and happened in time in the sense that they extend in time accumulating temporal parts. Events are considered as possible transformations from one portion of reality to another, i.e. they may change reality by changing the state of affairs from one situation to another [11].

Moreover, in the ontology design patterns of the UFO-B ontology, temporal properties of objects and spatial properties of events are derived from the existential dependence of events on the objects that participate in them. Properties that are only manifested in particular situations on the occurrence of certain triggering events are called *dispositions*. Dispositions are manifested through the occurrence of resulting events and state changes [15].

UFO-C incorporates *intentionality* to the basic core provided by UFO-A and UFO-B. In this context, UFO distinguishes between Agentive and Non-agentive substantial individuals, termed *agents* and *objects*, respectively. As opposed to objects, agents are capable of bearing special kind of intrinsic properties named *intentional moments*. Intentionality of agents should be understood as the capacity of their properties to refer to possible situations of reality. Every intentional moment has a type (e.g., *belief, desire, intention*) and a propositional content represented by a *proposition*. The latter being an abstract representation of a class of situations referred by that intentional moment.

*Intentions* are desired state of affairs for which the agent commits at pursuing (an intention is an internal commitment). For this reason, intentions cause the agent to perform *actions*. Actions are intentional events, i.e., events with the specific purpose of satisfying the propositional content of some intention of an agent. The propositional content of an intention is termed a *goal*. UFO contemplates a relation between situations and goals such that a situation may satisfy a goal.

*Communicative acts* (special kinds of actions) can be used to create *social moments* (*commitments* and *claims*). Thus, social moments are types of intentional moments that are created by the exchange of communicative acts between parties and the consequences of these exchanges. In this view, language not only represents the reality but also creates a part of reality. The later ontological claim tightly correlates with the LAP foundations of DEMO (ref. Sect. 2.2).

## 2.2   The DEMO Theory and Methodology of Enterprise Ontology

In the presented work, we employ the OntoUML [1] conceptual modeling language to extend real-world semantics of the modeling constructs of the DEMO Theory and Methodology of Enterprise Ontology [2]. Based on the strong theoretical basis, the DEMO methodology facilitates creation of ontological models that are essential, complete, free from logical contradictions, compact and succinct, independent of their realization and implementation issues [2].

The interpretive and intersubjective world view of the methodology results in considering an enterprise as a discrete dynamic system, of which the elements are social individuals or *actors*, capable to negotiate by performing *coordination acts* and to contribute to bringing about the goods or services by performing *production acts*. By performing coordination acts, actors express their *intensions* and comply with *commitments* towards each other regarding the performance of production acts [2]. By performing both kinds of acts, actors transfer the world into the new states characterized by resulted *coordination facts* and (if any) *production facts*.

The core concept in DEMO is the notion of the uniform communication patterns between autonomic actors involved in a business deal. These patterns, also called *transaction patterns*, always involve two *actor roles* (the initiator and the executor) and consist of certain coordination acts related to one production fact of a particular type. *Transaction* is a sequence of acts that is a path through the complete transaction pattern [2]. It goes off in three consecutive phases: the *order phase*, the *execution phase*, and the *result phase* [2].

The DEMO transaction concept distinguishes between the intersubjective (social) and the objective worlds. Thus, coordination acts and their results (coordination facts) relate to the intersubjective world. By performing production acts actors change the states of products or services related to the objective world. The distinction of these two worlds at the conceptual level gives an opportunity for a coherent modeling of both the information and the process worldviews on an enterprise.

Finally, the methodology builds a comprehensive view on the interaction and management processes of an enterprise in four Aspect Models [2]. Through these conceptual models expressed in an enterprise-specific modeling language, it is possible to achieve a solid understanding of business agent roles, their potential communications and fulfilled changes in the production world, the types of transactions taking place in an organization and relations between them, as well as the information processed and created in the course of transactions execution.

# 3   A Formal Enterprise Ontology Pattern Language

In this section, we elaborate on a set of enterprise ontology patterns built on a synthesis of UFO and DEMO. Due to lack of space, we left the description of the synthesis out of the scope of this paper. The patterns described in the following subsections are tightly interrelated with each other through their elements.

## 3.1   Participation in a Transaction

Enterprises are social systems whose elements (or social individuals) are human beings able to enter and comply with commitments [2]. Granted authority to perform particular acts in a responsible way, a social individual of an enterprise fulfills an *actor role* [2]. In his fulfillment of an actor role, a social individual becomes an actor. Obviously, a social individual may cease to be an actor without ceasing to exist. Moreover, an actor role can be instantiated by agents of different kinds, e.g. persons, organizations or organizational units. Thereby, *Actor Role* is a *Role Mixin* stereotyped by <<roleMixin>> in OntoUML model depicted in Fig. 1.

The notion of transaction discussed in DEMO [2] is articulated in the UFO categories as follows. At each time the business relation between two actors holds, the *transaction* is constituted by a mereological sum of all mutual commitments made by actors in their negotiation about a particular change in the production world (i.e., a production result). Thus, each transaction is a *relator* mediating two actors (Fig. 1). The actor that initiates a transaction is of the type *Initiator*. The actor that carries out a production act is of the type *Executor*. *Initiator* and *Executor* are subtypes of the type *Actor Role*.

In the broader sense, transactions are mereological sums of all their constituent relational qualities [14] inhering in one interacting actor and directly or indirectly existentially dependent on another one. These qualities and their changes can be specified in conceptual models by attributes of transactions. For example, a yearly membership registration (*Transaction*) of a customer (*Initiator*) in a company (*Executor*) can have a particular cost (an attribute), which changes over time.

Moreover, being an endurant, each transaction is an instance of a kind that can be specialized in various ways along the distinctions proposed by OntoUML (see Sect. 2.1). Hence, for each instance of *Transaction*, the phases *Transaction-Order*, *Transaction-Execution*, or *Transaction-Result* can be specified according to the coordination facts constituting this transaction.

Distinction of actor roles in an organization by means of the method described in [2] together with the Organization Arrangement patterns developed in [7, 16] could help the ontology engineer to treat problems related to the definition of *Kinds* for selected actor roles (see also Sect. 4).

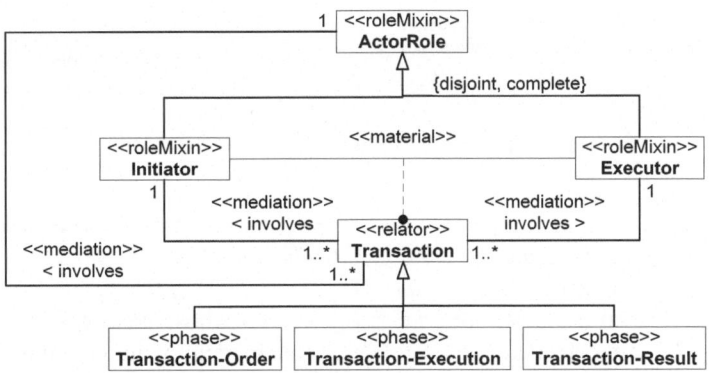

**Fig. 1.** The pattern of participation in a transaction

### 3.2 Coordination Acts and Facts

Each coordination act performed by an actor towards his addressee contains an intention and a proposition [2]. With the *intention*, an actor proclaims his 'social attitude' with respect to the *proposition*. The standard transaction may contain coordination acts with the following intentions: request, promise, state, accept, decline, quit, reject, and stop [2]. With the proposition, an actor proclaims an abstract representation of a class of desired situations [1]. In accordance with many standards, the portion of reality which is subject to changes, can be abstracted by the category *Work Product*.

The foregoing definition of coordination acts was formalized by the Coordination Act pattern. This pattern comprises the types: *Actor Role*, *C-act*, *C-act Intention*, *C-act Proposition*, *Work Product Disposition*, *Work Product*, as well as their interrelations depicted in Fig. 2.

We propose to model instances of the *Proposition* type as specializations (subtypes) of *Work Product Disposition*, where the extension of the latter is a class of desired situations such as creation or termination of an object, a relation between objects, or a qualitative property of an object. For example, the proposition of C-acts and C-facts

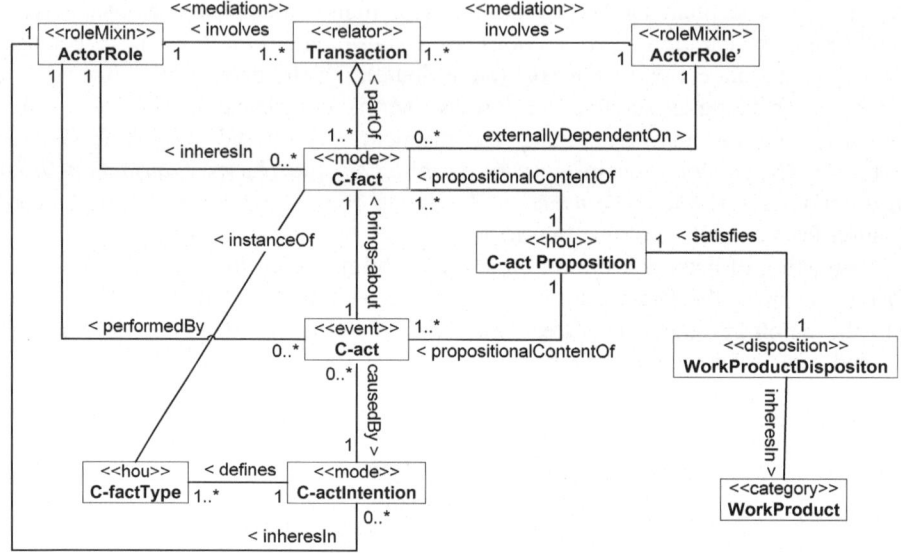

**Fig. 2.** The pattern of coordination acts and facts

appeared in a transaction of type *Membership Registration* can be formulated as '(new) membership has been started' or simply, '*Membership Started*', where the latter is a possible specialization of *Work Product Disposition*. Thus, the *Proposition* type is a high-order universal (a powertype), i.e. a rigid sortal whose instances are types [17]. Following [7], we extended the OntoUML metamodel by introducing the stereo-type <<hou>> to represent high-order universals.

A coordination act *brings about* a situation, which *triggers* a (social) *commitment* of one agent towards another regarding the proclaimed intention and the proposition. This commitment is a *coordination fact* (*C-fact*) [2]. Examples of coordination facts are: "*membership has been started* is requested asap", "*membership has been started* is promised asap", where "*membership has been started*" is the propositional content of both C-acts and their resulted C-facts, and "membership" is an identifiable instance of kind *Membership*, where *Membership* is a specialization of the category *Work Product*. For the sake of simplicity, in this version of patterns, we omit from consideration the time part of propositions.

As a social commitment, a *C-fact inheres* in one of the negotiating actors per-forming a C-act, and is *externally dependent* on the target actor. Hereby we consider a C-fact being a relational quality (a *mode*) that contributes to constitute the relationship between two actors, i.e., each *C-fact* is always a *part of* some *transaction*. Moreover, we assume that each C-fact inherits the (fact part of) C-act proposition from its acti-vating C-act.

C-acts with particular intention define a partition of the generalization set of C-fact types (*C-factType* powertype). In other words, all C-facts brought about by C-acts with particular intention, are instances of particular specialization of the *C-fact* type. For instance, *Work Product Disposition Requested* comprises instances of *C-fact* that result

C-acts with the intention 'request', or *Work Product Disposition Promised* comprises instances resulted C-acts with the intention 'promise'.

The foregoing definition of coordination facts was formalized by the Coordination Fact pattern. This pattern comprises the types: *Actor Role, Transaction, C-fact, C-fact Type, C-act Proposition, Work Product Disposition, Work Product* as well as their interrelations depicted in Fig. 2.

### 3.3 Production Acts

By performing material or immaterial production act (P-act), the executor of a transaction contributes to bringing about goods and/or services [2]. Thus, a *production act* may *bring about* a *work product disposition* (Fig. 3), which is a change of a qualitative property of an object, creation/termination of an object, or creation/termination of a relation between objects. A work product disposition inheres in a *work product*. The relator *Work Product Participation* establishes the participation of work products in a P-act [18]. This relator is modeled with its specializations for creation and change participation.

When the ontology engineer wants to represent the structure of work products, the Work Product Composition and the Work Product Nature patterns developed in [18] facilitate modeling of work product mereological decomposition and the types of work products respectively. Moreover, since the patterns in [18] are constructed using OntoUML, they can be easily merged with the pattern depicted in Fig. 3.

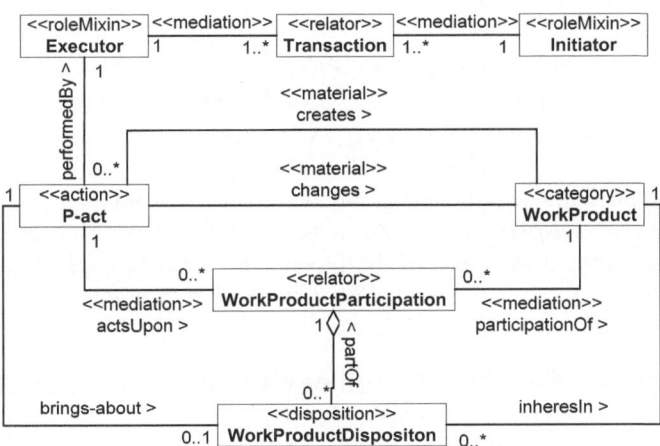

**Fig. 3.** The pattern of production acts

### 3.4 Production Facts

As pointed out in DEMO [2], all changes of a work product that have not been traced properly in a social world of an enterprise are not considered of being effective or usable in this world. Thus, only a work product change, which is stated and accepted by coordination acts of a particular transaction, becomes a *production fact* (*P-fact*) of an enterprise [2].

To put it more precisely, an individual *p* is a P-factum iff there is a work product disposition *p* which satisfies both the propositional content of the *statement* of this disposition by a C-fact, and the propositional content of the *acceptance* of this disposition by a C-fact. C-facts stating and accepting the disposition, are parts of the same transaction and instances of the types (or their specializations) *Work Product Disposition Stated* and *Work Product Disposition Accepted* respectively (Fig. 4).

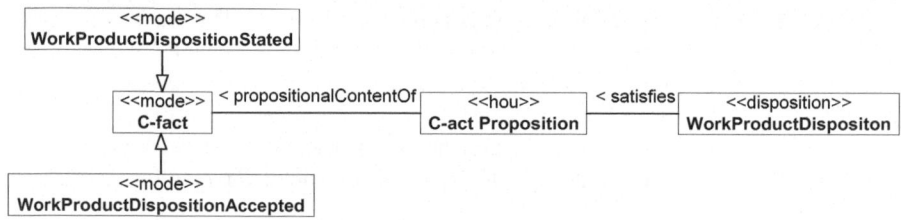

**Fig. 4.** The pattern of production facts

Since the conceptual model in Fig. 4 does not precisely express the given definition, hereafter we specify it more formally in first order logic. In the definition that follows, we use the notation x::U to represent the relation of instantiation between an individual x and a universal U.

$$P\text{-}fact(p) =_{def} WorkProductDisposition(p) \land \exists x\, (satisfies(x,p) \land x::C\text{-}actProposition)$$
$$\land \exists! y\, (propositionalContentOf(x,y) \land y::WorkProductDispositionStated) \land \exists! z$$
$$(propositionalContentOf\,(x,z) \land z::WorkProductDispositionAccepted)(1)$$

It is important to highlight that unambiguous articulation of types *C-act Proposition* and *Work Product Disposition* as well as their interrelations with the types of the coordination world and the types of the production world of an enterprise serves to provide a basis for the coherent modeling of states in both worlds.

## 4 Applying the Enterprise Ontology Patterns: A Case Study

Enterprise ontology patterns are modeling fragments to be used during enterprise conceptual modeling, and focus only on conceptual aspects, without any concern with the technology or language [8]. In this section, we shortly present a case study, applying the enterprise ontology patterns for the conceptual modeling of pizzas delivery.

One can imagine a simple Pizzeria where only pizzas are made on receiving a new order. Customers can have their pizzas delivered home. To realize this service, the owner of the company hired students, who deliver pizzas on bicycles. However, the students deliver pizzas only in the city region nearby the Pizzeria. For the delivery of orders to remote locations, the Pizzeria uses the transportation service of a third-party company. The owner of the Pizzeria decided to control the delivery process by means of ICT (Information and Communication Technology). He started from the conceptual modeling stage preliminary to the data modeling. In addition, we suppose that the owner have already analyzed his business by means of the DEMO methodology [2]. Thus, he analyzed the transactions, the actor roles, and the business processes of his company.

Figure 5 presents the conceptual model, which was constructed by applying the Participation in a Transaction pattern together with the Organization Arrangement patterns from [7] to a conceptualization of the *Delivery* transaction in the Pizzeria. In this domain-specific pattern, the roles *Initiator* and *Executor* are specified by *Order Manager* and *Deliverer* respectively. While *Order Manager* is a role that can be played by organizational units of the Pizzeria (instances of *Pizzeria Organizational Unit*), two kinds of actors can play a role of *Deliverer*, to wit: the Pizzeria's delivery unit and third-party delivery companies (instances of *Third-party Delivery Co*). Moreover, the domain-specific facts '*order id of [Delivery] is [ID]*', '*start date of [Delivery] is [Date]*', '*end date of [Delivery] is [Date]*' were represented respectively by the attributes *OrderId, startDate*, and *endDate* of the *Delivery* relator.

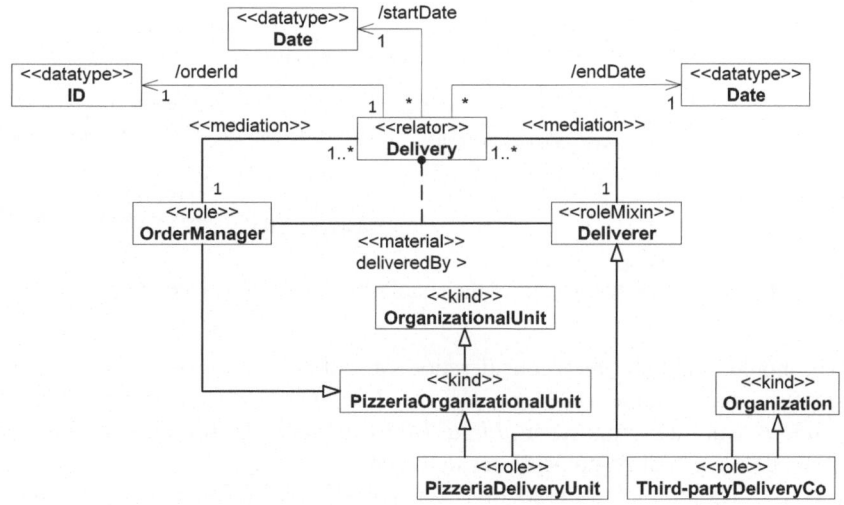

**Fig. 5.** Extended conceptual model of the *Delivery* transaction

The ontology engineer (the Pizzeria's owner) might need to track coordination facts appeared in the *Delivery* transactions by means of ICT. The pattern of Coordination Facts (Fig. 2) can be applied at the initial conceptual modeling stage. This pattern leads to the definition of a work product type, a type of inhered dispositions (*Work Product Disposition*), and the instances of *C-act Proposition* that allow making commitments about the desired disposition(s) before it comes to exist.

For the sake of simplicity, we suppose that a work product of the *Delivery* trans-actions is of the type *Pizza*, and the dispositions are instances of *Pizza Delivered* with the attribute *address* (Fig. 6). In Fig. 6, only one instance of *C-act Proposition* is depicted. According to the proposition made in Sect. 3.2, this instance is a type of dispositions (*Pizza Delivered*) constituting the fact part of delivery requests. However, in Fig. 6, the instance of *C-act Proposition* is depicted separately from the type *Pizza Delivered*. This example illustrates that a number of delivered pizza states (the instances of *Pizza Delivered*) may satisfy 'PizzaDelivered' instance of *C-act Proposition*.

C-facts resulted C-acts with different intentions constitute different phases of a transaction. Thus, the P-fact type *Delivery Requested* (Fig. 6) is a part of the order phase of *Delivery*.

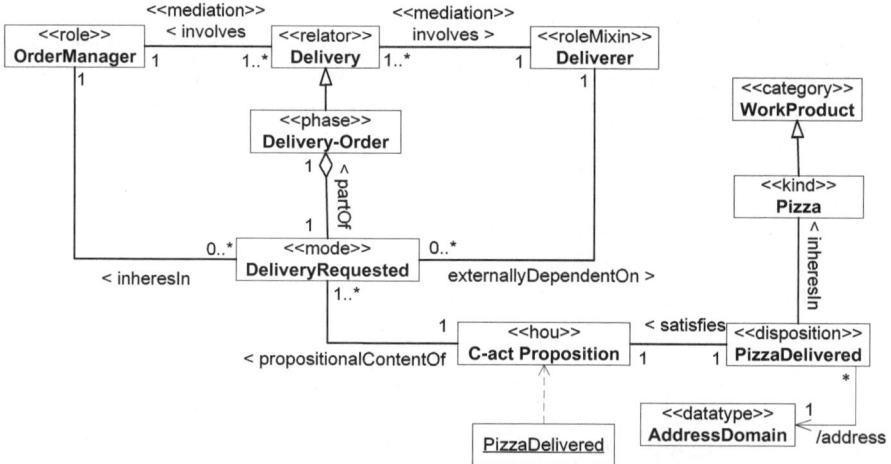

**Fig. 6.** Conceptual model of the coordination facts of delivery requests

We should highlight that consideration of different subtypes of *Deliverer* can require the specialization of *Pizza Delivered* as well as new instances of *C-act Proposition*, e.g. the proposition *Pizza Delivered Locally* for all requests to the Pizzeria's delivery unit responsible for deliveries.

The specification of the Production Acts pattern can be extended by the standard delivery metadata modeled by the attributes of a work product (Fig. 7). Further specification of the elements of the domain-specific pattern in Fig. 7 may be required to model special conditions of production acts.

In Fig. 8, the specification of the Production Fact pattern is depicted together with one exemplifying instance. For this particular case, the instances of the P-fact com-ponents were given names reflected their datalogical representations. If the domain-specific pattern is used for creation of meta-data in Pizzeria's database, then these instances illustrate possible data elements.

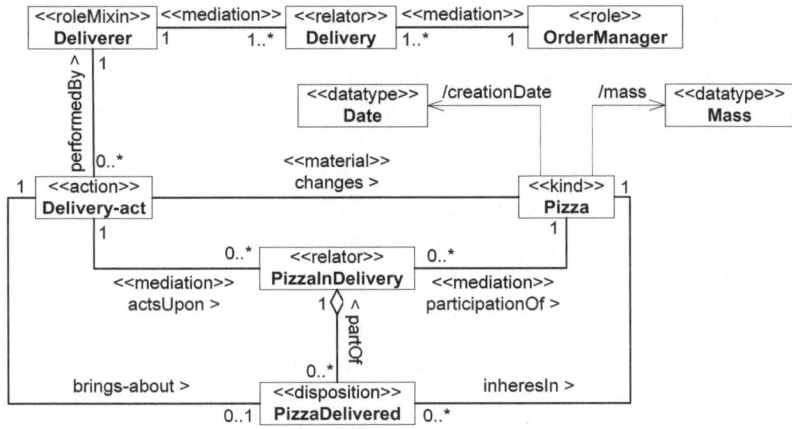

**Fig. 7.** Extended conceptual model of the *Delivery* production acts

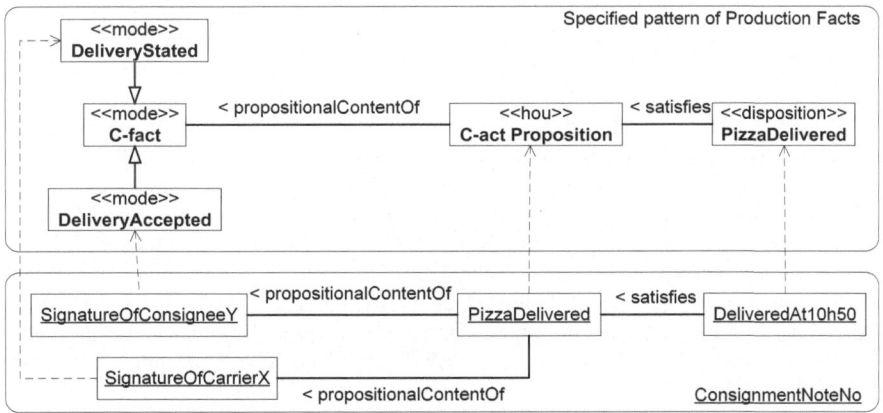

**Fig. 8.** Conceptual model of the *Delivery* production facts and one exemplifying instance of this model

## 5    Final Considerations

Enterprise conceptual modeling is not an easy task. In this work, we proposed an initial version of the Formal Enterprise Ontology Pattern Language aimed at facilitating enterprise conceptual modeling. Since the patterns constituting this language are expressed in OntoUML, they carry out the ontological and formal semantics of OntoUML's modeling constructs inherited from the foundational ontology UFO [1]. On the other hand, since the proposed patterns were built in accordance with the DEMO theory of enterprise ontology [2], they inherit the real-world semantics of the enterprise domain.

We argue that the proposed enterprise ontology patterns tend to bring the following benefits for enterprise conceptual modeling: (i) the coherent models of the coordination and the production world of an enterprise; (ii) the conceptual modeling process of particular enterprises tends to be accelerated by reuse of these patterns; (iii) an easy integration with the domain-specific ontological patterns expressed in OntoUML.

Following the directives on how to map conceptual models in OntoUML to their implementation and less-expressive computationally-oriented codification languages [19], our future research direction is the mapping of the proposed ontology patterns to the constructs of the Web Ontology Language (OWL) and to the rules expressed in the Semantic Web Rule Language[1] (SWRL). Codification of the proposed patterns will result in a core enterprise data metamodel.

**Acknowledgments.** The reported study was funded by RFBR according to the research project № 16-06-00300 a. This research was also partly funded by the CLASSE ("Les Corridors Logistiques: Application a la Vallee de la Seine et son Environnement") project of the Grand Research Network of in Upper Normandy (Grand Réseaux de Recherche de Haute-Normandie). The authors would like to express their gratitude to Dr. Giancarlo Guizzardi for his invaluable advice and inspiring discussions.

# References

1. Guizzardi, G.: Ontological foundations for structural conceptual models. Telematics Instituut Fundamental Research Series, No. 015, The Netherlands (2005). ISSN 1388-1795
2. Dietz, J.L.G.: Enterprise Ontology – Theory and Methodology. Springer, Heidelberg (2006)
3. Barjis, J., Dietz, J.L.G., Liu, K.: Combining the DEMO methodology with semiotic methods in business process modeling. In: Liu, K., Clarke, R.J., Andersen, P.B., Stamper, R.K. (eds.) Information, Organisation and Technology: Studies in Organisational Semiotics. Information and Organization Design Series, vol. 1, pp. 213–246 (2001)
4. de Jong, J.: Designing the Information Organization from Ontological Perspective. In: Albani, A., Dietz, J.L., Verelst, J. (eds.) EEWC 2011. LNBIP, vol. 79, pp. 1–15. Springer, Heidelberg (2011)
5. de Kinderen, S., Gaaloul, K., Proper, H.A.: Transforming Transaction Models into ArchiMate. In: CAiSE 2012 Forum at the 24th International Conference on Advanced Information Systems Engineering (CAiSE). CEUR-WS, vol. 855, pp. 114–121 (2012)
6. Krouwel, M.R., Op 't Land, M.: Combining DEMO and Normalized Systems for Developing Agile Enterprise Information Systems. In: Albani, A., Dietz, J.L., Verelst, J. (eds.) EEWC 2011. LNBIP, vol. 79, pp. 31–45. Springer, Heidelberg (2011)
7. Falbo, R.A., Ruy, F.B., Guizzardi, G., Barcellos, M.P., Almeida, J.P.A.: Towards an enterprise ontology pattern language. In: 29th Annual ACM Symposium on Applied Computing, pp. 323–330. ACM (2014)
8. de Almeida Falbo, R., Guizzardi, G., Gangemi, A., Presutti, V.: Ontology patterns: clarifying concepts and terminology. In: 4th Workshop on Ontology and Semantic Web Patterns. Sydney, Australia (2013)

---

[1] The Web Ontology Language (OWL) and the Semantic Web Rule Language (SWRL) are Semantic Web languages recommended by the W3C for knowledge representation.

9. Guizzardi, G.: Logical, ontological and cognitive aspects of object types and cross-world identity with applications to the theory of conceptual spaces. In: Zenker, F., Gärdenfors, P. (eds.) Applications of Conceptual Spaces: The Case for Geometric Knowledge Representation, Part III. Synthese Library, vol. 359, pp. 165–186. Springer, Switzerland (2015)

10. Guizzardi, G., Wagner, G.: Using the Unified Foundational Ontology (UFO) as a foundation for general conceptual modeling languages. In: Poli, R., Healy, M., Kameas, A. (eds.) Theory and Applications of Ontology: Computer Applications, pp. 175–196. Springer, Netherlands (2010)

11. Guizzardi, G., Wagner, G., de Almeida Falbo, R., Guizzardi, R.S., Almeida, J.P.A.: Towards ontological foundations for the conceptual modeling of events. In: Ng, W., Storey, V.C., Trujillo, J.C. (eds.) ER 2013. LNCS, vol. 8217, pp. 327–341. Springer, Heidelberg (2013)

12. Guizzardi, G., Falbo, R.A., Guizzardi, R.S.S.: Grounding software domain ontologies in the Unified Foundational Ontology (UFO): the case of the ODE software process ontology. In: XI Iberoamerican Workshop on Requirements Engineering and Software Environments, pp. 244–251 (2008)

13. Nardi, J.C., De Almeida Falbo, R., Almeida, J.P.A., Guizzardi, G., Ferreira Pires, L., Van Sinderen, M.J., Guarino, N., Fonseca, C.M.: A Commitment-based Reference Ontology for Services. Information Systems, vol. 54, pp. 263–288. Elsevier Ltd. (2015)

14. Guarino, N., Guizzardi, G.: "We need to discuss the relationship": revisiting relationships as modeling constructs. In: Zdravkovic, J., Kirikova, M., Johannesson, P. (eds.) CAiSE 2015. LNCS, vol. 9097, pp. 279–294. Springer, Heidelberg (2015)

15. Guizzardi, G., Wagner, G.: Dispositions and causal laws as the ontological foundation of transition rules in simulation models. In: 2013 Winter Simulation Conference, pp. 1335–1346. IEEE (2013)

16. Quirino, G.K., et al.: Towards a service ontology pattern language. In: Johannesson, P., Lee, M.L., Liddle, S.W., Opdahl, A.L., Pastor López, Ó. (eds.) ER 2015. LNCS, vol. 9381, pp. 187–195. Springer, Heidelberg (2015). doi:10.1007/978-3-319-25264-3_14

17. Guizzardi, G., Almeida, J.P.A., Guarino, N., Carvalho, V.A.: Towards an ontological analysis of powertypes. In: International Workshop on Formal Ontologies for Artificial Intelligence (FOFAI 2015), 24th International Joint Conference on Artificial Intelligence (IJCAI 2015). CEUR-WS, vol. 1517 (2015)

18. Ruy, F.B., Falbo, R.A., Barcellos, M.P., Guizzardi, G.: Towards an ontology pattern language for harmonizing software process related ISO standards. In: 29th Annual ACM Symposium on Applied Computing, pp. 388–395 (2015)

19. Guizzardi, G., Zamborlini, V.: Using a trope-based foundational ontology for bridging different areas of concern in ontology-driven conceptual modeling. In: Science of Computer Programming, vol. 96, Part 4, pp. 417–443. Elsevier B.V. (2014)

# Extended Viable System Model

Alexey Sergeev[1,2(✉)] and José Tribolet[3,4]

[1] Department of Information Systems and Technologies,
National Research University – Higher School of Economics,
Bol. Pecherskaya 25, 603155 Nizhny Novgorod, Russia
aisergeev@yahoo.com
[2] Department of Engineering and Management, Instituto Superior Técnico,
University of Lisbon, Lisbon, Portugal
[3] Department of Computer Science and Engineering, Instituto Superior Técnico,
University of Lisbon, Lisbon, Portugal
[4] Instituto de Engenharia de Sistemas e Computadores,
Investigação e Desenvolvimento em Lisboa (INESC-ID), Lisbon, Portugal
Jose.Tribolet@inesc.pt

**Abstract.** Viable System Model (VSM) is a well-known and widely used concept when working with enterprise as a viable system. However, research shows that VSM does not include all the required elements to correctly model enterprise as a viable system. This paper proposes extensions to VSM which help to model enterprise in a more complete way. The proposal is illustrated using case study of a real company. Authors propose to tie extended VSM to the notion of Enterprise Operating System in future research.

**Keywords:** Viable system model · Enterprise operating system · Enterprise architecture · Enterprise engineering

## 1 Introduction

In this work we follow view of Tribolet [1] on the enterprise as "a semantic web" of active servers (agents), either silicon based or carbon based, running "internally" their own apps and interacting "externally" through such "web", in real-time. Silicon based servers are represented by actual computing devices such as laptops, PCs, servers. Carbon based servers are human beings, which are performing certain roles within the organization and interacting with each other and silicon based servers. Certainly carbon based servers and silicon based servers are not equal – human beings exclusively have cognitive abilities, authority and competence to make decisions which they are responsible for. Notions of authority, competence and responsibility are not applicable to silicon based servers. Since both types of servers are interacting with each other, exchange information and share tasks, they represent certain type of network, or web of servers.

Continuing the metaphor, as long as an enterprise is a web of servers, and servers are interconnected and communicating with each other, and running their own operating systems, we can consider that such enterprise has its own operating system, which we call the Enterprise Operating System (EOS).

© Springer International Publishing Switzerland 2016
D. Aveiro et al. (Eds.): EEWC 2016, LNBIP 252, pp. 132–147, 2016.
DOI: 10.1007/978-3-319-39567-8_9

We propose the following definition of Enterprise Operating System, which is the adaptation of the definition of computer OS applied to the enterprise:

*Enterprise operating system is the essential component of enterprise system that supports system's basic functions, controls the way a system works, manages system resources and their allocation among actors to make it possible for them to function and work together, adapt to changes and recover after critical situations.*

Since EOS includes parts of interconnected stand-alone operating systems, EOS is not a stand-alone OS by itself, it is a distributed OS. The notion of EOS is not new in the literature, however, notion of EOS is typically tied to the software implementation. For example, Guerreiro, van Kervel and Babkin define EOS as an Enterprise Information System, which controls the business transactions operation in an organization [3, 4]. In contrary to such focused and narrow view of an EOS, our understanding of EOS is considerably wider. We view EOS not as a software system with certain functions, but as the set of different processes and mechanisms which are essential for the enterprise existence, adaptation and overall viability. While EOS might include certain processes implemented in software, in general it has nothing to do with software or computer operating systems – the term is used only as a metaphor of the artefact within the enterprise with the functions which OS plays for computer. The relevant (albeit not exactly the same) understanding of EOS can be found in this work [33], where authors call the similar concept "Organizational Operating System".

As the enterprise is a dynamic real time network of actor-servers interacting in real time, all the time, a key question is: what are the key dynamic interactions among the enterprise servers, and what is the most adequate control architectural model to represent them. The most usual control architectures used in classical engineering systems seem to not have enough capabilities to capture and control the complex and diverse interactions among enterprise servers. A more appealing approach is the one of Maturana and Varela [5] using the biological systems paradigms with "autopoiesis" capabilities to capture the nature of reflexive feedback mechanisms in living systems, and concepts such as structural determinism and structure coupling, and one of Beer [2] introducing the notion of viable system.

As soon as we compare enterprise to a living system, we must more broadly consider enterprise to be a viable system. By definition, a viable system is any system organized in such a way as to meet the demands of surviving in the changing environment [2]. It is obvious then that enterprise by its nature is a viable system, therefore, existence and viability (i.e. maintaining existence) are the essential characteristics of any enterprise, and hence enterprise structure can be represented by a viable system model (VSM), which by definition is a model of the organizational structure of any viable or autonomous system [6]. Many works starting with the founding book of Beer [2] also view the enterprise as a viable system [6–20]. However, research shows that often VSM is not applicable to real world enterprises (see Sect. 3 for the literature review), so the main goal of this paper is to analyze drawbacks of classical viable system model and propose its extended version which is able to better describe real world enterprises. This paper works as a basis for future research which will include further exploration of EOS concept based on extended VSM construction and mechanisms.

This paper is organized as follows: Sect. 2 provides description of VSM and its parts, Sect. 3 includes literature review on VSM criticism and introduces our proposal for VSM extension, Sect. 4 describes case study whose purpose was to find examples of VSM drawbacks and practical illustration of the extended VSM applicability. Section 5 concludes the paper and provides plans for future research.

## 2   VSM Description

Enterprise structure can be represented by a viable system model (VSM), which by definition is a model of the organizational structure of any viable or autonomous system.

VSM considers an enterprise interacting with its environment [6, 20, 31] in two ways:

- Operation – the primary functions where all basic works are being done (like production, distribution, etc.);
- Metasystem - the secondary functions which support all units working together in an integrated way (accounting, scheduling, strategic planning, etc.)

Figure 1 illustrates the basic VSM [20, 31]:

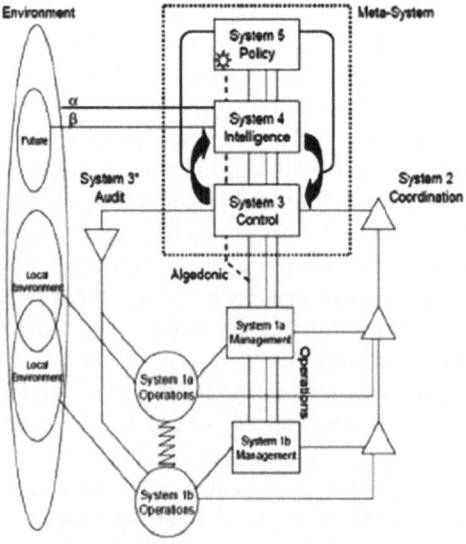

**Fig. 1.** VSM basic model.

VSM has five key systems, one at the Operation and four at the Metasystem (adopted from [2, 6, 20, 31]).

We can find at the Operation:

**System 1** – Implementation/Operational Units

Operational units where primary activities are done. The Operational units are responsible for producing the products or services.

We can find at the Metasystem:

**System 2** - Co-ordination/Conflict solver

The system responsible for stability/resolving conflict between Operational units and to co-ordinate the interfaces of its value-adding functions and the operations of its primary sub-units.

Examples of the services in a complex organization that may come under System 2 [7]:

− Computer/ICT services
− Documentation
− Purchasing
− Scheduling of common facilities
− Safety and Security
− Tax compliance
− Training in existing practices

**System 3** − Control/Optimizer

The system responsible for optimization/generating synergy between Operational units via a two-way communication between the Operation and the Metasystem.

Management accounting, budgeting and production control are typical of functions provided by System 3 [7].

**System 3\*** − Auditing

This systems fulfills the need for an audit channel that can delve into detail without taking over and micromanaging. The financial audit is the most obvious example, but there could be an energy audit, a security audit, an IT compatibility audit, a study of customer complaints and others. Sporadic employee satisfaction surveys and needs analyses are other examples [7].

Taken together, the management functions of Systems 1, 2, 3 and 3\* account for the as-is run time operations of the organization. Note that the only direct connection to the environment exists in the linkage between it and the System 1 operations. Note also that these are functions, not names on an organization chart. It is possible, even likely, that an individual could play a role in delivering a product or a service to a customer and in managing that operation. System 3 often includes representatives from management at System 1 and almost everyone enacts roles in System 2, at least by observing the protocols [7].

**System 4** − Intelligence, Planning, Strategy and Adaptation

The system responsible for the future plans and strategies and adaptation to a changing environment, it implements the two-way link between the Viable System and its external environment getting continuous feedback from the exterior and projecting the organization identity to the exterior.

Recruitment, staff development, benchmarking, participation in trade shows and conferences, market research and lobbying are concerned with learning about and affecting the outside and future. Research and development, strategic planning, borrowing policies and marketing use that knowledge to make internal modifications to be ready for coming changes [7].

**System 5** - Policy

The system responsible to guarantee that the organization works as a whole making the policies and providing clarity about the overall direction, values and purpose of the unit.

VSM scheme can be redrawn in the following way (Fig. 2):

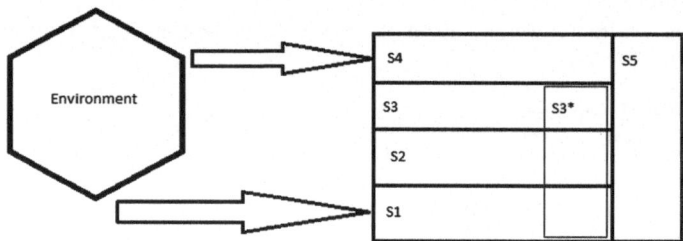

**Fig. 2.** VSM basic model - adaptation.

Arrows mean information gathering flows, they are purposefully unidirectional since we are interested only on gathering information from the environment in order to understand how environment affects enterprise operation. Information gathering flow from System 1 to environment is important for System 1 only, while flow from System 4 is crucial for the whole enterprise.

Since System 5 defines policy for the whole enterprise, it is positioned vertically to touch every other System of VSM.

## 3   VSM Extension

While plenty works show that standard VSM is applicable to real life enterprises [2, 7–17], there are many which point out the drawbacks of standard VSM and its inapplicability for real world enterprises.

Contemporary applications of VSM show that an enterprise has to have good environment scanning capabilities [8, 10, 11, 18].

Espejo and Reyes in [10, Chap. 2] discuss the notion of homeostat – a special case of a feedback system which helps to maintain a set of variables among expected values regardless of the nature of perturbations that may affect them. It means that organization must have capability to monitor certain variables ("sensors") and have mechanisms to react to changes beyond normal value range ("triggers" which causing organization to react). The similar concept of feedback system which requires sensors and triggers is described in [32].

In [10, Chap. 2], Espejo and Reyes also highlight the crucial importance of communication. They state that it is not possible to separate control from communication, therefore communication problems may cost much for any organization. Shannon's model of communication discussed by authors highlights that in order to transmit message, there should be efficient and secure communication channel, and decodifier on receiver's side should be able to decode messages from sender, codified by codifier. It brings the first possible problem of communication – transmitting the message through the noisy channel, and the requirement for codifier and decodifier to understand each other. Second possible problem of communication is that receiver must not only receive, but also understand the message. In order to do this, both sender and receiver must share the same vocabulary. Third problem of communication, as highlighted by authors, is that receiver must understand the intention of the sender – therefore, both sender and receiver must share the same context of their communication. It all brings the idea that communication channel, shared vocabulary and context must be explicitly modelled in VSM, while standard VSM assumes these parts as existing in implicit manner.

Perez Rios in [11, Chap. 1] states that organization must have information at the precise moment when one must decide and take appropriate measures, which means that organization must be getting real time information and react upon it. It again brings the idea of explicit specification of "sensors" and "triggers" in VSM. He also stresses attention on the fact that communication is an essential part of VSM, which means that all those elements affecting communication processes among individuals (the sending and receiving of information) should be explicitly taken into consideration.

Following Espejo and Reyes [10], Perez Rios in [11, Chap. 1] describes the same model of communication and highlights the same communication problem. Author explicitly defines the main communication channels that should exist and be dealt with in the design and/or diagnosis of the organization which intends to be viable. It is stated that the number of channels linking functions in the VSM is very large, since every connection between two elements is in fact a channel of communication. Consequently, author limits his comments to the six essential "vertical" channels, whose function is to jointly absorb all the variety (complexity) facing the system in focus. These channels are the following (Hildbrand and Bodhanya follow the same explicit definition of channels in [15]):

- Channel 1 (C1). Channel connecting and absorbing variety between the environments of each elementary operational unit.
- Channel 2 (C2). Channel connecting the various elemental operations (operational units making up System 1).
- Channel 3 (C3). Corporate intervention channel (System 3–System 1).
- Channel 4 (C4). Resources bargaining channel (System 3–System 1).
- Channel 5 (C5). Anti-oscillatory channel (Co-ordination) (System 2).
- Channel 6 (C6). Monitor channel (Auditor).

Another channel that also deserves special consideration is the Algedonic Channel.

All this describes the same attempt to explicitly specify communication part in VSM, hence extending standard VSM structure. To add to this, in [11, Chap. 2] Perez Rios puts a lot of stress on specification of "sensors" and how to process information from them, which correlates to our intention for VSM extension proposed in this paper. It is further justified in [11, Chap. 3], where author describes pathologies of organizations which include pathologies caused by underdeveloped communication channels and sensors (hence lack of explicit specification of them).

Nechansky in [19] highlights that VSM's Systems are specified as interrelated black boxes without any functional and structural details, i.e. without explicit specification of many crucial parts of VSM. Author argues that standard VSM is not applicable for some real world examples of enterprises – e.g. that larger systems like large companies or societies, seem not to be unequivocally determined and may deviate from VSM, while nevertheless being viable. Author finds empirical evidence for viable systems with organizational structures which are more complex than standard VSM scheme. He states that it is needed to explicitly define the system for top-down control independent from S5. Example of such system – department conducting Six Sigma project for the whole organization, reporting directly to S5 while not being part of other hierarchical organizational structure. Author also states that there should be bottom-up system for correction of performance problems, which he calls "immune system". Continuing Beer's metaphor of VSM being analogous to the human brain, immune system is a widely independent system, which cannot be directly steered from the brain. The immune system detects lower level problems, which cannot even be recognized by the nervous system and the brain, initiates and carries out actions to correct them, and may even make the highest level system redistribute resources to fight severe problems. The immune system is a stand by subsystem with no direct input from the top level of the whole system. It has the ability to observe and intervene on lower levels, and has a bottom-up channel to initiate corrections on the top level, if necessary. It can react quickly and pass by all middle hierarchical levels to overcome delays or even resistance, which might occur there. Examples of such immune system, as author points out, are Kaizen and other forms of continuous improvement, company shareholders' meetings, as well as works councils which are coordinating hierarchies to unite the interests of employees – they discuss them, aside the corporate hierarchy, directly with top managers, board members or even shareholders, and, if necessary, pursue them even against them. Examples from broader society are antimonopoly committees and free press, which step in when something is wrong with the market or society at large.

Authors of [20] review other works with some specific criticisms of VSM [21]. One of these criticisms asserts that the VSM underplays the purposeful role of individuals in organizations [22], which results in the failure to consider the social and political dimensions of organizations [21]. It is an essential fact that the component parts of organizations are human beings, "who can attribute meaning to their situations and can therefore see in organizations whatever purposes they wish and make of organizations whatever they will" [23]. The role of people and politics is crucial in EA [20], but the VSM has been shown to be weak in dealing with this issue.

Summarizing this literature review on VSM inefficiencies, we propose the following extended VSM (Fig. 3).

The proposal is to explicitly specify Immune System, Language, Competence, Tools and Sensors/triggers.

1. Immune System

    The set of deep crucial mechanisms which can intervene into any System's operation and make changes to Systems in the situation of crisis. On one hand, such mechanisms are created by S3, S4 or S5, but on the other hand they can change parent System.

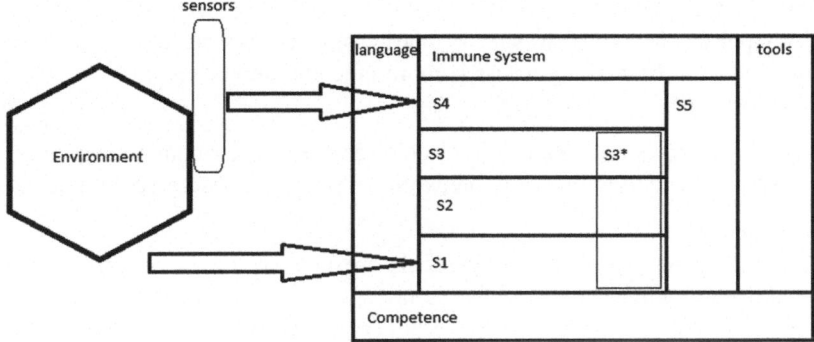

**Fig. 3.** Extended VSM.

Examples within enterprise:

- Board of Directors of a company
- Shareholder meeting
- Legal attorney can veto any activity if it contradicts with the law

2. Language

Everything which helps enterprise members (including VSM Systems) to communicate and understand each other. Based on the literature review, it is needed to explicitly specify:

(a) Communication channels – ways, format and media for communication. Examples of defined communication channels may be:

- Meeting minutes should be sent via email
- Interview with job applicant should be done either face to face or via phone

(b) Shared vocabulary – enterprise (and departments within enterprise) may have certain specific terms for certain specific things. It is highly important that communicating subjects are sharing the same vocabulary. Examples:

- Specific terms for yearly performance review sessions with managers
- Specific terms for the level of employee on the career ladder (e.g. junior engineer – engineer – senior engineer – principal engineer)

(c) Context – understanding of the meaning of the message is dependent on the context. It is important to explicitly define context for certain communication channels and information flows. Examples of the importance of context:

- Term "BMC" may mean "Baseboard Management Controller" for hardware engineer, while for manager it may mean "Business Model Canvas"

3. Tools

It is important to explicitly specify hardware and software tools which enhance communication by making it faster, more efficient, and/or secure. Examples:

- Access to corporate email from mobile devices (faster communication)
- VPN connection to corporate network assets (more secure communication)

4. Competence

Literature review shows that individuals are not taken into account when using standard VSM, while people are the essential part of every enterprise. One of the main attribute of employees from employer's perspective is their competences [24–28]. Review in [29] shows that competences are not explicitly considered in enterprise engineering field of research as well. The proposal is to add explicit specification of competences to the extended VSM. Using terms from the Four Stages of Competency model [16], the goal is to make enterprise consciously competent about its employees and about itself.

5. Sensors/triggers

We want to replace and extend the notion of homeostat by explicit specification of:

Sensors – mechanisms for information gathering and state monitoring.
Triggers – thresholds for sensor values and reactive actions for thresholds violation.

Importance of sensors is highlighted in [32], where authors state that sensors are crucial for the system to be observable. In order to be controllable, system must be observable and have mechanisms which react on certain sensor outputs – i.e. triggers are necessary. Having sensors and triggers is a mandatory condition to steer the organization.

Example:

Sensor: regular monitoring of governmental legislation for changes which may affect enterprise operation.

Trigger: if there is a new legislation which may affect enterprise operation, legal department must review it and propose respective changes to comply with new legislation.

It may sound obvious, but there are real world examples of lack of such simple mechanisms within enterprises which lead to significant issues.

## 4 Case Study

In order to illustrate that extension for VSM is viable, case study is being conducted. It is based on real life example, while some details were changed to comply with confidentiality requirements. We must note that the brief description of case study is provided for two reasons: firstly, case study is not finished yet – its completion is planned as the next step in this research, secondly, the goal of including this case study into this paper is only to illustrate that proposed VSM extensions can be found in real organization.

Case describes European customer support department of a multinational company. Customer support is outsourced to 3$^{rd}$-party vendor providing technical and warranty support services to company's customers in the region. The goal of the case study was not to build VSM for this department (which is impossible since the department is not a separate viable system by itself), but to review employees' roles and processes within this department in order to find those which cannot be categorized according to standard VSM.

Vendor support center includes:

- Technical support agents – responsible for first-line technical support for customers
- Technical support experts - responsible for second-line technical support for customers
- Technical support team leaders – responsible for technical teams management
- Warranty support agents - responsible for first-line warranty support for customers
- Warranty support team leaders - responsible for warranty teams management
- Reporting specialist – responsible for all reporting activities both internally within vendor support center and externally to company customer support department
- Support center manager – responsible for support center operation from vendor side.

Customer support department includes company employees:

- Regional customer support manager – responsible for all customer support activities in the region
- Escalations handling manager – responsible for handling all non-technical and non-IT escalations from vendor support center (including warranty exceptions approval, dealing with angry customers, etc.) and for all exceptional situations in the region (e.g. lawsuits, customer escalations directly to company executive office, etc.)
- Product support engineers – responsible for handling all technical escalations from vendor support center, technical trainings to technical agents and are involved into new products support planning; playing the role of interface between vendor support center and product developers within the company.

It appeared that some processes in this department cannot be categorized as belonging to some System of standard VSM. However, preliminary results of the case study show that they are fitting into extended VSM structure, as proposed in this paper.

Examples of processes and artefacts, which are categorized in accordance to extended VSM:

1. Language:
   (a) Communication channels

       - Meeting minutes should be sent via email
       - Job offer must be sent via email
       - Job interview must be conducted either via phone or as a face-to-face meeting
       - Contract termination notice must be sent via paper mail

All these rules for communication channels are not explicitly included into VSM, while it was argued that explicit definition of communication channels is needed. In particular, aforementioned rules have direct influence on Tools part of extended VSM, also if they are violated, it may lead to communication problems within the organization (e.g. when meeting minutes are not distributed at all, which may lead to misunderstanding between different actors or even VSM Systems) or may have impact on organization viability as a whole (e.g. if job offer is not sent via email, it might have legal actions in certain countries). The list is not exhaustive and provided only as an example of extended VSM application.

(b) Shared vocabulary

- "AR" means "Action Required"
- "Grade" means level of professionalism of employee
- "Focal" means yearly employee performance review process

As well as with communication channels, the lack of explicit definition of shared vocabulary may lead to issues within the organization. It is especially critical for communication between Systems of VSM. E.g. during Focal process, both employees of business units (System 1) and managers (System 3) must have common understanding of the term and the process to avoid potential issues such as managers are not ready to rate employee's performance which leads to lack of salary increase and hence employee dissatisfaction up to leaving the company. Standard VSM does not explicitly specify shared vocabulary, while literature review in Sect. 3 shows it is necessary.

c) Context

- Company is going to acquire company X – knowing this fact is changing context of certain conversations and decision making processes.
- Term "BMC" means "Baseboard Management Controller" for product support engineer, while for higher management it may also mean "Business Model Canvas"

Similar to the communication channels and shared vocabulary, lack of explicit definition of context of communication can lead to misunderstanding issues. E.g. if someone within the company does not know that company is in the process of company X acquisition, this someone may inadvertently tell something wrong to the journalists during press conference.

2. Tools:

- Email being the basic tool of communication with email on mobile devices, secure email and access to email from outside of corporate VPN being enhanced versions of this tool.
- Phone being basic tool of communication while phone with the highest quality connection and ability to do conferencing and voice mails being enhanced versions and IP-phone being cheaper and more flexible version.
- CRM – enhanced communication tool, since it is more secure, approved by legal department and faster way of communication with customers for difficult projects.

Explicit definition of tools helps to enable and enhance communication channels. For example, knowledge that CRM is an approved tool removes the necessity to check with legal department every time someone wants to share certain confidential document with customer via email. Standard VSM lacks capability to define tools explicitly as they are not part of any VSM System.

3. Immune System:

- Legal department can stop any activity at any time
- Crisis team can stop production lines at factories
- Board of Directors and Shareholders' meeting can change company course and replace CEO (and whole S5)

Understanding of parts of immune system across the whole organization is crucial. E.g. if someone within business unit is not aware that legal department can stop business unit operation in the crisis situation, they may disobey, which potentially may lead to the end of existence of this particular organization, hence breaks its viability. Examples provided here are not fitting to any other System of VSM, so can be explicitly specified only as part of extended VSM.

4. Competence:

- Competence to be an interface between product developers and business managers
- Product competence to train technical agents

If product competence is not specified explicitly as a requirement for business unit employees, System 1 may fail to conduct its functions. Lack of competence to be an interface between product developers and business managers may lead to broken communication between System 1 and 3. It explains why explicit definition of competence is needed on particular example (after it was argued by literature review in Sect. 3).

5. Sensors/triggers:

- Sensor: monitoring social networks for negative posts; trigger: if number of negative posts grew > 100 % vs yesterday, need to report to regional marketing immediately.
- Sensor: monitoring warranty returns; trigger: if number of warranty returns grew > 30 % vs last week, need to review associated support tickets and report to respective business unit.

Without explicit definition of sensors and triggers these mechanisms may be lacking. E.g. if process of monitoring of social networks is not explicitly specified in enough detail, company may fail to recognize severe PR issues which may have direct impact on company's brand and stock price.

These are just some examples from the case study which is not finished yet, but already provide some insight into the viability of the proposed VSM extensions. The completion of the case study is planned as the next step of this research.

# 5  Conclusion

In this paper we provided description of viable system model as a method of viable system representation. We also provided literature review which highlighted that while plenty works show that standard VSM is applicable to real life enterprises, there are many which point out the drawbacks of standard VSM and its inapplicability for real world enterprises. Hence, based on this literature review and case study in progress, we proposed extended version of VSM with Immune System, Language, Tools, Competence and Sensors/triggers added. Case study also illustrated that extended VSM is applicable for real world enterprise representation.

We must admit that proposed extensions to VSM were designed to be applied to the enterprise only (following the original purpose of viable system definition as per Beer [2]), and illustrated using case study centered on the enterprise. Usage of VSM in other areas such as biology, social sciences, and so on may prove extended VSM to be inapplicable, however, those fields of study are beyond the scope of this paper.

Similar effort was done in the past by Aveiro et al. in [34]. In that paper authors applied the Design and Engineering Methodology for Organizations (DEMO) [35] to specify an ontological model for the generic Control Organization that they argue that exists in every organization. With their proposal, DEMO was extended so that they claim to specify critical properties of an organization – which they call *measures* – whose value must respect certain restrictions imposed by other properties of the organization – which they call *viability norms*. Aveiro et al. stated that they precisely specified defined *resilience strategies* that control and eliminate *dysfunctions* – violations of viability norms caused by *exceptions*. The notion of measures as defined by authors has similar purpose as our notion of sensors, but applied only inside the organization. As measures are "critical properties of an organization", they do not allow to monitor the environment, which is the crucial part to support organization viability. Hence, our definition of sensors is wider than the notion of measures as proposed by Aveiro et al., since sensors are designed for events and changes both inside and outside the organization. The notion of viability norms which is paired with notion of measures and the concept of resilience strategies are combined in our notion of triggers. As long as applied only inside the organization, the term "resilience" may not be fully appropriate since does not tie the concept to the adaptation to external changes. Word "trigger" was chosen as widely used in environmental studies, biology and medicine (e.g. in collocation "environmental trigger"), as well as in computer science, and tied to the notion of sensor. Our notion of triggers is wider than combined notions of viability norms and resilience strategies since applied both inside and outside the organization. Our notion of immune system utilizes sensors and triggers (therefore is somewhat related to resilience strategies as defined by Aveiro et al.), but works on top and beyond Systems 1 through 5, being able to control them, hence separately defined in explicit way (therefore wider than the concept of resilience strategies as understood by Aveiro et al.). Authors of [34] claim that their proposal of the Control Organization seems to fit in part of Beer's System 3 (also named control) of the VSM. As was mentioned in Sect. 2 of our paper, System 3 accounts only for the as-is run time operations of the organization, and does not directly communicate to the environment.

In contrast, our proposal relates to the organization as a whole (across all systems of the VSM) and enables organization not only monitor and control the as-is run time operations using internal measures and viability norms, but also monitor the environment and react to its changes.

Future research plans include three stages.

The first one is to finish the case study and publish its full description in the net paper.

The second one is to find similarities between viable systems in general and distributed systems. Some authors [30] provide opinion that autonomy and adaptation are essential for distributed systems, which makes them viable systems, so VSM should be applicable to them as well. Some authors show that enterprises are similar to distributed systems [19]. The theory of distributed systems, especially distributed computing systems and distributed operating systems, is very well developed, and distributed systems have their own mechanisms to support viability. The idea is to apply these mechanisms to VSM and possibly find more room for VSM extension and improvement. The hypothesis is that distributed systems (especially distributed operating systems) have explicit specifications of certain mechanisms which are implicitly included or not at all included into VSM. This research will also help to validate extensions to VSM proposed in this paper.

The third one is to explicitly define parts of EOS – currently EOS is only a high level concept, whose existence is indirectly confirmed by our literature review. Hypothesis is that EOS includes parts of extended VSM plus some other mechanisms. The idea is to merge extended VSM with model of distributed operating system and so create reference model of Enterprise Operating System.

# References

1. Tribolet, J.: An Engineering Approach to Natural Enterprise Dynamics - From Top-down Purposeful Systemic Steering to Bottom-up Adaptive Guidance Control/J. Tribolet - ICEIS 2014 keynote. http://www.iceis.org/KeynoteSpeakers.aspx?y=2014#4
2. Beer, S.: Brain of the Firm/S. Beer - Allen Lane, The Penguin Press, London, Herder and Herder, USA (1972)
3. Guerreiro, S., van Kervel, S., Babkin, E.: Towards devising an architectural framework for enterprise operating systems. In: Proceedings of the 8th International Joint Conference on Software Technologies, pp. 578–585
4. van Kervel, S.: Ontology driven Enterprise Information Systems Engineering. SIKS Dissertation series nr. 2012-50. ISBN: 978-90-9027133-0
5. Maturana, H.R., Varela, F.J.: The cognitive process. Autopoiesis and cognition: The realization of the living. Springer Science & Business Media. p. 13. (1980). ISBN 978-9-027-71016-1
6. Walker, J.: The VSM Guide/J. Walker (2006). http://www.esrad.org.uk/resources/vsmg_3/screen.php?page=1qguide [available online on the 25th of September 2014]
7. Leonard, A.: The viable system model and its application to complex organizations. Syst. Pract. Action Res. **22**, 223–233 (2009)

8. Hoverstadt, P.: The fractal organization: creating sustainable organizations with the Viable System Model. Wiley (2008)
9. Pfiffner, M.: Five experiences with the viable system model. Kybernetes **39**(9/10), 1615–1626 (2010)
10. Espejo, R., Reyes, A.: Organizational Systems: Managing Complexity with the Viable System Model. Springer, Heidelberg (2011). ISBN: 978-3-642-19108-4
11. Perez Rios, J.: Design and Diagnosis for Sustainable Organizations: The Viable System Method. Springer, Heidelberg (2012). ISBN: 978-3-642-22317-4
12. Alqurashi, E., Wills, G., Gilbert, L.: A viable system model for information security governance: establishing a baseline of the current information security operations system. In: Janczewski, L.J., Wolfe, H.B., Shenoi, S. (eds.) SEC 2013. IFIP AICT, vol. 405, pp. 245–256. Springer, Heidelberg (2013)
13. Herrmann, C., Bergmann, L., Halubek, P., Thiede, S.: Lean production system design from the perspective of the viable system model. In: The 41st CIRP Conference on Manufacturing Systems (2008)
14. Julio, C.P.R.: Extending the viable system model scope on ICT-sector software projects in Castilla y León. Kybernetes 43(2), 192–209 (2014)
15. Hildbrand, S., Bodhanya, S.: The potential value of the Viable System Model as a managerial tool. Manage. Dyn. **22**(2) (2013)
16. Stephens, J., Haslett, T.: A set of conventions, a model: an application of stafford beer's viable systems model to the strategic planning process. Syst. Pract. Action. Res. **24**, 429–452 (2011)
17. Burgess, N., Wake, N.: The applicability of the Viable Systems Model as a diagnostic for small to medium sized enterprises. Int. J. Prod. Performance Manage. **62**(1), 29–46 (2013)
18. Kirikova, M.: Work systems paradigm and frames for fractal architecture of information systems. In: Nurcan, S., Pimenidis, E. (eds.) CAiSE Forum 2014. LNBIP, vol. 204, pp. 165–180. Springer, Heidelberg (2015)
19. Nechansky, H.: Issues of organizational cybernetics and viability beyond Beer's viable systems model. Int. J. Gen Syst **42**(8), 838–859 (2013)
20. Zadeh, M.E., Lewis, E., Millar, G., Yang, Y., Thorne, C.: The use of viable system model to develop guidelines for generating enterprise architecture principles. In: 2014 IEEE International Conference on Systems, Man, and Cybernetics, 5–8 October 2014, San Diego, CA, USA
21. Checkland, P.: Are organisations machines? Futures **12**, 421–424 (1980)
22. Ulrich, W.: A critique of pure cybernetic reason: the Chilean experience with cybernetics. J. Appl. Syst. Anal. **8**, 33–59 (1981)
23. Flood, R.L., Carson, E.R.: Dealing with complexity: an introduction to the theory and application of systems science, 2nd edn. Plenum Press, New York (1993)
24. Munkvold, B.E., Hustad, E.: IT-supported competence management: a case study at ericsson. Inf. Syst. Manage. **22**, 78–88 (2005)
25. Nordhaug, O.: Human Capital in Organizations. Scandinavian University Press, Oslo (1993)
26. Hachicha, R.M., Dafaoui, E.M., Mhamedi, A.E.: Competence evaluation approach based on 2-tuple linguistic representation model. 978-1-4244-3672-9/09/$25.00 ©2009 IEEE
27. Czelusniak, J., Abreu, A., Dergint, D., Hatakeyama, K.: Proposal of agent's software for support competence management process. In: PICMET 2010 Conference (2010)
28. Sanghi, S.: The Handbook of Competence Mapping: Understanding Designing and Implementing Competency Models in Organizations. Sage Publications, London (2004)
29. Sergeev, A., Babkin, E.: Towards competence-based enterprise restructuring using ontologies. In: Aveiro, D., Pergl, R., Valenta, M. (eds.) EEWC 2015. LNBIP, vol. 211, pp. 34–46. Springer, Heidelberg (2015)

30. Herring, C., Kaplan, S.: The viable system architecture. In: Proceedings of the 34th Hawaii International Conference on System Sciences – 2001 (2001)

31. Millar, G.: The Viable Governance Model: a Theoretical Model of IT Governance within a Corporate Setting. DIT Unpublished doctoral dissertation, University of New South Wales, Canberra (2009)

32. Abraham, R., Tribolet, J., Winter, R.: Transformation of multi-level systems – theoretical grounding and consequences for enterprise architecture management. In: Proper, H.A., Aveiro, D., Gaaloul, K. (eds.) EEWC 2013. LNBIP, vol. 146, pp. 73–87. Springer, Heidelberg (2013)

33. Páscoa, C., Tribolet, J.: Organizational Operating Systems, an Approach. In: CENTERIS 2015 - Conference on ENTERprise Information Systems, 7–9 October 2015, pp. 521–528, Elsevier (2015)

34. Aveiro, D., Silva, A.R., Tribolet, J.: Control organization: A DEMO based specification and extension. In: Albani, A., Dietz, J.L., Verelst, J. (eds.) EEWC 2011. LNBIP, vol. 79, pp. 16–30. Springer, Heidelberg (2011)

35. Dietz, J.L.G.: Enterprise Ontology: Theory and Methodology. Springer, Heidelberg (2006). ISBN: 3-540-29169-5

# Foundations of Enterprise Engineering

# Towards the Ontological Foundations for the Software Executable DEMO Action and Fact Models

Marek Skotnica[1](✉), Steven J.H. van Kervel[2], and Robert Pergl[1]

[1] Czech Technical University, Prague, Czech Republic
skotnicam@gmail.com, robert.pergl@fit.cvut.cz
[2] Formetis, Boxtel, The Netherlands
steven.van.kervel@formetis.nl

**Abstract.** The discipline of enterprise engineering and the DEMO methodology enable a model-driven approach to enterprise software systems development.

Apart from the graphical notation, the DEMO models may be fully specified in the DEMOSL language, which may become a basis for an workflow software system implementation. However, the current specification of DEMOSL has been designed mostly for the reasoning between human stakeholders.

In this paper a formal calculation construct called a DEMO Machine is proposed and basic ontological foundations of this machine are elaborated based on the alignment with the theories of enterprise engineering, various ontological and formal quality criteria and the application of the Generic Systems Development Process for Model Driven Engineering (GSDP-MDE methodology).

**Keywords:** Enterprise engineering · DEMO · DEMO machine · Enterprise operation system · Ontological foundations

## 1 Introduction

The domain of this paper encompasses enterprises, ontological foundations and enterprise information systems. Enterprises, as defined in [1], are social systems composed of human actors communicating about their productions to serve some external entity, typically called the "customer". An enterprise is an engineering artefact, designed and implemented for a specific purpose. An enterprise information system [2] is an information system (IS) that provides (i) some valuable descriptive perspective on the operation of an enterprise, for example: financial, personnel, inventory, production monitoring systems; or (ii) executes a prescriptive role, a control system that steers the operation of an enterprise, driven by the execution of a model of that enterprise. An example of such a prescriptive control system is a workflow system.

© Springer International Publishing Switzerland 2016
D. Aveiro et al. (Eds.): EEWC 2016, LNBIP 252, pp. 151–165, 2016.
DOI: 10.1007/978-3-319-39567-8_10

For the engineering of enterprises and the supporting information systems (ISs), appropriate scientific foundations are provided by the DoEE [1] and other theories, as described in Sect. 2. A promising approach is to derive IS directly from conceptual models of enterprises, eliminating manual programming, i.e. a manual translation of software specifications into propositions of a computer programme expressed in a programming language. This approach is proposed and generally elaborated by the Model-Driven Engineering [3].

The relevance of the MDE approach to derive ISs is very high, given that the majority of IT projects in the professional world fails or are "challenged" [4,5]. There is no evidence available that MDE is a panacea to this situation, however the MDE approach based on the DEMO methodology is scientifically interesting due to its strong theoretical foundations (Sect. 2) and a good empirical degree of appropriateness [6–8].

DEMO models are engineering specifications with the C4-ness qualities (models are Concise, Coherent, Consistent and Comprehensive [9]). The approach to implementation of ISs directly derived from DEMO models [10] is a novel topic. However, published professional results [7] document feasibility of this approach that addresses several serious problems:

(i) The elimination of programming due to the fact that the DEMO model is the source code for a native DEMO model executing software engine.
(ii) A substantially better business-IT alignment, enabled by automatic model verification, early model validation, followed by incremental model improvements, eliminating most of the human errors induced by manual programming.
(iii) Reduction of complexity due to highly expressive specifications and abstraction layers.

The paper is organized as follows: In Sect. 2, the underlying scientific foundations are briefly discussed. In Sect. 3, the research question is more precisely defined. In Sect. 4, the axioms of the theory are proposed, investigated and represented in a formal notation. In Sect. 6, the related work is discussed. In Sect. 7, the current results are summarised and further research is mentioned.

## 2    Scientific Theories and Methodologies Applied

We understand the notion of ontology as a "formal, explicit specification of a conceptualization shared between stakeholders" [11]. The most important criteria regarding the quality of any ontology [12] are (i) ontological truthfulness, an ontology providing a truthful representation of the real world; (ii) ontological completeness, completeness of expression for any phenomenon that may exist in our domain of the real world; and (iii) ontological appropriateness, good support for shared reasoning between stakeholders. The mentioned C4-ness quality criteria must be also met.

Other important concepts regarding ontologies, conceptual languages and models are formulated by Guizzardi in [13].

Enterprise Ontology [9] is a theory for enterprises, composed of human actors that communicate and cooperate about some production fact, to meet the requirements of some external entity, typically called a "customer".

The DEMO methodology [9] is an engineering methodology, based on the theory of enterprise ontology, to devise conceptual models of enterprises.

The notion of the model quality is represented by the already mentioned C4-ness criteria, as well as three cardinality laws [10,13,14].

MDE essentially means using ontologies for designing artefacts, which is the domain of The Design Science Paradigm described by [15], who provides a framework to devise engineering artefacts.

The Normalised Systems Theory formulates rules that software systems[1] must adhere to, to be evolvable and maintainable over time [16].

The Generic Systems Development Process for Model Driven Engineering (GSDP-MDE) [10,14] provides a methodology to devise a conceptual language and a model-executing software system based on a domain ontology. The GSDP-MDE is a special case of the Generic System Development Methodology, which is based on the General Systems Theory [17]. GSDP-MDE provides a model-instance driven approach where for each phenomenon instance in the real world, there is one unique instance of a model that is a precise *descriptive* representation of the specific phenomenon instance in the real world. At the same time, the model instance provides a *prescriptive* representation of the allowed state transitions of this real world phenomenon instance. The model-instance driven approach is the foundation for the descriptive and prescriptive ISs.

## 3   Formulation of the Research Question

### 3.1   The DEMO Machine Concept

The currently latest version of the DEMO 3 specifications of models and representations [18] is based on DEMOSL, an acronym of DEMO Specification Language. DEMOSL is specified using EBNF (extended Backus-Naur Form) [19]. This language is derived from reasoning on rules and facts from a modeller's perspective, primarily used for shared reasoning between stakeholders. The main research question is: **How should a DEMO Machine be designed that can be used to interpret DEMOSL?** Such a machine should take as its input a specification based on DEMOSL and enhanced by necessary execution semantics. As this is a very broad topic, we will limit ourselves here to discussing just a fragment of this machine, as specified further. Moreover, the DEMO Machine is meant as a formal computation model (similar to the e.g. Turing Machine), i.e. we do not elaborate on software implementation.

### 3.2   Appropriateness of the DEMOSL for DEMO Machine Implementation

The DEMO Machine needs to take into account the following challenges that are induced by the execution level and thus not addressed in DEMOSL:

---

[1] But not limited to.

1. *Integration.* DEMOSL concepts are either new (to be carried out) or existing concepts already present in the enterprise. DEMOSL does not deal with this separation.
2. *Facts duplication.* The facts representation must be physically present in one place to assure the consistency of enterprise systems [20]. This point is related to *Integration,* but it is also valid on its own.
3. *Lack of expressiveness.* At the execution level, there are many domains, where DEMOSL is not expressive enough to describe it, like scientific computations.
4. *Modularity.* DEMOSL does not specify, how the solution is modularised, which is at the same time a crucial execution concern.
5. *Lack of version transparency.* DEMOSL does not deal with evolvability of the models with the respect to the running instances.
6. *Execution semantics of DEMOSL.* Currently, the execution semantics of DEMOSL is not fully specified. Let us demonstrate this on a simple example:

```
when T01(M) is requested with member(new M) = P
  if age(P) < minimal_age then decline T01(M)
  else promise T01(M)
```

The following semantics is not defined:

– How with should be executed?
– What does age(P) mean, where and how should it be calculated?
– What does minimal_age mean, where and how should it be stored?

This list of topics is probably not complete, however it names the key challenges that definitely need addressing.

### 3.3 Formulation of Ontology for DEMO Machine

Based on these observations, we narrow our research question to: How to formulate a domain ontology for Facts, Agenda and Rules (FAR)? We started building the DEMO Machine ontology from this topic, because facts, agenda and rules are the "heart" of a DEMOSL execution. This ontology should address the points listed above and it should exhibit the necessary qualities:

(i) To be based on and compliant with the FI, TAO and PSI theories of EE.
(ii) Truthfulness and good appropriateness qualities and compliance with the three cardinality laws [13].
(iii) Maintaining the strict C4-ness criteria.

As for the notions of "Way of thinking" and "Way of working" distinguished in the DEMO method and theories, the FAR ontology is rather a way of working, as we come from the existing way of thinking (the PSI theory) and formulate how to enhance it for the execution.

### 3.4   Verification and Validation Questions of the Research Question

The FAR domain ontology is proposed below that enables the construction of executable Fact and Rule expressions that operate on Agenda. As for the model verification, we must make sure that it is free of anomalies that may enable a construction of rules and expressions that cannot exist in the world of phenomena.

## 4   Axiomatic Specifications of the Fact, Agenda and Rule Ontology

### 4.1   Addressing the DEMOSL-DEMO Machine Deficiencies

Let us elaborate, how the FAR Ontology (as well as the whole DEMO Machine) may address the challenges stated above.

1. *Integration* and *Facts duplication.* Based on the *Separation of Concerns Principle* from the Normalised Systems Theory [16], the DEMO Machine should not supply the functionality of the already-existing enterprise systems, such as a database. Also, the DEMO Machine should not specify scales, dimensions, sorts, units such as time, money and others.
2. *Lack of expressiveness.* For areas, where there are already established solutions (like mathematical libraries), these should not be represented in a DEMO Machine, to maintain the separation of concerns and the C4-ness criteria.
3. *Modularity* and *Version transparency* are complex topics that cannot be easily commented. They are a subject for future work that should be based on the studies of Normalised Systems Theory mentioned above.
4. *Execution semantics of DEMOSL.* The execution semantics should be specified by the DEMO Machine. The FAR Ontology focuses on the subset of execution, namely the facts, agenda and rules concepts.

Let us now dive into the specific part of the DEMO Machine, the FAR Ontology, which will be specified as a set of axiomatic definitions.

### 4.2   Fact Axioms

The DEMO theory builds on the $\Phi$ theory. The letter $\Phi$ stands for "FI", an acronym for Fact and Information about a "world", being a specific part of the universe we are interested in, and of which we require factual information or knowledge [9]. Our world of interest is "the world of enterprises". A world of interest is assumed to be composed of Acta, Facta and Stata. **Stata** are things or phenomena that existed before the beginning of our observation. A **Fact** is a proposition about something that exists in the real world and provides us with *factual knowledge* about the world. Facts can be about either *concrete* or *abstract* things or phenomena. They are the results of **Acta**, being actions or acts, undertaken by an entity. Facts come to being by carrying out acts. Once they originate, they cannot disappear; they can be only ignored.

During the design time, we deal with facts as *propositions* about the real world. They exist just as a symbolic structure and we cannot decide its truthfulness. Then, once the DEMO Machine executes (i.e. the fact "happens"), we may *valuate* it as true, false or undefined. Undefined means that the subjects of the proposition does not exist, yet, or we do not know the valuation, as a result of e.g. a technical failure. The valuation may (and typically does) change during the execution. Any calculations based on facts should take this into account. Stata also represent factual knowledge about our world of interest that exist since the beginning of time. Obviously any facts about Stata are always either true or false.

Let us present the definitions here using the standard mathematical constructs.

**Definition 1. *Fact*** *A fact is an ordered tuple:*

$$Fact := (Identifier, Type, Proposition) \tag{1}$$

*Identifier – A unique identifier of the fact.*
*Type $\in \{Internal, External, Composed\}$*
*Proposition – A specification[2] of the statement about the real world.*

**Definition 2. *Value of a fact*** *is a valuation function:*

$$FactValue : (TransactionInstance, Fact) \rightarrow \{True, False, Undefined\} \tag{2}$$

**Definition 3. *Transaction Instance Linking (TIL)*** *is a ternary relation that relates certain transaction instances to each other. This relation is defined outside of the DEMO Machine, which requests this relation for the evaluation of the rules.*

$$TransactionInstanceLinking(TIL) :=$$
$$TransactionInstance \times TransactionInstance \times LinkingIdentifier \tag{3}$$

*TransactionInstance – A transaction instance unique identifier.*
*LinkingIdentifier – A name of the relation that holds between the transaction instances.*

*Example 1.* Two transaction instances are sharing the same membership:
("T01_1", "T02_2", "Membership")

**Definition 4. *Internal Fact*** *is a factual statement about a DEMO model instance.*

$$InternalFact := (Fact, InternalFactExpression) \tag{4}$$

---

[2] FAR does not specify the language, it may be a natural language or any other language.

**Definition 5.**

$$InternalFactExpression :=$$
$$(singleTransactionComparison)|(multiTransactionComparison) \quad (5)$$

$singleTransactionComparison = (transaction).state\ (operator)$
$((transaction).state\ |\ (state))$
$multiTransactionComparison = (transactionSelector).(selectorFunction)$
$(t => (singleTransactionComparison))$
$transaction = this\ |\ this.parent$
$state =$ perfect tense intention" as defined in DEMOSL
$operator =\quad ==\quad |\ !=$
$variable = (transaction).(attribute)$
$selectorFunction = all\ |\ any$
$transactionSelector = transactionType < (linkingIdentifier) > |$
$this.children < transactionType >$
$transactionType =$ existing transaction type defined in the model
$linkingIdentifier =$ identifier of the relation between transactions

This grammar is using the Extended Backus-Naur Form (EBNF). Round brackets denote non-terminals. Note that the presented grammar is very basic and it is not able to capture all facts about the DEMO model instance or its history. Complete grammar is a subject for further research.

*Example 2.* Let us show an example by formalising the fact F02 "Are invoices paid?", which is the situation when all instances of T03 that are linked to the current transaction are in the same state as the current transaction.

F02 = (("F02","Are invoices paid?"), T03< *"Invoice"* >.all(t => t.state == this.state))

**Definition 6. *External Fact*** *is a Fact about the world outside the DEMO Machine*

$$ExternalFact := (Fact, CalculationEngine) \quad (6)$$

*CalculationEngine – Identifier of the external system function evaluating the fact.*

Data in external data banks are represented as external facts, for instance. External facts represent knowledge of phenomena in the environment that may change over time and have no (known) calculation specification. We operate just with a further unspecified reference to external system function that is able to valuate the fact, thus carrying out the separation of concerns principle.

*Example 3.* A fact that evaluates that the person attached to the transaction instance is older than 18 years

F01 = (("F01","Is person older than 18 years?"), CalculationEngine)

CalculationEngine may be implemented in any computer technology such as a web service (SOAP or REST), or locally as a system library. In the following code, we implement it as a class in a standard programming language. The calculation of a F01 would be realized as its method:

```
public class CalculationEngine {
[DEMOEngineExternalFact(FactId="F01")]
public FactValue IsPersonEligible (TransactionInstance t) {
var person = DAL.GetPersonByTransactionInstanceId(t.Id);
if(person == null) return FactValue.Undefined;
else return person.Age > 18 ? FactValue.True : FactValue.False;
}}
```

**Definition 7. *Composed Fact*** *is a fact composed from internal and external facts.*

$$ComposedFact := (Fact, ComposedFactExpression) \qquad (7)$$

**Definition 8. *Composed Fact Expression***

1. *InternalFactIdentifier and ExternalFactIdentifier are composed fact expressions.*
2. *If x and y are composed fact expressions, then following expressions are also composed fact expressions:*
   (a) *(x and y)*
   (b) *(x or y)*
   (c) *not (x)*

*For valuation of composed facts, the Kleene and Priest three-valued logics is used.*

*Example 4.* A person is older than 18 years and he is accepted as a applicant in a membership approval process of the Volley tennis club:

```
F01 = (("F01","Is person older than 18 years?"),
  VolleyCalculationEngine)
F02 = (("F02","Is person accepted in the approval process?"),
  VoleyCalculationEngine)
F03 = (("F03","Is person eligible for membership?"),
  ("F01 and F02"))
```

The resulting truth table is then:

| F01 | F02 | F03 Result |
|-----|-----|-----|
| True | True | True |
| True | False | False |
| True | Undefined | Undefined |
| False | True | False |
| False | False | False |
| False | Undefined | False |
| Undefined | True | Undefined |
| Undefined | False | False |
| Undefined | Undefined | Undefined |

## 4.3   Agenda Axioms

An agenda is set of possible coordination acts (agendum) that is presented to the actor. These are well-defined concepts in the PSI theory. An actor involved in a transaction is offered, according to the transaction axiom, to choose one of the valid options to perform coordination acts, which happens in asynchronous time. Example: After a Request from the initiator, the executor may issue either a Promise or a Decline, but other coordination acts such as a Reject are now forbidden, to comply with the Transaction Axiom.

An agenda for an actor must be (re)calculated completely at run time by the DEMO Machine of the model instance, after each state change of the model instance. It will be shown that the allowed options for coordination acts are restricted by causal and conditional dependencies and rules. It means that application of rules is present to guarantee the compliance with the PSI theory. Any extension, enlargement, of the transaction transition space or the state space is impossible since this would violate the PSI theory axioms.

**Definition 9. *Coordination Act (cAct)*** *is a proposed or intended action for an actor.*

$$cAct := (Transaction, TransactionInstance, \\ ActorInstance, Intention, SettlementType) \tag{8}$$

*Transaction = Transaction kind as defined in DEMOSL.*[3]
*TransactionInstance = Associated transaction instance. May be empty.*
*ActorInstance = Associated actor instance.*
*Intention $\in$ {Create(T, n), Promise, Decline, Request, Quit, Accept, Reject, State, Stop, RevokeRequest, AllowRevokeRequest, RefuseRevokeRequest, Revoke-Promise, AllowRevokePromise, RefuseRevokePromise, RevokeState, AllowRevoke State, RefuseRevokeState, RevokeAccept, AllowRevokeAccept, RefuseRevokeAccept}*
*SettlementType $\in$ { Allow, Enforce, Restrict }*

There are two additions to the definition given by the DEMO theory. One is the possibility to create a new transaction (generated by the composition axiom) which will be used by the rules. $Create(T, n)$ means "Create $n$ transactions of type $T$", where $n$ is a positive whole number. The second is the settlement type which says how the cAct should be dealt with. Allow means that an actor is allowed to perform the intention. Enforce cAct says that the given intention should be actually performed, unless there is a Restrict cAct with the same intention for the same transaction instance. Practically, the Restrict cAct also informs the actor, why such an intention cannot be performed. In the DEMO theory, an actor is allowed to perform an act even when it is restricted. However, in the enterprise practice, legal and other compliance is a crucial aspect of execution. Thus, we enable this feature in the DEMO Machine.

---

[3] Transaction is also defined by the TransactionInstance if present.

Please note that in Definition 9 we do not take into account any additional information from inside or outside of the organization. This is due to the separation of concerns principle addressing the Facts duplication (Sect. 4.1). All external information (facts) are handled outside of the DEMO Machine.

**Definition 10.** *Agenda is a function that calculates a set of actor's possible actions based on the current state of the model taking into account the composition axiom and the respective rules.*

$$Agenda : (ModelInstance, ActorInstance) \rightarrow \{cAct\} \tag{9}$$

**Definition 11.** *Perform cAct*

$$PerformCAct : (ModelInstance, ActorInstance, CActToEnforce) \rightarrow Agenda \tag{10}$$

*To perform a cAct means that the actor makes a selection of an allowed cAct from its agenda and it enforces it.*

## 4.4 Rules and Dependencies Axioms

Rules and dependencies are specifications of either a prescriptive execution of a coordination act, or a conditional prohibition of a coordination act for an actor, depending on the evaluation of a fact.

A rule and a dependency restrict the available freedom of an actor to issue coordination acts at the execution time. The evaluation, if the rule or dependency applies, takes place at runtime, depending on the state of that model instance. The transaction instance state space and the state transition space of a model instance is further restricted (made smaller). It is impossible to add new options for coordination acts since that would violate the axiomatic specifications derived from the PSI theory.

**Definition 12.** *Causal Rule and Dependency are defined as the application of a rule that results in a transaction state change.*

$$CausalRule = (Transaction, TransactionState, Fact, cActTrue, cActFalse) \tag{11}$$

**Definition 13.** *Evaluation of Causal Rule and Dependency*

```
if TransactionInstance.State == TransactionState
  and FactValue(TransactionInstance, Fact) == True
then anAgenda.Add(cAct(cActTrue, Enforce))
else if False then anAgenda.Add(cAct(cActFalse, Enforce))
```

**Definition 14.** *Conditional Rule and Dependency are defined as the application of a rule that results in a restriction of an agendum, in such a way that one of the allowed coordination acts is prohibited while the rule applies.*

$$ConditionalRule = (Transaction, Fact, cActToRestrict) \tag{12}$$

Since facts may change over time during execution, a condition that inhibits a specific cAct can be met, and the specific cAct is permitted. If one of two cActs is prohibited in the agenda, then the opposite cAct can be performed in asynchronous time by the actor. As long as the fact in the conditional rule holds, it is not possible for the actor to perform the cAct.

**Definition 15.** *Evaluation of Conditional Rule and Dependency*

```
if anAgenda(TransactionInstance).Contains(cActToRestrict(Allow))
   and FactValue(TransactionInstance, Fact) != True
then anAgenda.Add(cActToRestrict(Restrict))
```

**Prohibition or Prescription of an Agenda.** From the above follows that rules and dependencies operate on an agenda by prohibition or prescription. They reduce the model instance state space and the model instance transition space, which causes a desired limitation of complexity. It is impossible to increase the state and transition spaces by "adding" new options for coordination acts which would be violation of the PSI theory. Rules and dependencies are calculated immediately during the calculation of the agenda.

## 5    Discussion and Evaluation of the FAR Ontology

The relation between the FAR Ontology and the DEMO models is as follows. The DEMO models provide a formal specification of the rules and facts, created and accepted by stakeholders, that represent the enterprise interaction with its environment. The DEMO Machine specifies the construction of an artefact (a software system) that must fulfil the requirements of the created DEMO models. The FAR Ontology is a crucial part of the DEMO Machine.

The following reasoning is provided to assure:

 (i) A compliance with the PSI theory, the causal and conditional dependencies, and the application of explicitly specified causal and conditional AM rules.
(ii) A reduction of complexity while maintaining guaranteed ontological conciseness and comprehensiveness.

Assume a model composed of actors and transactions. The application of the Transaction Axiom reduces the number of states of each transaction and the number of states in the model state space, which results in a reduction of complexity.

The application of the Composition Axiom demands that before any production fact can be performed, all child production facts must have been produced, i.e. Stated and Accepted. This further reduces the number of states in the model state space. The ontological conciseness and comprehensiveness of the PSI theory has been shown in [2].

The application of the causal dependencies reduce the state transition space of the model instance, since a specific option of an agenda must be chosen, while the other agenda options are forbidden.

Conditional dependencies disable specific agenda options, until a specific condition has been met. In this way, the state transition space is reduced further and the state space is also reduced, without a loss of ontological conciseness and comprehensiveness.

The DEMO Action Model conditional and causal rules modify the agenda similarly to causal and conditional dependencies and they reduce the state space and the state transition space further, without any loss of ontological conciseness and comprehensiveness.

For a DEMO Machine based solely but precisely on the PSI theory, it has been argued and shown that there is minimized expression, or zero entropy in expression quality [14]. Any enterprise that may possibly exist in the real world can then be represented by one and only one model. In addition, anything that is not an enterprise cannot be represented. Based on this reasoning, it is argued that such DEMO Machine based on a proper implementation of the FAR Ontology will keep these qualities.

### 5.1   Falsifiable Proposition of the FAR Ontology

As any domain ontology is a hypothesis that provides falsifiable propositions about the world of phenomena [21]. The following hypothetical assumptions have been made:

1. "The PSI theory is a domain ontology, a falsifiable hypothesis about the world of coordination between actors". There is much empirical evidence for a good degree of confidence in the ontological truthfulness and appropriateness of the PSI theory. The C4-ness qualities have been proven. The construction of the DEMO engine using the GSDP-MDE has been proven.
2. "Any business rule that may exist in the real world can be expressed in restriction(s) of actor agenda, by conditional or causal rules". This proposition is directly derived from the PSI theory, hence with a good confidence.
3. "Any fact that can be defined in the real world may be used in a rule to express any business rule in an enterprise". As the facts are either Internal or External, which is a complete list of fact types in the world, we may assume that any given rule may be expressed using a Composed Fact.
4. The hypothesis that any imaginable fact represented using the DEMOSL representation can be expressed in an appropriate way using the FAR Ontology, needs further theoretical research and empirical validation.

## 6   Related Work

### 6.1   Model-Driven Development

Model-Driven Development (MDD) is a very popular approach in the recent years realising the ideas of Model-Driven Engineering for implementing software systems. It is a software development approach based on modelling and transformations [22]. The product to be developed is described using various types of models specifying the requirements, functions, structure and deployment of the product. These models are used to construct the product using transformations between models and code generation. MDD was originally based on Model-Driven Architecture (MDA) developed by the Object Management Group (OMG) [23] defining these types of models: Computation Independent Model (CIM), Platform Independent Model (PIM), Platform Specific Model (PSM), Implementation Specific Model (ISM).

The most usual part of the MDD approach is the process of forward engineering to represent the transformations of more abstract models into more specific ones. The most common use-case of such a process is the development of conceptual data models and their transformation into source codes or database scripts.

Our approach shares the idea of driving the development by models. DEMOSL models represent CIM, DEMO Machine and the FAR Ontology brings in execution semantics, which may be related to PIM. However, our approach is to directly interpret the PIM model. In this respect, our approach is similar to the following effort.

## 6.2   XModel

The solution of devising a workflow software system based on model presented by Johanndeiter et al. in [24] is based on the OrgML modelling language, a part of the MEMO framework, and the XMF metaprogramming platform. The idea is also based on applying the MDE approach, while avoiding the error-prone manual coding stage. The idea is based on applying multiple levels of meta-modelling and utilising XMF's unique features to support multiple dynamic levels of abstraction. The approach seems very interesting, however it seems to lack a proper evaluation in enterprise. Our approach also differs in a careful selection of ontologically well-founded methodologies that exhibit necessary qualities and benefits, as discussed in Sects. 2 and 5.

## 6.3   The DEMO Engine and the Enterprise Operating System

DEMO Engine of the ForMetis Consultants company is a software system for designing DEMO models with the ability to simulate DEMO models for validation and to provide model execution in full production [7]. Construction of DEMO models is done using the graphical representation of the DEMO ATD in a graphical environment. In the current implementation, the DEMO Process Model is primarily calculated from the ATD. Response links and waiting links (causal and conditional dependencies) can be then specified using the graphical representation of the PSD. There is a limited and not well-engineered support for even simple Action Model rules, which is the aim of our FAR Ontology.

The Enterprise Operating System [10] is software system composed of a set of DEMO models and a DEMO model executing software engine, the DEMO Engine. The EOS captures and controls all phenomena that occur in operation of the organizational business transactions. This is very similar to an operating system of a computer that reads from and writes to binary registers of a CPU and peripheral controllers and supports many tasks. Using a computer without an operating system is extremely difficult and error-prone. This seems to apply also to controlling and monitoring enterprises without an appropriate enterprise operating system. Many of the engineering challenges of this effort are directly related to the DEMO Machine and open questions described in Sect. 3.

# 7    Conclusions and Further Research

We proposed the concept of a DEMO Machine as a theoretical construct for DEMO models execution. We then proposed the FAR Ontology as a key part of the DEMO Machine. The proposed further research topics are present in the respective parts of the paper.

The FAR Ontology using the GSDP-MDE approach for model-driven information systems provides an approach for enterprise information systems implementation with considerable benefits (Sect. 3). Some of the concepts have been already implemented in DEMO Engine described in Sect. 6.3.

As for future work, the remaining parts of the DEMO Machine need to be formulated, so that every DEMOSL model may be executed. This comprises an exact formulation how the Transaction and Composition Axioms are applied for the model execution. The work should address the concerns named in Sect. 3. As for the FAR Ontology itself, algorithms with proper qualities implementing the proposed functions need to be elaborated and a broader empirical research on the appropriateness in the professional world is suitable. A single empirical business case with inappropriate expressiveness would invalidate our hypothesis and provide valuable clues for improvement of the FAR Ontology.

# References

1. Dietz, J.L.G., Hoogervorst, J.A.P.: The discipline of enterprise engineering. Int. J. Organ. Des. Eng. **3**(1) (2013)
2. Guerreiro, S., Kervel, S., Babkin, E.: Towards devising an architectural framework for enterprise operating systems. In: Proceedings of ICsoft 2013 8th International Conference on Software Paradigm Trends. SciTePress (2013)
3. Bzivin, J., Gerb, O.: Towards a precise definition of the OMG/MDA framework. In: IEEE International Conference on Automated Software Engineering (2001)
4. Sauer, C., Cuthbertson, C.: The State of IT Project Management in the UK. Templeton College, Oxford University, Oxford (2003)
5. Budzier, A., Flyvbjerg, B.: Double Whammy, How ICT projects are fooled by randomness and screwed by political intend. In: CRASHH Conference, University of Oxford (2011). Draft v5
6. Mulder, J.B.F.: Rapid enterprise design. Ph.D. thesis, Delft University of Technology (2006)
7. Hintzen, J., van Kervel, S.J.H., van Meeuwen, T., Vermolen, J.A.J., Zijlstra, B.: A professional case management system in production, modeled and implemented using DEMO. In: Proceedings of 16th IEEE Conference on Business Informatics (CBI) (2014)

8. Op 't Land, M.: Applying architecture and ontology to the splitting and allying of enterprises. Ph.D. thesis, University of Technology Delft (2008)
9. Dietz, J.: Enterprise Ontology Theory and Methodology. Springer, New York (2006). ISBN: 3-540-29169-5
10. van Kervel, S.J.H., Dietz, J.L.G., Hintzen, J., van Meeuwen, T., Zijlstra, B.: Enterprise ontology driven software engineering. In: Proceedings of ICsoft 2012 7th International Conference on Software Paradigm Trends. SciTePress (2012)
11. Gruber, T.R.: A translation approach to portable ontology specifications. Knowl. Acquis. **5**(2), 199–220 (1993). Knowledge Systems Laboratorium, Computer Science Department, Stanford University
12. Guizzardi, G., Ferreira Pires, L., van Sinderen, M.: An ontology-based approach for evaluating the *domain appropriateness* and *comprehensibility appropriateness* of modeling languages. In: Briand, L.C., Williams, C. (eds.) MoDELS 2005. LNCS, vol. 3713, pp. 691–705. Springer, Heidelberg (2005)
13. Guizzardi, G.: Ontological foundations for structural conceptual models. Ph.D. thesis, University of Twente (2005)
14. van Kervel, S.J.H.: Ontology driven enterprise information systems engineering: Ph.D. thesis, University of Technology Delft (2012)
15. Hevner, A.: A three cycle view of design science research. Scand. J. Inf. Syst. **19**(2), 87–92 (2007). Information systems and Decision Sciences, University of South Floria, USA
16. Mannaert, H., Verelst, J.: Normalized Systems Re-creating Information Technology Based on Laws for Software Evolvability. Koppa, Belgium (2009)
17. von Bertalanffy, L.: General System Theory: Foundations, Development, Applications. George Braziller, New York (1968)
18. Dietz, J.: DEMOSL-specification: version 3.4, CIAO! enterprise engineering. Network (2016). doi:10.5281/zenodo.47471
19. ISO, Geneva: ISO 14977. Information technology Syntactic metalanguage Extended BNF, Norm (1996)
20. Coronel, C., Morris, S.: Database Systems: Design, Implementation, & Management, 11th edn. Course Technology, Cambridge (2014)
21. Popper, K.R.: Zwei Bedeutungen von Falsifizierbarkeit [Two meanings of falsifiability]. In: Seiffert, H., Radnitzky, G. (eds.) Handlexikon der Wissenschaftstheorie (in German), pp. 82–85. Deutscher Taschenbuch Verlag, Mnchen (1994). ISBN: 3-423-04586-8
22. Mellor, S.J., Clark, A., Futagami, T.: Model-driven development. IEEE Softw. **20**(5), 14–18 (2003)
23. OMG: Model driven architecture (MDA): The MDA guide rev 2.0. online. http://www.omg.org/cgi-bin/doc?ormsc/14-06-01
24. Johanndeiter, T., Goldstein, A., Frank, U.: Towards Business Process Models at Runtime, pp. 13–25. MoDELS@ Run. time 1079 (2013)

# Cross Channel Communication Design Critical Literature Review

M.A.T. Mulder$^{(\boxtimes)}$

M.A.T. Mulder, Leusden, The Netherlands
mark@mulderrr.nl

**Abstract.** Literature on cross channel communication design shows that customer interaction is too often implemented from a technology viewpoint which keeps us from a fundamental design of the problem and solution. Implementations that have started from a technical or business case point of view have not been very successful.

Customer interaction is using processes, Customer Relationship Management (CRM) or portals from a functional viewpoint but is not constructed from a Performance in Social Interaction theory ($\Psi$-theory) In literature we have found channel characteristics and a maturity model that can help us reach the cross communication goal. With these findings in mind, we have defined our channel and service concepts. We summed up the usable concepts we need, to change the perception of multichannel and introduce a design that starts from communication and realises a cost effective way of integration existing and emerging channels.

## 1 Introduction

In recent years communication channels between companies and customers have evolved from spoken language to magazines, phone, text, chat and social media. Each channel has its superb properties that were supposed to conquer the world. However, in the end it seems that we need multiple channels to accommodate the customers [15]. Although several single, multi and omnichannel solutions have been built, none has been completely successful. Therefore, we will emphasize the importance of a theoretical approach to solve problems with the customer changing channels in social communication and transactions.

Research on customer experience has observed the importance of engaging the customer and following the right process [21]. In addition, communicating with the customer using preferred channels with desired properties or characteristics is important [26]. Regrettably, current designs are technology or business case oriented and multichannel strategies are built from existing ways we do business. We will study communication from a transaction point of view as suggested by the $\Psi$-theory [8]. This theory defines communication in 20 steps with clear responsibilities for both actors but does not guide implementation.

In order to study the cross channel communication issues as found in practice, we need a sound theory. The trend, as shortly presented above, is based on literature on omnichannel, multichannel and CRM.

© Springer International Publishing Switzerland 2016
D. Aveiro et al. (Eds.): EEWC 2016, LNBIP 252, pp. 166–180, 2016.
DOI: 10.1007/978-3-319-39567-8_11

Omnichannel has become a sales buzzword over the past years. Unfortunately, little technical and theoretical foundation is present in the implementations. We need to create a solid foundation. We suggest that by adopting the cross channel communication idea, which states that the transaction is the central point in customer communication, we can design the cross communication model according to the $\Psi$-theory and implement this model.

In Sect. 2 we evaluate the literature on communication from a customer and a company centric view. We continue in Sect. 3 with an evaluation of channel characteristics, issues, notions and implementations. Section 4 addresses transactions, whereas the last Sect. 5 focusses on strategies and implementation. We end this paper with the conclusions in Sect. 6.

## 2 Communication Viewpoints

In this section we will evaluate two different viewpoints on cross channel communication. The customer centric viewpoint takes as a starting point customer experience and behaviour and quality of service. The company centric viewpoint starts from customer value management, customer analysis, CRM standpoint, processes and customer portals.

### 2.1 Customer Centric Viewpoint

The service-centred paradigm [21] postulates that value is created by customers through product usage. The service-centred paradigm defines a service interface and service experience that can be used to create a service design to facilitate service operations. This suggested approach focusses on interaction implementation but before this interaction implementation can be constructed, it has to be further defined. [8] suggests that starting from an implementation free communication concept as defined in $\Psi$-theory, can add desired customer experience aspects.

Customer engagement behaviours may be defined as "a customer's behavioural manifestations that have a brand or company focus, beyond purchase, resulting from motivational drivers" [34, p. 248]. Missing this behaviour may give the company a wrong valuation of customers. The proposed conceptual model also considers some barriers to customer engagement: CRM and customer intelligence strategies, channel strategies, and media strategies. Actually, these components may influence customer engagement or sober the effects of customer engagement [34].

Understanding the communication part of customer experience is a start for better understanding requirements to improve customer interaction. Most customer experience improvements are dealing with understanding the sent message, for instance, by reordering fields or processes or reformulating sentences. Therefore, aside from the message, the $\Psi$-theory teaches us to understand the communication steps building the complete transaction. When the transaction is completely implemented, recognition of the communication will increase, thus, improving customer experience.

Another framework [27] tries to capture the multichannel services quality using at least one virtual component delivered through a virtual channel. Actually, capturing the quality of a service is subjective. Nevertheless, we agree that customer experience is formed through all channels.

Some other issues should be taken into consideration when taking the customer viewpoint. Trust is the most important decisive antecedent for buying on the internet [31]. In addition, the rise of social media has to be taken seriously because companies can learn from their customers [18]. Aside from companies, governments should also take into account the right channels through which their services are delivered. The barriers found for accepting services are internet usage, channel penetration and user readiness, lack of appropriate know-how and channel appropriateness for specific services [33]. The issues on trust and social media customers are important and should be taken seriously by companies. Readiness for new channels is underestimated by government and overestimated by companies. Therefore, a sound look at this aspect using a business case should be considered. The more integrated the channels, the more communication with the same potential customers will cost. Nevertheless, new channels are likely to improve the customer experience when customers are not satisfied with the channels on offer.

## 2.2  Company Centric Viewpoint

In customer value management, customers are valued for their transactions with a company. In customer engagement customers are valued for their positive behaviour towards a company [2] (e.g. buying, advertising). The channel cost can be used to decide to target specific customers. High end customers can be targeted with expensive programs, whereas the rest is targeted with a low cost channel [15]. Nevertheless, loyalty programs are not able to deliver a return on investment. Customers do not buy more [35]. When focussing on customer value, the way companies communicate with customers becomes important. The completion of transactions can improve the customer value.

For the sake of customer analysis, several models are used to anticipate customer behaviour, based on past experiences and assumptions. Models exist for customer engagement, development and retention [2]. Predicting customer behaviour has become more difficult because of incomplete and incorrect data collection and analytics, or inappropriate marketing actions [35]. Therefore, a correct handling of customers is important to reduce customer churn [2]. With a high data volume, data interpretation and measuring a model is difficult [35]. From [8] we know that there are universal transaction patterns in a systematic way which means that the information about steps and context in communication can be measured.

The multichannel strategy can also be an iterative process with many stakeholders resulting in a compromise [15]. This is often implemented using CRM. The implementation of CRM is something that can easily fail. Multichannel communication can improve customer profitability by offering a variety of transaction options [35]. From a customer point of view, CRM is often considered the starting point of communication with the customer and of customer knowledge. However, communication is something that comes ahead of and on top of CRM.

The Service Experience Blueprint (SEB) [21] method allows for a flexible and modular process design across the different interfaces compared to the single mapping of service blueprinting (SB). It first focusses on different service activities followed by service design at the multi-interface level and subsequently at the concrete interface level. Although this method focusses on multiple interfaces, it starts at an implementation level blocking the use of this method for changing interfaces.

A company customer experience requirement (CER) [21] is not always equivalent to the customer requirements. Therefore, service interfaces act as activity substitutes but complement each other in providing an overall experience. The SEB method enables a design of the service experience. Through SEB, each channel is designed using service links to contribute to the overall service experience. This technical approach to multichannel communication contributes to the solution of combining channels for customer experience. Nevertheless, it does not take into account the state of the transaction and, therefore, does not know the next possible action. Without a transactional model, the customer experience is solely dependent on the companies' practical communication abilities. Worse still, companies mitigate this problem by allocating the most skilled people which, with more channels to operate, could finally fail.

The nexus of mobile, social, cloud and information forces is compelling organizations to rethink their portal initiatives, designs and products. Portal technology and methodologies [19] must change radically to address the exponentially expanding demands. A portal is a personalized point of access to relevant information, processes and people. Portals have value when multiple sources have to be delivered to multiple channels to access the right information or application. Single point of access no longer means single means of access and all access will be people oriented [19]. The portal concept does not interfere with the cross channel design. Cross channel communication needs a way to authenticate the customer and especially portals have implemented a usable solution to that problem.

Self-service technologys (SSTs) [7] can help companies to reduce labour costs while providing more channel options. A convenient SST can provide more flexibility in the transaction process along with a reduction in the amount of effort needed to initiate and complete a transaction. When using a portal or other SST, we must be sure that the customer understands the steps he can take. The transactions that can be done on the portal and the state the transaction is in should be clear to the customer.

## 3   Channels

In this section we will evaluate the channel characteristics, channel issues and channel organization, and we will conclude with channel implementation.

## 3.1  Channel Characteristics

Channel characteristics are those properties that influence the effectiveness and possibilities of channel communication. We will highlight a few characteristics.

An interesting topic of channel management is the customer context. Without a loyalty program it is difficult, although crucial, to know the customer context (e.g. situation, location, identity) [35]. The way in which the context is handled is dependent on the interaction style, e.g. Web, SMS, mobile app [15]. This topic is subject to change as the technology advances. Also, the target devices are very much subject to change, leaving us with only the customer context as usable characteristic.

Due to the explosion of channels, the variations in customer preferences towards channels have increased. Together with other changes, marketing communication has changed significantly [16]. We cannot manage every channel individually because this would result in a combinatorial explosion of effort. We need a conceptual design that handles every channel as an interchangeable and expandable element in the design.

From a variety of channel characteristics one set of characteristics is selected using service delivered, business goals, customer context, paradigm (interaction style) and target devices [15]. Assuming that the channels characteristics are well chosen, the business goal in combination with the service delivered are usable characteristics as the other characteristics are implementation characteristics which we do not need in this phase.

Aside from characteristics, channel maturity is important. A maturity model of channels has been proposed showing five maturity levels [36].

- Creating presence (channel is up and running);
- Aligning fundamentals (basic value propositions are coordinated);
- Achieving proficiency (capable of function integration of customer processes)
- Leveraging across channels (exploiting channel-capabilities and collaboration)
- Optimizing operating mode (achieving repeatable cross-channel processes).

We conjecture that a theoretically founded, transaction model based communication design, which has a cross channel start and perspective will end up in the highest maturity level. In this highest maturity level, we can add more channels whenever they become available.

The existing literature offers little help in how to develop a multichannel strategy. Nevertheless, channel chain analysis is a good candidate. The term used most frequently to develop this strategy is CRM. In our context CRM is a management approach that wants to establish relationships with customers to maximise customer value [22]. Another strategy is service delivery systems (SDS) [27]. When a communication failure occurs, the key challenge for the SDS is to be able to detect customer mistakes and to offer support in a timely manner. Unfortunately, neither CRM nor SDS contributes directly to cross communication channel design.

Technological advancements have altered the pattern of commercial communication. The number of players in any media category has increased and is expected to increase even more in the coming years [16]. For commercial communication one should consider changing business processes. However, no information on integration of channels is mentioned in existing literature. Business processes should be created from within communication theory instead of integrating new, incompatible channels into existing processes.

The greater the perceived integration of online and in-store operations, the smaller the impact of availability on channel selection with regard to those options. Given an availability failure, it is less likely customers will seek out channel options provided by competing companies (e.g. When a form is not available on the web, the customer can send an email.) [1]. In short, when a customer has started a transaction with a company, it is likely that he will complete the transaction when it is possible.

Channels can be categorized. An older categorization list categorizes channels in sales force, outlets, telephony, direct marketing, e-commerce and m-commerce. Which channel the customer uses depends on the implemented channels in the categorization. This categorization is easily overtaken by time.

## 3.2   Channel Issues

The iPhone started a new era in which a mix of communication media is introduced [6]. As multiple channels become available, companies need to develop channel strategies. The responsiveness of channels also influences the products involved [34]. Unfortunately, using multiple channels generates issues and these increase when channels are integrated. For example, channels are not isolated but are used in overlap (channel multiplicity) causing maturity differences problems. Where some devices can be used for one channel, other devices can be used for multiple channels; thus, channels and devices become indirectly integrated as well. A strategy can be to use a specific channel to target specific customers to reduce cost. When cost per channel reduces, the strategy may have to change resulting in an iterative multichannel strategy with many stakeholders. These strategy changes can be a technical challenge [15]. Therefore, the implementation of multichannel communication can be a huge problem when the implementation is done from a technical perspective (without a theory).

Not all channels are efficient. An experiment showed that the telephone is not performing at any dimension [21, p. 322]. Measurements should be possible within the cross channel communication design, thus allowing for efficiency measurement during use.

Multitasking is switching between tasks in a sequential way and involves a performance penalty unless done on different types of channels (written, spoken, seen) [28]. Currently, chat channels within organisations have a low message rate and, therefore, multitasking looks like an efficient solution. When customers move to a channel in cross channel communication, multitasking gives a different customer experience. For example, two customers talking to the same employee, switching to a video channel means that multi-communication becomes impossible for the company.

## 3.3    Channel Organization

Every 50 years sales undergoes a major change, also known as a paradigm shift [23]. First the department stores were introduced, next was mass production, and then speciality retailers in the suburbs. Therefore, customer expectation changed every time beyond recognition [23]. Companies are now expected to have a full 360 degrees view of their customer and all data present at all times [3]. All changes that are happening using many channels make this the road to omnichannel.

The biggest challenge in omnichannel is channel conflicts where new channels threaten traditional channels. For example, as a reaction to the lower price in competing channels, stores feel compelled to lower cost and cut service. This makes the problem worse because the store does not have any benefits for customers anymore [23]. Moreover, the change from single to multi and omnichannel models requires a stronger link between business and technology capabilities. These capabilities can be used to change business models [30]. From an academic view, the focus has been on either customers as assets and assigning resources to customers or on how to embed CRM in the organisation [34]. The solution lies within the focus on communication with the customers in addition to embedding a customer centric approach in the CRM.

Product-centric strategies are no longer capable of dealing with advanced communication requirements, resulting in customer-centric strategies. However, the new scenario requires a formidable communication design that can integrate these changing business dimensions to develop multichannel, multimedia communication [16]. MultiChannel Customer Management (MCCM) is "the design, deployment, coordination, and evaluation of channels for enhancing customer value through effective customer management" [20]. This is a customer-centric viewpoint and not a channel-centric viewpoint [16]. Actually, the customer-centric viewpoint is good from a business point-of-view. When we think about communication, a transaction-centric viewpoint becomes necessary. One side of the channel is customer-centric, the other side is the company, resulting in a transaction or communication centric approach.

Finally, the organisation forms the biggest challenge in becoming omnichannel. Moreover, current organizational structures are aimed at silos. An organisation has to be built around *change* to survive [3]. Therefore, when organisations are built around change, there must be a constant factor to build the change upon. An organisation construction model as included in Design and Engineering Method for Organisations (DEMO) can provide the essential transactions that are the base for the change of products, implementation, channels and organizational form.

## 3.4    The Notion of Channel

In order to understand channels better, we need notions to categorize and organise channels. One can distinguish, for example, between the virtual and physical nature of channels [27]. This research differentiates between a **virtual channel** and a **physical channel** on the physical infrastructure. Furthermore, they differentiate between **Complementary channels** and **Parallel channels** on the customer's ability to choose channel. These definitions give a scope to the notion of channel. Although these definition is ambiguous because, for example, virtual and physical are not that different. Therefore, we use these definitions to define our own, higher level definitions.

**Definition 1.** *A **Channel** is a protocol description used for communication over a medium during the execution of a transaction.*

Though the definition does not cover all previous examples we choose to start the notion of channel from the $\Psi$-theory in order to rebuild the structure. We realise that the notion of protocol and communication need to be further defined whereas a transaction is defined in the $\Psi$-theory [8]. Furthermore, we intentionally abstract from the physical channel and will limit the notion of implementation to the conceptual design of the channel at this moment because these definitions need further research. Examples of channel implementations are: Chat which is a protocol of alternated exchanges of short messages over the internet; Phone which is a protocol of alternated exchange of spoken text over fixed lines, mobile or VoIP; e-mail is a protocol of asynchronous sent messages over the internet.

Aside from the implementation medium, channels can be seen from a service point of view [27]. This research uses **Virtual service** when no human intervenes as opposed to a **Physical service**. Additionally it defines a **Multichannel service** when multiple channels are used. Subsequently, we combine the definition of a transaction from DEMO as discussed in [12]: A **Transaction** "is a generic pattern of coordination and production, carried out by two distinct actor roles that create an original result... [12]" We will use this definition in the abstract (e.g. the theoretical foundation of communication design) and implementation (e.g. applied communication design) cases. The definition mentions the results (e.g. information, paid order, transported book) that are created during a transaction. In addition, a definition of service within the context of DEMO is given for service oriented systems [32]: A **Service** "is a pattern of coordination and production acts, performed by the executor of a transaction for the benefit of its initiator, in the order as stated in the complete, universal pattern of a transaction". When implemented it has the ability (1) to get to know the coordination facts produced by the initiator and (2) to make available to the initiator the coordination facts produced by itself. Actually, this definition limits the service to the process steps involved during a transaction, only for the execution part of the transaction. It does not include information exchange within the transaction other than required for the process itself. Therefore, this definition does not fully suit our concept of service where we want to see customer-centric behaviour. When we combine the definitions to emphasis on the information and customer centric part in the service we define:

**Definition 2.** *A **Service** is the experienced behaviour of information and process components of a carried out transaction.*

This definition allow us to evaluate the experienced service in later research. Examples of service implementations (behaviour, information and process) are: Getting a product (b) under terms and conditions (i), and the products that are delivered(p) during a transaction; The feeling (b) about the amount that is to be paid (i) and the payment itself (p) in the payment transaction.

## 3.5   Channel Implementation

There are many pros and cons reasons for retailers to go multichannel [36]. In addition, consumers are seeking new media and are willing to pay for the right content on these media. Therefore, content management systems that support multichannel output are required for new business models that support paid subscriptions [11]. This business case driven implementation of multichannel output is often regarded as omnichannel implementation. In our opinion, the omnichannel implementation involves the complete communication and not only the information output or increased sale.

Customers have increasing interest in mobile applications and from 2018 on, multichannel Application Developments (AD) will become common and a consistent set of tools will be available for mobile AD [5]. In this context multichannel application development is defined as a means to use multiple interaction paradigms over multiple platforms over multiple delivery methods. User interfaces will become more human centric and will need no training [6]. Implementing new channels within the customer communication is pointless without taking these developments into account.

Characteristics of one channel may be disruptive to other channels. Using the right combination of channels is crucial [35]. At any rate, companies may want to use multiple different and comparable channels to retain customers when channel availability fails [1]. Factors that affect the customer's choice of channel [26] include economic goals, quest for affirmation and social interaction. Moreover, research has also shown that the positive customer's experience needs to be promoted [1]. Therefore, in determining whether a service should be delivered through multiple channels (and which these channels are), a six-step methodology has been created [10] that provides a global guidance to enhance the probability to multichannel strategy success. In short, all these implementation factors need to be considered when implementing channels and services. Even then, the concept of cross channel communications does not say anything about the applicability of channels in the context of a company.

One factor in channel implementation is the degree to which customers can choose alternative channels for a given service (parallel-channels mode) and the degree to which customers can accomplish preferred tasks through each available channel (complementary channels mode) [27]. A framework [16] classifies customer tasks into six types: new product/service information, product/service assistance, product/service purchase, upgrade request, complaints/feedback, product returns. Even though this list sums up all tasks, we suggest that some of them are not essential. Using Dietz [8] we might reduce this list to: new product/service information, assistance and feedback, product/service purchase and upgrade request (transaction). Reducing process steps to transactions must result in essentially the same as the implemented processes from the framework mentioned above [16]. Moreover, transactions contain the return and cancellation requests by default. Focus is on the processes that require a transaction because the information and assistance is enclosed within a transaction.

## 4   Transactions

In this section we will evaluate channel switching during transactions, the transactions aspect trust and human interaction and close with transaction results.

Studies suggest that customers buy more when using more channels. Moreover, if consumers have a positive experience on an online channel, they are less likely to go to another company [4]. Therefore, providing the right information on a channel might not be enough to let the customer do a transaction. Being able to provide the customer with an alternative channel that takes away the obstacle to complete a transaction can be the positive factor in customer interaction.

The customer centric multichannel framework suggested in [16] proposes a comprehensive communication loop and is novel in two aspects: the framework uses customer-centric company responses and they can use this information to adapt their products and services. Even though it is a business oriented framework, this model does help us to implement the cross channel communication into customer-centric thinking. The closed loop communication matches the transaction idea for communication. In both systems we follow all communication steps and know every response to every request in the multichannel environment.

A conceptual model has been developed [29] to explain why customers choose a specific channel. A pragmatic shopper will more often buy online instead of in the store. Unfortunately, the impact on companies when customers change channel, is not clear. Thus, when we use a cross channel communication design for this type of online customers, the customers are able to continue their shopping on a different channel to complete the transaction. In traditional implementations the customer will loose the transaction on the other channel and must restart the transaction which might be a show stopper.

The need for human interaction is a construct defined as the desire for human contact by the customer during a service experience. Furthermore, in any transaction where the customer is using some technology, the idea of accuracy is imperative to a successful transaction [7]. Subsequently, according to Dietz [8], using the $\Psi$-theory, we can build a transaction concept that closely resembles the human way of communicating. The experience should feel natural when we use all normal steps of communication.

To evaluate the effectiveness of a communication system, we must analyse the results [2]. To measure the process, the Transaction Costs Economics (TCE) model [25] can be used to value each channel for their contribution to the transaction result. When reasoning from the essential model of an organisation [8], in relation to the communication, we need to measure the implementation of each step.

## 5    Design and Implementation

In this section we will evaluate multichannel strategies, design properties and multichannel implementation issues.

### 5.1    Multichannel Strategies

The maturity of channel strategies can be ordered by the number and integration of channels [22]: Single channel, segmented, graduated, migrator (moving customers to other channels), activity based (channel per type of activity), integrated. In the last, highest, order the customer can use any channel. Unfortunately, the maturity model does not provide information whether you can change channels and whether that change is disruptive to a transaction. Nevertheless, the list provides a clear insight into the maturity steps a company can use to implement cross channel communication.

The advantage of multichannel is better reach, improved customer service, and higher customer satisfaction. There are six stages in the presented framework: coverage, profitability, number of channels, decision rules, strategic channels and optimal channel strategy. Firms need to determine the profits on various properties from each channel member [26]. Therefore, the multichannel strategy is only concerned with the profitability of the customer. In contrast with the customer-centric strategy, this will rule out the use of more channels.

### 5.2    Design Challenges

Although companies tend to all-in-one solutions, the best-of-breed are still relevant for specific solutions or compliance [14]. Thus, from an integration perspective, every design should be modular in such a way that specialized parts can be exchanged. This is a prerequisite for integrating cross communication modules.

To correctly analyse customer behaviour, we need enough data of good quality with clear ownership [2] which is a problem in current operational automated system. Contrarily, when modelling transactions using DEMO, the ownership is clear. The executor owns the created data. In this way, precisely data ownership can be defined and used for analysis.

The component model in [13] focusses on building information systems by combining components. The main characteristics of these components are: unique functionality, matching logical and software components, request-response interfaces, encapsulation and reusability. These findings suggest that the more components are used the more difficult it will be to maintain the system. This requires a high level overview of the whole system where the knowledge is structured in the same way as the system itself, reducing the knowledge needed to the part that needs to be changed.

### 5.3    Multichannel Implementation Issues

Retailers have four issues in multichannel strategies [36]: organizational structure, data integration, consumer analytics and evaluation and performance metrics. These challenges show that the cross channel communication design not only has to focus on the technical side of communication but also on the business side. Therefore, DEMO can help modelling the business part of the cross channel communication. We expect the DELTA ($\delta$-theory) [9] to cover the translation from the social to technical transaction systems.

Several companies in the business to business (B2B) sector use multiple channels that are needed by the company to serve its customers. Integrating all channels to create the complete customer experience is the ideal situation. In practice, however, we need a way to mitigate cross channel conflicts [24]. Yet, a sound model of transactions can help us address the cross channel conflicts and solve or mitigate these issues.

Multi-Channel Management (MCM) [25] addresses the coordination and management of the channel (coordination) mix for business to consumer (B2C) communication. Even though this approach focusses on the marketing and revenue part of multichannel, the customer is not even mentioned. Therefore, this management model is not usable for our transaction viewpoint.

Interaction is, as suggested in [16], about a sales transaction, instead of communication. In this context, multichannel is "the variety of channels that customers use to interact and transact with the company" [16]. Therefore, changing channels is necessary for a multichannel framework. Although in this study only multichannel retailing is considered, we agree on the transactional focus.

A knowledge-based approach [33] is defined for automatically creating delivery channel specific services. Nevertheless, solving the transaction from a technical point of view almost always results in an approach that emphasises one of the existing techniques without the possibility to expand on all issues. The service content issues are relevant though.

As each channel has it own characteristics, organisations struggle with channel synchronisation because it is a technical and also an organizational problem. Furthermore, the problem with multichannel is in the multiplicity of channels. In [17] a functional pattern based architecture is presented for the found structures, patterns and characteristics. Actually, when we model channel synchronisation from the transactional view, we can focus on the similarities of the channels instead of the different characteristics. This allows us to focus on the services on completing the transaction. Therefore, the channel properties can then be optimised around the transactions.

## 6  Conclusions

The customer and company centric viewpoint, which research often approaches from the customer value viewpoint [2], teaches us that we need an implementation free communication concept [8] that has also to be based on trust [31]. Also, understanding communication [34] will improve interaction and customer experience [27] through all channels. This customer experience can be designed [21] upon the customer understanding [7] of the interface. In this design of cross channel communication, we need customer authentication and authorization [19] to have a usable solution from a customer and company viewpoint.

Channel characteristics that seem usable are customer context [35], the delivered service [15] and multitasking properties [28]. Multichannel communication can be arranged in maturity levels [36] and the used channel communication should be seen as transaction centric [16]. When implementing channels, the focus must be on the communication within the channels [30] in addition to a customer centric approach [34]. But first of all, organisations implementing multichannel should have a solid base to support the change [3]. From existing channel definitions [27], we derived our definition of channel and service.

The interaction experience should feel natural [7] to customers when they use all normal steps of communication [8] and should have a partial implementation in closed loop communication [16]. Moreover, the outcome [25] should be measurable.

From a strategy point of view, maturity [22] is looked upon as a whole. The cross channel communication design should take into account modularity [14], ownership and maintenance when the system becomes more complex [13]. Here, future research should focus on technical as well as organisational aspects [36]. When we model channel synchronisation [17] from the transactional view, we can focus on the similarities of the channels.

All relevant papers report on the current state of affairs regarding multichannel. When we want to change this state we need to change the perception of multichannel and introduce a design that starts from communication and covers the customer and company point of view and realises a cost effective way of integration existing and emerging channels. Case studies with this $\Psi$-theory theory in mind have to be performed where $\Psi$-theory is set as a base and the communication implementation is performed from that starting point.

Enterprise Engineering is about communication, organisation and information. Current multichannel designs and implementations focus too much on information. We will continue research to show that the integration of the aforementioned aspects in multichannel communication can lead to the proper design of cross channel communication.

# References

1. Bendoly, E., Blocher, J.D., Bretthauer, K.M., Krishnan, S., Venkataramanan, M.A.: Online/in-store integration and customer retention. J. Serv. Res. **7**(4), 313–327 (2005)
2. Bijmolt, T.H.A., Leeflang, P.S.H., Block, F., Eisenbeiss, M., Hardie, B.G.S., Lemmens, A., Saffert, P.: Analytics for customer engagement. J. Serv. Res. **13**(3), 341–356 (2010)
3. Chan, J.P.: The promise of digital technology in brick and mortar retail (2013)
4. Chiu, H.-C., Hsieh, Y.-C., Roan, J., Tseng, K.-J., Hsieh, J.-K.: The challenge for multichannel services: cross-channel free-riding behavior. Electron. Commer. Res. Appl. **10**(2), 268–277 (2011)
5. Clark, W.: New directions for mobile enterprise application platforms: convergence 2012, multichannel 2018. Gartner (2012)
6. Clark, W., Cearley, D.W.: Mobile applications and interfaces: new approaches for a multichannel future. Gartner (2012)

7. Collier, J.E., Kimes, S.E.: Only if it is convenient understanding how convenience influences self-service technology evaluation. J. Serv. Res. **16**(1), 39–51 (2013)
8. Dietz, J.L.: Enterprise Ontology: Theory and Methodology. Springer, Heidelberg (2006)
9. Dietz, J.L.: Delta. Technical report TR-FIT-15-05, Czech Technical University (2015)
10. Enterprise, D.G.: Multi-channel delivery of egovernment services. IDA (2004)
11. Frank, A., Weiner, A., McGuire, M.: Agenda overview for media, 2013. Gartner (2013)
12. Guerreiro, S., van Kervel, S.J.H., Vasconcelos, A., Tribolet, J.: Executing enterprise dynamic systems control with the demo processor: the business transactions transition space validation. In: Rahman, H., Mesquita, A., Ramos, I., Pernici, B. (eds.) MCIS 2012. LNBIP, vol. 129, pp. 97–112. Springer, Heidelberg (2012)
13. Janssen, M., Wagenaar, R., Beerens, J.: Towards a flexible ICT-architecture for multi-channel e-government service provisioning. In: 2003 Proceedings of the 36th Annual Hawaii International Conference on System Sciences, 10 p. IEEE (2003)
14. Johnson, G., Kraus, D., Boold, S.: Critical capabilities for contact center infrastructure. Gartner (2012)
15. Jones, N.: Fit mobility into a multichannel and multiplatform strategy. Gartner (2012)
16. Kumar, V.: A customer lifetime value-based approach to marketing in the multichannel, multimedia retailing environment. J. Interact. Mark. **24**(2), 71–85 (2010)
17. Lankhorst, M.M., Oude Luttighuis, P.H.: Enterprise architecture patterns for multichannel management. In: Patterns in Enterprise Architecture Management (PEAM2009) Workshop. Presented at the Patterns in Enterprise Architecture Management (PEAM2009) Workshop, Kaiserslautern, Germany (2009)
18. Meredith, M.J.: Strategic communication and social media an mba course from a business communication perspective. Bus. Commun. Quart. **75**(1), 89–95 (2012)
19. Murphy, J.: Portals unbound: how the nexus of forces is reshaping enterprise portals. Gartner (2012)
20. Neslin, S.A., Grewal, D., Leghorn, R., Shankar, V., Teerling, M.L., Thomas, J.S., Verhoef, P.C.: Challenges and opportunities in multichannel customer management. J. Serv. Res. **9**(2), 95–112 (2006)
21. Patrício, L., Fisk, R.P., Falcão e Cunha, J.: Designing multi-interface service experiences the service experience blueprint. J. Serv. Res. **10**(4), 318–334 (2008)
22. Payne, A., Frow, P.: The role of multichannel integration in customer relationship management. Ind. Mark. Manage. **33**(6), 527–538 (2004)
23. Rigby, D.: The future of shopping. Harvard Bus. Rev. **89**(12), 65–76 (2011)
24. Rosenbloom, B.: Multi-channel strategy in business-to-business markets: prospects and problems. Ind. Mark. Manage. **36**(1), 4–9 (2007)
25. Schierholz, R., Glissmann, S., Kolbe, L.M., Brenner, W., Ostrowski, A.: Don't call us, we'll call you-performance measurement in multi-channel environments. J. Inf. Sci. Technol. **3**(2), 44–61 (2006)
26. Sharma, A., Mehrotra, A.: Choosing an optimal channel mix in multichannel environments. Ind. Mark. Manage. **36**(1), 21–28 (2007)
27. Sousa, R., Voss, C.A.: Service quality in multichannel services employing virtual channels. J. Serv. Res. **8**(4), 356–371 (2006)
28. Stephens, K.K.: Multiple conversations during organizational meetings development of the multicommunicating scale. Manage. Commun. Quart. **26**(2), 195–223 (2012)

29. McIver, P., Luxton, S., Sands, S.: Multichannel shopping: the relationship between search and purchase channel choice. In: ANZMAC (2009)
30. Sullivan, P.J.: Hype cycle for application services, 2012. Gartner (2012)
31. Teltzrow, M., Meyer, B., Lenz, H.-J.: Multi-channel consumer perceptions. J. Electron. Commer. Res. **8**(1), 18–31 (2007)
32. Terlouw, L.: Modularization and specification of service-oriented systems. Ph.D. thesis, Delft Technical University, Delft, The Netherlands (2011)
33. Vassilakis, C., Lepouras, G., Halatsis, C.: A knowledge-based approach for developing multi-channel e-government services. Electron. Commer. Res. Appl. **6**(1), 113–124 (2007)
34. Verhoef, P.C., Reinartz, W.J., Krafft, M.: Customer engagement as a new perspective in customer management. J. Serv. Res. **13**(3), 247–252 (2010)
35. Verhoef, P.C., Venkatesan, R., McAlister, L., Malthouse, E.C., Krafft, M., Ganesan, S.: Crm in data-rich multichannel retailing environments: a review and future research directions. J. Interact. Mark. **24**(2), 121–137 (2010)
36. Zhang, J., Farris, P.W., Irvin, J.W., Kushwaha, T., Steenburgh, T.J., Weitz, B.A.: Crafting integrated multichannel retailing strategies. J. Interact. Mark. **24**(2), 168–180 (2010)

# Things, References, Connectors, Types, Variables, Relations and Attributes – A Contribution to the FI and MU Theories

Duarte Gouveia[(✉)] and David Aveiro

University of Madeira and Madeira Interactive Technologies Institute,
Caminho da Penteada, 9020-105 Funchal, Portugal
duarte.gouveia@m-iti.org, daveiro@uma.pt

**Abstract.** This work builds upon the FI [1] and MU [2] theories, that belong to the 2015 ensemble of theories from the discipline of enterprise engineering [3]. We critique several aspects of those theories and build upon them proposing a modelling ontology to represent the world, having an asynchronous network of actors, as a requirement. This modelling ontology has seven building blocks to enable modelling data and structures of the world (Things, References, Connectors, Types, Variables, Relations and Attributes). Things address the problem of identity. References introduce the notion of Pointer, extending the FI Theory [1] and clarifying concepts. Connectors address the problem of linking mutable and immutable Things in a network environment. The most innovative contribution is the usage of Types as a dynamic expression of constraints over attributes. Variables and Relations are defined using the revised Relational Theory [4, 5]. Variables are mutable structures that hold values using temporal logic. Relations can be assigned to Variables that also follow the temporal logic. Attributes are Variables within the closure context of a Thing. Together these seven building blocks allow for better modeling in line with the FI and MU theory.

**Keywords:** Enterprise engineering · Organizational engineering · Model theory · Asynchronous networks · Temporal relational theory

## 1 Introduction

Society can be modelled as a network of asynchronous actors [6], that share information and establish agreements to provide the supporting infrastructure for the creation and distribution of goods and services. We use the preliminary assumption that such an asynchronous network of actors is the correct way to model the world [7].

In 2015, the enterprise engineering community published an ensemble of theories to model organisations in their structural and functional perspectives. This work focus on two of those theories: The FI theory [1], which is a philosophical theory that addresses knowledge, in general, and facts and information, in particular. The MU theory [2], which is a technological theory, that addresses modeling in general, and modeling theory in particular.

This work has a very simple structure. In Sect. 2 we critique some aspects of the FI and MU theories, as the problem statement.

© Springer International Publishing Switzerland 2016
D. Aveiro et al. (Eds.): EEWC 2016, LNBIP 252, pp. 181–195, 2016.
DOI: 10.1007/978-3-319-39567-8_12

In Sect. 3 we contribute with a proposed modeling ontology with seven building blocks. Our aim is to solve stated problems and others stated in previous work [7], devising a model ontology that is more powerful, concise and coherent. Not all of the implications of the chosen options could be addressed in this gestalt presentation due to lack of space. Some implications were mentioned and referenced to future work in Sect. 5. The conclusion is presented in Sect. 4.

## 2    Problems Identified in FI and MU Theories

**In the MU Theory** [2]:

1. In the extended adapted model triangle, the concrete complex can be material (like cars) or immaterial (like contracts). This can be a quite confusing as "concrete immaterial things" is a very strange concept.
2. "Conceptual complexes are aggregates of thoughts, more specifically of facts." I believe that thoughts are not just mere aggregates, they have an inherent structure. Besides, there is more than mere facts in conceptual complexes.
3. Not all things that exist in conceptual complexes are models of things that exist in the concrete world. We can conceive things that do not exist. "The precondition for the creation of any (conceptual) fact in the mind is that the form of a thing (…) conforms to the prescription of form of some type."
4. I don't agree that a thing cannot exist without a type. An unknown thing can be perceived as existing and we might not understand what it is, what is for, why is it there, etc. A thing can also exist simultaneously complying with several types at the same time (see Sect. 3.4.1 for an example). A type should not be a single prescription of form as many concepts can be expressed in multiple forms with the same meaning.
5. The chosen paradigm for the general modelling language is not the only one that exists and I argue for the benefits of two different ones in this work.

**In FI Theory** [1]:

6. Not all information is perceived and stored with the purpose of being transmitted to others. Some information is for internal use only. Therefore, although information that is transmitted between human minds needs to be converted into symbols, that is a practical need that does not affect the ontological nature of information. Therefore I do not agree that information has a dyadic notion: content and form.
7. The extended adapted model triangle lacks the notion of pointers, that is, a way to express references in the conceptual world to other things, either physical (concrete complex) or conceptual (conceptual complex).
8. "The basic assumption in world ontology is that a world consists of distinguishable concrete things." There are many examples that contradict this assumption. This is discussed in Sect. 3.1.
9. Regarding the creation of type, it is stated that we can have types created by declaration and by construction. I agree with this, but then, there is a huge step stating that the way to do those constructions is either by specialization, generalization or aggregation. There are many other ways to create types, namely by adding, removing or updating constraints as presented in Sect. 3.4.

# 3   The Building Blocks to Model the World

This model ontology has seven building blocks: Things, References, Connectors, Types, Variables, Relations and Attributes. Each has its own sub-section, as follows.

## 3.1   Things

A Thing is something that has an identity. We believe that an identity is what gets in our minds when a Thing is perceived, either because of its identifiable attributes or by its unique relations with other identifiable Things over structure, space or time (provenance). Identity is a hidden Attribute of Things that in an Information System would be represented by a unique identifier. Therefore we adhere to the notion of "bare individual", as proposed by Bunge [8] for the problem of "sameness" and "change". This means a Thing has a persistent identity, even with changing properties, Some examples of Things:

- **The red apple in the fruit basket**
  To be a proper identifier, there should be only one red apple in the fruit basket. We use features (color, shape) to describe the apple; space relations - object inside another identifiable object, the basket, as well as object near to others of a special type - fruits.
- **The next element in a sequence**
  A sequence is a data structure with an implicit order in elements. Knowing the current element, the next relation operator gives a clear result when applied to a specific structure.
- **That specific grain of sand in my thumb**
  Unlike the red apple in the fruit basket, a grain of sand does not have unique features that enable unique identification by the naked eye. We may be able to identify in relation to other identifiable things if they are concrete enough to the example at hand.
- **The glass with water that was on this Table 5 min ago**
  We are able to give identity to things even if they don't exist in reality at present. The glass of water that was on the table acquired an identity and a way to be referenced for those who were in that context.
- **The ship that belonged to Theseus** [1, 9]
  The ship of Theseus is a well-known paradox from ancient Greece that addresses the fundamental issue of identity. If all parts of the ship are replaced, one by one, is it still the ship of Theseus? When is it no longer the ship of Theseus? In this way to model the world, we address this issue by using as identifiable property to the Thing "ship of Theseus" using an ownership binary relationship. As long as social conventions assume ownership, the identity is kept, independently of the number of replacements in its components. The identity of a thing is more than the sum of its component parts – is has its usage history, location over time, and all other relations established with other identifiable Things or Types of Things (which are also Things in this modelling).

A Thing starts to exist, and gains an internal unique identifier, by simple declaration as in predicate logic, not requiring any justification about the features that made it identifiable or its relations with other Things. This simplification is required in order to bound the world being represented into a workable model. The internal unique identifier will be presented in Sect. 3.3.

A Thing can exist without a name, as long as it has an identity, that is, an unique internal identifier given by the system. On the contrary, there can be several distinct names referring to the same Thing.

Although we can have a Thing with no Attributes, we choose to always have one Attribute to allow the distinction between "concrete" (something that exists in the real world) or "conceptual" (something that exists in our minds and in the social world), due to its structural importance. We will name this attribute "nature", as can be seen in Fig. 1, but other names could be used to reference this property or use no identifier at all.

In Fig. 1, 4 kinds of elements are shown: Attributes ("nature"), Relations ("is a"), Connectors (→) and Constraints ("restrictions"), which will be presented respectively in Sects. 3.7, 3.6, 3.3 and 3.4.

Many times we refer to Things in the world and in our minds indistinguishably, therefore, the "nature" attribute will be of type OR (where both values can be true), instead of the more common type XOR (exclusive or - where only one of the alternatives can be true). This is easy to implement as we store the values assigned to an attribute in a Relation, according to the revised Relation Theory [5]. This way we are able to use an aggregated concrete/conceptual Thing, or use them separetely as needed.

By distinguishing things that exist in the concrete real world, those that exist in our individual minds and those that emerge from social agreements, we move away from the current FI theory that joins concrete things and social things in concrete complexes, as described in the problem statement in Sect. 2.

In order to better present each core construction element we introduce a novel graphical representation syntax, as can be seen in Fig. 1.

At the core of the graphical syntax are the Attributes, represented with green boxes. As previously described, a Thing is something with an identity, which is a hidden attribute, and that may have zero or many visible attributes. Each attribute is either an identifiable feature or a relation with other Things.

There is no implicit order in the attributes, although they must have one when we present then in graphical form.

The green box with an ellipsis ("...") indicates that a Thing can always have additional attributes added over time.

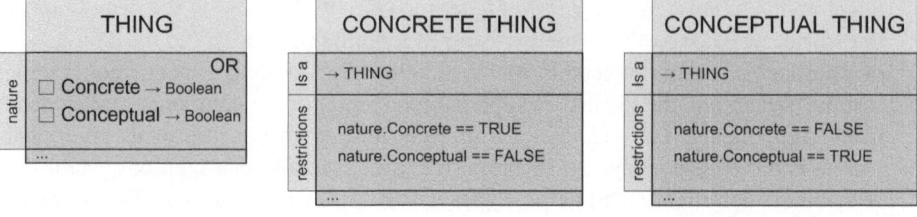

**Fig. 1.** Core construction elements: thing, concrete thing and conceptual thing (Color figure online)

We need to distinguish names of Things and names of Attributes from Things and Attributes. Names are not Things, nor Attributes. Names are references. References are fully described in Sect. 3.2. They aren't strongly attached to the Thing. Over time a reference can be changed or removed, and additional references can be added without interfering with the Thing's identity.

The blue boxes depicted in Fig. 1 are references (or names), presented as extrusions from the individual attributes – to the left to name the attributes, or to the top of the Thing itself – to name the Thing.

By convention, we use capital letters to distinguish Thing references, from Attribute references, although references work the same in both cases.

There can be more than one reference that targets the same Thing or the same Attribute. In that case, they will be added to the left or to the top of existing ones as an additional extrusion box.

All Things can be compared with other Things through the equal operator (==). Two things are equal iff they have the same unique internal identifier number. Having the same values in Attributes is not enough to answer True to the equality operator between two Things. Therefore, the equal operator is reflexive, as it only returns True if both operands are (or refer to) the same Thing. This is very important property as a Thing, in a distributed environment may be copied between several local execution environments and therefore exist in many locations at the same time. What gives a unique identity to Things is it's internal identifier number, that is not visible to users, and that will be presented further in Sect. 3.3.

The alternative option, Things that have equal values in their attributes are equal Things although appealing, can be a source of many logical problems. Since the unique internal identifiers are not visible to users, i.e., that property cannot be perceived, we are not able to distinguish two different Things that appear the same. Like two grains of sand or two molecules of water.

## 3.2 References

A Reference is a Thing that points to/refers to a Thing, other than itself. The attribute for this is "referer". Both the Reference Thing and the referred Thing can be either a concrete thing or a conceptual thing, as depicted in Fig. 2.

These two kinds of Reference "inherit" the Attribute "nature" from Thing. If a specific Reference is a concrete thing, then it can be called a Sign Reference. If it is a conceptual thing, then it can be called a Pointer Reference.

Just like Things can be concrete or conceptual, there are two kinds of references: Concrete References and Conceptual References.

In Fig. 2, the Conceptual and the Concrete Things are within the Thing graphic element just to illustrate the idea that they are derived through "inheritance" from Thing.

The Meaning Triangle [10], presented in Ogden and Richards in 1923, and adapted in Fig. 3 using the options presented in [1], defines three kinds of elements: the physical "Sign", the physical "Referent", and the conceptual "Thought".

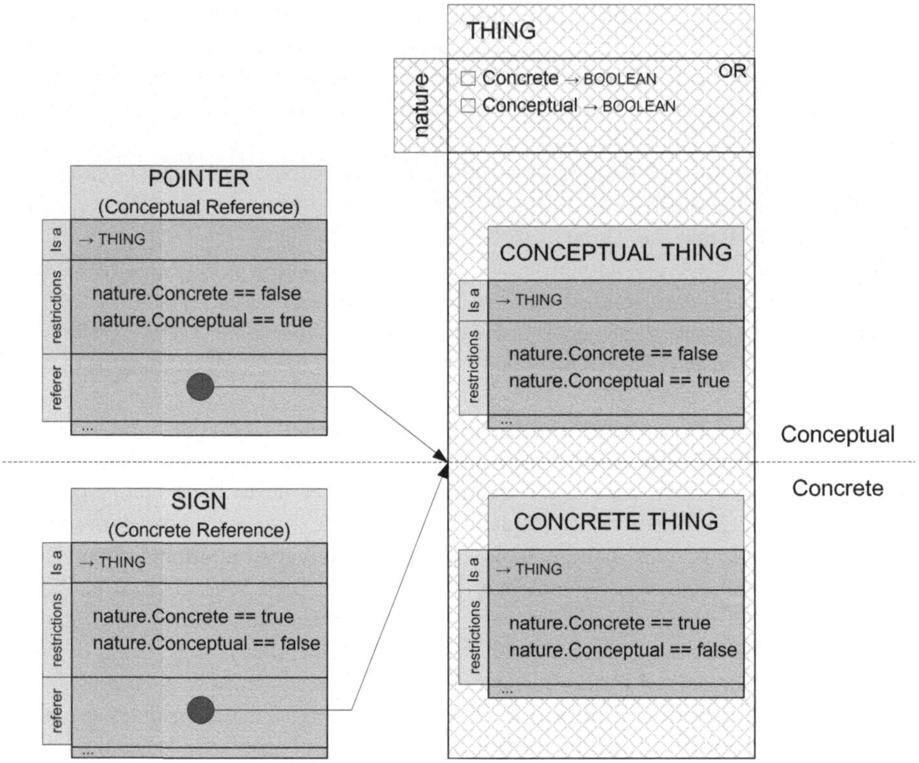

THING

☐ Concrete → BOOLEAN     OR
☐ Conceptual → BOOLEAN

nature

POINTER
(Conceptual Reference)

Is a | → THING

restrictions | nature.Concrete == false
nature.Conceptual == true

referer | ●

...

CONCEPTUAL THING

Is a | → THING

restrictions | nature.Concrete == false
nature.Conceptual == true

...

Conceptual

Concrete

SIGN
(Concrete Reference)

Is a | → THING

restrictions | nature.Concrete == true
nature.Conceptual == false

referer | ●

...

CONCRETE THING

Is a | → THING

restrictions | nature.Concrete == true
nature.Conceptual == false

...

**Fig. 2.** Core construction elements: Pointer and sign

The elements shown in Fig. 2 map the one in Fig. 1 in the following way: The "Thought" is a "Conceptual Thing"; The "Referent" is a "Concrete Thing"; The "Sign" is a "Sign" (Concrete Reference).

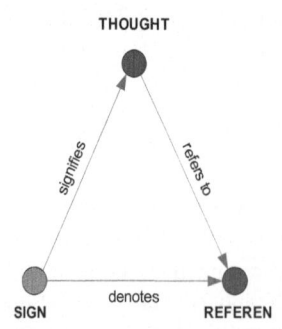

**Fig. 3.** The meaning triangle [1]

We extend this definition by including the notion of Pointer (Conceptual Reference), as presented in Fig. 2, which is a Conceptual Thing that can refer to a Thing (either Conceptual or Concrete).

Let's see an example of a Pointer – Conceptual Reference, applied to a sequence of a few physical elements. Imagine that there is a reference in your mind that refers to the current element in that sequence, which initially is the one in the first position. That Thing that tracks the current position in your mind is a Pointer. You can change the element being pointed to without changing the identity of the sequence, nor the identity of the Pointer. Now imagine a similar sequence of Things in your head. You can still have a Pointer to a Conceptual Thing, in this case, one elements of a mental sequence.

You can even name that Pointer that only exists in your mind as "next in line", and that naming would be a Pointer referring the Pointer that holds the current position. We can rename the label "next in line" without changing the current position pointer identity. This is another example as why names are not an inherent part of the Thing nor Attributes. Naming will be fully explained in Sect. 3.2.

Unlike all other kinds of Things, when an equality action is being performed with References, what is compared is not the identifier of the Reference Thing, but the identifier of the referer. This is a design option for this work. This allows using indirection with References. If we have a Reference R1 that points to a Reference R2, that points to a Thing T, then evaluating R1==R2, R1==T, R2==T will result in True in all of them.

## 3.3   Connectors

When we draw an arrow to connect different Things in a diagram, like the one in Fig. 2, we are using the topological features of the boxes and arrows on a plane to establish a connection between Things. In an information system we do not have such concrete material links to establish similar connections. All Things need an identifier to enable the system to map that unique identifier to concrete Things expressed as blocks of memory stored somewhere, in cache, in memory or in disk, locally or remotely.

Since our goal is an asynchronous network model based on the Actor Model [11], where there is no guarantee of permanent network connection between local executing environments in the network. The same Thing may exist in several copies (caches) over the network. There is an absolute need of global unique identifiers, but the description of how these might be implemented, through which mechanisms and in which format will be a matter for future work.

There are actually three kinds of Connectors: connector-origin, connector-destination and connector-relation. Connections can be directed, when origin and destination are different roles, or undirected, when both connected parts are of the same kind.

Connectors can have one of four cardinality options: one-to-one (1-1), one-to-many (1-N), many-to-one (N-1) and many to many (N-M).

While one-to-one relations could be implemented without connector-relation, we actually believe that we should always use the four kinds of connectors to make evolution easier [4]. Upgrading a 1-1 cardinality option to a higher cardinality is a quite common change.

Connector-origin and connector-destination can be implemented as views over connector-relations as prescribed in relational theory [4]. Additionally, another common change is qualifying relations, that is, giving attributes to the relation itself. Therefore we choose to always consider the connections between Things to be Things in order to simplify the way we handle connections between things and to be prepared to possible future evolutions, according to the good practices of Normalized Systems [12].

Another very important function of connections is keeping track of references. Being able to reference Things from both sides is useful, as it allows to know when a Thing is no longer connected to anything else, and therefore the connector can evoke the apoptosis. Like in programmed cell death, apoptosis allows freeing the identifier and the elimination of any memory space reserved to that Thing. This option makes garbage collection useless, as all connections (to mutable) elements are always directly managed.

The fundamental question in keeping consistency across distinct local execution environments is if Things are mutable or immutable.

Immutable Things can be freely shared with multiple copies, for example with a Gossip protocol [13], because the only challenge that needs to be addressed is how many Things are referencing it, so that when none exists apoptosis can be called.

Having immutable Things can greatly improve memory storage space, as well as communication, as repeated equal Things can be reduced to a single one. Finding duplicated tuples can be a time-consuming task, but when they are found, the system should gradually reduce them.

On the other hand, mutable things have to keep read/write privilege control which is a very significant overhead in communication, and a big source of problems.

The ideal situation would be that, over time, the information system would be able to grow on the amount of data it holds without growing more than loglinear way (N*log N) in the size needed to store it, taking advantage of the inherent redundancy of data. Therefore, immutable Things cannot be changed by the users of the IS, but they can be optimized by the IS by using mathematically equivalent Things. This might be a relief for Big Data problems, as more things can be described using immutable things.

Notice that the amount of information that needs to be transferred between executing environments greatly depends on the amount of information they already agreed upon. For example, if instead of characters we used syllables to represent strings we would greatly reduce strings as the possible combinations of characters are much less than the existing syllables. If words are made of syllables and sentences are made of words, then a big natural compression can occur in strings just by using the appropriate grouping of elements.

Another example, Google announced in 2008 [14] that they had indexed over 1 trillion images' URL. If two execution environments could agree on a specific ordering for those images, and therefore on a sequential number for each of them, then only 40 bits would be enough to identify any image already stored, as $2^{40}$ is bigger than 1 trillion.

For Things that are mutable, that is, can change value over time, the amount of necessary control significantly increases as they need to authorize read/write operations. This problem has already been solved in computer architectures to share memory between different cores, but we will not address this issue here. It is an implementation issue that will be addressed in future work.

As a general rule we should try to use the least possible amount of shared Things, and within shared Things, use immutable Things as much as possible, to decrease the amount of control and promote reusability.

## 3.4 Types

### 3.4.1 What Types Should Not Be

In our opinion, one of the most conceptually constraining issues in programming languages is the today's notion of Type. Types are usually presented, as in MU Theory [2], as a prescription of form. We believe this is the wrong option for two reasons.

First, some concepts like numbers or date/time exist in a scalar dimension independently of the form they are represented. For example, numbers, can be expressed in Roman literals, decimal format, hexadecimal format, binary format, unsigned long integers, short signed integers, floating point format, product of primes, and several others. We can perform operations over numbers independently of the way they are represented. Limiting results to specific representations generates overflow exceptions that could be avoided through a conceptual number model. The same can happen with date/time, as multiple formats can be used, although the same scalar phenomenon is lying underneath representation. Both these representation issues will be addressed in future work.

Second, Types are used in Object Oriented languages as a constraint that limits instances to a very unpleasant straight jacket, keeping the definitions established to its class along the life cycle. Some programming languages, like C++, allow objects to have multiple inheritance from several classes at the same time (allowing solutions for duplicate names in attributes), but others, like in Java, tighten the straight jacket further by only allowing a Thing to be an instance of a single Type.

This option creates several problems. First, it creates, for the full life cycle of the instance, a dependency to its class, which is contrary to the good principle of independence of concerns stated by Normalized Systems, by limiting evolvability. Second, it does not conform to reality, as Things can be of several Types at the same time. For example, a horse can be an instance of "Means of transportation", an instance of "Athlete" and an instance of "Animal". All three of these classes have different attributes and operations available. Having to choose just one class creates problems ahead.

In the case of Java programming language, in order to solve those problem several concepts were added, and instead of making things easier, made it worst. Mixins aggregate two (or more) instances of specific class into a single object, and allow a single point of access to both instances. Interfaces aggregate functions without any attributes. Interfaces don't have instances, but objects/classes can comply with interfaces without establishing the inheritance relationship. Generic types for data structures try to alleviate the burden of strong typing by establishing the content values at creation time, which creates all sorts on unnecessary complexities for programmers.

The strongest constraint for Types was introduced in 2003 by [15], by stating that all structures must follow three a fixed four level of type constraints: instance level (M0), class level (M1), MOF constructs (M2) and MOF metamodel (M4). This type theory paradigm is still the dominant paradigm, and is the proposed type model in the MU theory [2].

Aristoteles said that there are two kinds of problems: the ones that emerge from the complex nature of things, and the ones we make more complex by the way we choose to handle them.

An alternative Type Theory paradigm is the one proposed in xModeler [16]. Instead of distinguishing classes and instances, we can have clabjects that assume both roles at the same time. You can always create a new clabject from another one, through copy of their current properties and methods. Inheritance is therefore a once in a time assignment operation that does now create the dependencies that make evolvability harder.

Although this approach is refreshing, regarding types, it is still not flexible enough, as it limits inheritance operations to the moment of the creation of new objects. We believe that the Type of a Thing should be able to change over execution time, not as a generic type, but as an adaptive type that constrains or broadens the possible values according to programmer needs.

Most programming languages assume the existence of some primitive data types, typically: Boolean, Integer, Float and String. We believe this modelling ontology shouldn't have any primitive data types. Booleans can be modeled as nominal categories (sets of value Things). Strings can be modeled as sequences – a quite basic data structure. Integers and Floats, as well as all other types of scalars can be modeled as numbers. Everything else can be modeled using the principles of universal algebra [17, 18], and can be represented in a consistent way. Advanced data structures representation will be addressed in future work.

### 3.4.2    What Types Should Be

We wish to generalize Types into a reusable concept, so that we can use it whenever needed in an easy way. In our novel definition, a Type is a logical expression of Restrictions that when evaluated for a specific Thing results in True or False. Evaluations shall be performed before assignments either to variables or to parameters in function calls.

Types may be named (using References) to simplify referencing to complex and very long logical expressions. As logical expressions we include the option of first order logic, allowing qualifiers (for all, exist), or even higher order logic.

A Restriction can establish constrains over names, values, relationships with other Things, cardinality of relation attributes, representation and eventually others.

- **Constraints over names**

A Restriction might specify that: "A Thing should have an attribute named X". Or, on a negative perspective, "A Thing cannot have an attribute named X". Notice that attributes can hold values or references to other Things or functions. Functions are first-class citizens in this modelling ontology, but will only be addressed in future work.

- **Constraints over values**

A Restriction might specify: "The attribute X of the Thing in question can only take values Y and Z of the nominal category W". For a numeric attribute it can also establish ranges of valid values, either with inclusive or exclusive border values.

- **Constraints over relationships**

A Restriction might specify that: "There is an attribute named X that is a relation Y, that conforms to type Z." With first-order logic a Type can combine several constraints to express.

- **Constraints over representation form**

A Restriction might specify: "There is an attribute X that conforms to type Y using hexadecimals as representation form."

For advanced data structures we could express constraints over its typical properties of each data structure like "Sequences of size two", "Trees with depth between 2 and

3", "Graphs with average in-degree of 2", "Bag with 10 Integer numbers, with average 7.2 and standard deviation of 2.8".

All these constraints have to be able to be expressed with a formal language (or model representation). This shall be addressed in future work.

These restrictions may appear to be even more restrictive that usual programming languages if used all at the same time. But actually there is no required minimal number of restrictions. It is perfectly valid to establish as a type "Attribute X may hold all natural numbers that have a 3 in the least significant digit."

We should distinguish the definition of a Type and the ability of easily discovering all possible instances that can be valid. Natural numbers are infinite, but even so we are able to use them in a general way even without managing all instances of possible natural numbers.

Being able to deduce all possible valid evaluations of a Type is very useful because it enables reasoning by exclusion using the "Closed World Assumption".

We argue in favor of dynamic modelling where each variable can, over its life cycle, change, not only the value it holds, but also its type expressed through constraints. Current programming languages use a fixed model for variables, only allowing for changing the value within the possible values in the domain of the Type established at creation time.

Unlike common programming languages where variables, parameters and all other containers use a fixed model, in this modelling ontology, Things are not forced to have Types, but they may adhere simultaneously to multiple types, in a double bind relation between Types, and change the Type restrictions over time, either by adding additional constraints, or by removing or updating existing ones.

The idea of named type is just a set of constraints we may wish to impose on Things.

Constrains are always applied to the Attributes of Things, not to the Thing itself. The constraints limit the possible assignment operations to an Attribute, that is, checking if a concrete value is acceptable at that time.

A Thing can comply with several sets of constraints, and apply each of them to several of their Attributes. In that sense, this modelling ontology is multi-type by nature.

The idea of inheritance is quite disconnected from the idea of constraints. One Thing can choose to inherit an Attribute and not inherit the constraints that are associated with that Attribute.

This modelling ontology is dynamically typed in the sense that the applicable constraints applied to an Attribute can change over execution time.

As a consequence of this novel definition of Type we can program in novel ways

(a) Even if we don't know all Things that can be evaluated as true for a Type, we may use stochastic problem solving techniques by trying to discover known Things that fulfill the type constrains and discover possible solutions

(b) We may have a variable X with undefined value, but with a type definition restricting its possible values, for example, to natural numbers between 1 and 6. The assignment expression $Y = X + X$, even without having a value assigned to X, should establish the possible values of Y between 2 and 12 on its Type, and even better, could establish a likelihood of each of its possible values, since the likelihood of getting 7 is far greater than the likelihood of getting 12. We are of course modelling 2 dices…

Type reasoning can improve programming models as they might enable optimizations in function calls by knowing in advance that certain values are more likely than others. In current programming models we just evaluate what the parameter is at call time. The implications of these options have a far reach that cannot be fully addressed with the space constraints on this introductory gestalt presentation. They will be addressed in future work.

### 3.5   Variables

For most programing languages, there is little difference between a Variable and a Reference, except on the format of their value content. That is not the case in this modelling ontology. There is a substantial qualitative difference between a Pointer and a Variable. Although they are both mutable, a Pointer only holds the value of the last assignment, while a Variable is a much more powerful conceptual construction that keeps track of all the values assigned to it over time with a valid time/date, either from the past or to the future using temporal logic.

Due to space limitations, we shall refer further explanations about Variables to future work, that will synthesize the full revised temporal relational theory [4, 5].

### 3.6   Relations

A Relation is the complex data structure that supports the revised Relation Theory [4]. Each relation has a head and a body. The head is a set of attributes, each combining a name and a type. The body is a set of tuples adhering to the type in the corresponding attribute.

We can get a relational algebra [4] if we combining a Relation with typical operations over relations like: rename, restrict, project, union, intersect, minus, join, extend, group and ungroup.

Due to space limitations we shall refer further explanations about Relations to previous work [20], that synthesizes the full revised temporal relational theory [4, 5].

### 3.7   Attributes

An attribute is a Variable withing the context of a Thing. An attribute is not a Thing and therefore it does not stand on its own – it needs the Thing as a support for its full identity.

Attributes don't need types. In their more generic form, they can store a sequence of symbols in a format that the system might not even understand. That is actually what happens when strings are stored. Only the users really understand what those symbols mean. Other times, the symbols that attributes hold follow a very specific grammar or representation form. Attributes can also just point to other Things.

Attributes don't need names. Changing the name of the attribute does not change it's nature, or the value held. It can change only the perception of its use. Naming attributes can be a very troubling, as can been seen in the discussion of the FI theory [1]. This happens because names are used in a functional perspective, and therefore they are subjective, and there is no correct way to name attributes. Sometimes the best way is to name them based on the format, sometimes on the use case, sometimes we need very long names in order for them to make sense to the user. As names are references, we can have multiple names to the same attribute without any problem, namely, translating the attributes to different languages.

## 4   Conclusion

Choosing the foundation building blocks for modelling is a difficult job because of the infinite amount of alternative definitions, that all seem to fit due to our innate brain plasticity. With this work we aimed at critiquing some concept definitions, presenting alternative ones and therefore hoping to promote discussion regarding these foundations concepts.

We believe our major contributions are: A novel definition for Type as a dynamic expression of constraints; The clarification of the concept of identity in things; The introduction of the common concept of Pointer in the FI theory [1]; the discussion of practical but inevitable implementation problems regarding Connectors; The combination of the novel notions brought by the revised Temporal Relational Theory [4, 5] regarding Variables and Relations. And finally, we clarified the notion of Attribute as a clustering concept – a dependent concept of Thing, that relates Variables, Relations, References, Types and Connectors.

## 5   Future Work

During this work several references were made about future work. We summarize then in the following six topics:

- Handling global unique identifiers – which entity assigns them, what structure shall they have (single or dual identifier parts), which transactions are needed to operate them and share them for immutable and mutable data.
- When a mutable Thing is shared across several local execution environments on a asynchronous network, how can the ownership, read/write permissions and state control can be established, assuming that a permanent connection to the network is not guaranteed.
- Numbers and Time/Date are scalar phenomenons that, for historical reasons, have very complex representation forms. We should have a consistent ontology to model these concepts at an abstract level, and then be able to use distinct representation formats, as long as we are able to have equal and order efficient functions between different representation formats.
- Complex data structures are actually quite regular when you use a universal algebra approach to describe their components. We believe that all data structures are quite the same, and can be described in a simple canonical way.

- Functions are a very old construction for abstracting sections of code. They have a set of limitations that should not still be constraining programmers. Namely, they have only one result, mixing error codes and responses, or worse, throwing exceptions that diverge the execution in hard to control and recover ways. They only have one response value or, even worse, they require the construction of a new class to return several results combined. Functions are typically called in synchronous ways – the caller will block until an answer is given. Some programming languages, like Node.js, allow calling functions in asynchronous ways using the call-back paradigm. We think we should go a step further and define functions as a social interaction following the PSI grammar. This would allow to provide partial results as they are found, provide less accurate results sooner when possible, allow cancellation from the requester releasing resources sooner. We also think that functions could keep an internal state and continue execution from last result yielded, like in Python and Ruby. Functions could be defined in such a way to execute calls in lazy, eager or smart way, evaluating the parameters and providing the result in a just-in-time way. Finally, functions should be able to join the Logical Programming, Declarative Programming, Imperative Programming, Stochastic Programming, Linear Programming and other programming paradigms into a coherent solution.
- The implications of Type Theory hereby presented are far greater that it was possible to present. We need a formal language and a deductive procedure to extract the full potential of having Types established as boolean expressions of constraints, instead of life-cycle fixed inherited constraints.

**Acknowledgement.** This work was developed with financial support from ARDITI (Agência Regional para o Desenvolvimento da Investigação, Tecnologia e Inovação), in the context of program Madeira 14-20 –FSE.

# References

1. Dietz, J.L.G.: The FI Theory – Understanding Information and Factual Knowledge (2015)
2. Dietz, J.L.G.: The MU Theory – Understanding Models and Modelling (2015)
3. Dietz, J.L.G.: Enterprise Engineering Theories Overview – version 2.3 (2015)
4. Date, C.J., Darwen, H., Lorentzos, N.: Time and Relational Theory: Temporal Databases in the Relational Model and SQL. Morgan Kaufmann, Waltham (2014)
5. Date, C.J.: Time and Relational Theory (video). O'Reilly Media, Inc. (2015). http://my.safaribooksonline.com/video/databases/9781491917763 (last visited 8 March 2016)
6. Neto, A.B., Gouveia, D., Silva, M.J.: ACE: um agente de compras na Internet (1998)
7. Gouveia, D.P.B.: Organizations Redesign and Building of Information Systems (2014)
8. Bunge, M.: Treatise on Basic Philosophy: Volume 3: Ontology 1: The Furniture of the World. Reidel, Boston (1977)
9. https://en.wikipedia.org/wiki/Ship_of_Theseus (last visited 13 March 2016)

10. Ogden, C.K., Richards, I.A.: The Meaning of Meaning: A Study of the Influence Od Language Upon Thought and of the Science of Symbolism. Routledge & Kegan Paul Limited, London (1949)
11. Hewitt, C.: The Actor Model. Massachusetts Inst of Tech, Cambridge (1993)
12. Mannaert, H., Verelst, J.: Normalized Systems: Re-Creating Information Technology Based on Laws for Software Evolvability (2009)
13. Jenkins, K., Hopkinson, K., Birman, K.: A gossip protocol for subgroup multicast. In: 2001 International Conference on Distributed Computing Systems Workshop, pp. 25–30. IEEE, April 2001
14. https://googleblog.blogspot.pt/2008/07/we-knew-web-was-big.html (last visited 13 March 2016)
15. David, F.S.: Model Driven Architecture: Applying MDA to Enterprise Computing (2003)
16. Clark, T., Willans, J.: Software language engineering with XMF and XModeler. In: Formal and Practical Aspects of Domain Specific Languages: Recent Developments. IGI Global, USA (2012)
17. Burris, S., Sankappanavar, H.P.: A Course in Universal Algebra, vol. 78. Springer-Verlag, New York (1981)
18. Goguen, J., Malcolm, G.: A hidden agenda. Theoret. Comput. Sci. **245**(1), 55–101 (2000)

# Author Index